THE
SWEETEST

A
BOXER'S
MEMOIR

THING

THE SWEET- EST THING

A BOXER'S MEMOIR

MISCHA MERZ

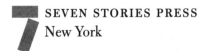

SEVEN STORIES PRESS
New York

SEVEN STORIES PRESS
140 Watts Street
New York, NY 10013
www.sevenstories.com

College professors may order examination copies of
Seven Stories Press titles for a free six-month trial period.
To order, visit www.sevenstories.com/textbook
or send a fax on school letterhead to (212) 226-1411.

Library of Congress Cataloging-in-Publication Data
Merz, Mischa, 1964–
The sweetest thing : a boxer's memoir / Mischa Merz. —1st ed.
p. cm.
Summary: "Mischa Merz takes a wild and unpredictable journey
through the fascinating world of womens boxing in America"
— Provided by publisher.
ISBN 978-1-58322-928-6 (pbk.)
1. Merz, Mischa, 1964– 2. Women boxers—Australia--Biography.
3. Boxing—United States. 4. Women boxers—United States. I. Title.
GV1132.M47A3 2011
796.082—dc22
2010048504

BOOK DESIGN BY POLLEN, NEW YORK
FRONTIS PHOTOGRAPH © JESS D'CRUZE, 2009

PRINTED IN THE UNITED STATES

2 4 6 8 9 7 5 3 1

For my husband Peter Holding, with love and gratitude

CONTENTS

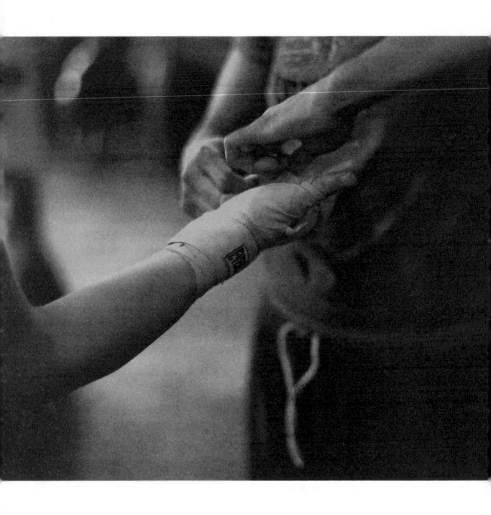

Wrapping hands before sparring. MONIKA MERVA.

PREFACE

MY RELATIONSHIP with boxing has been like one you would have with another human being. I have loathed it and adored it. It has both invaded my dreams and turned my stomach. I have resolved to reduce its significance in my life only to see my passion for it intensify. Boxing is my man. Even my husband will tell you so.

Boxing has rewarded my dogged persistence with fleeting moments of grace and flair, and I have collected these moments like love letters to be kept securely locked away and savored in later years.

I was such a hopeless case when I first began to box—so slow and unresponsive—that each and every admiring comment made on my jab or footwork was forever etched in my consciousness.

By the time I first walked up the steps of Gleason's, the famous New York City gym that is the heart of the women's boxing renaissance, the sport was part of the rhythm of my soul. The metronome of the skipping rope and the spank of leather mitts on a heavy bag ignited my engine. By then I was no longer amused by the paradox of my presence in such a place. Instead, I was comforted by the familiarity of it: the round bell; the heavy swinging bags; the snort of the shadowboxers, their idiosyncrasies, aliveness, and common purpose. The ring is preeminent here, the most hallowed of spaces, like an altar, a stage, or a sacred site. All gyms contain these elements. All gyms are home to a boxer, and fighters as well as former fighters are welcomed without hesitation. That I can call myself a fighter now is something that I treasure more than I would the title Doctor or Professor. In fact, I have spent more time in contemplation of the sport than most people spend on a PhD.

These days, sparring—which used to drain my legs of sensation, dry my mouth to dust, and overstimulate my bladder—is second nature. I regard having someone try to hit me in the head as an almost friendly gesture. I have made friends this way and lost them only when we stopped hitting each other.

"Are you still boxing?" people ask me from time to time, possibly expecting to hear that I have finally come to my senses. "More than ever," I tell them now. There's no doubt that I am a better boxer than I ever hoped I could be. I practice the sport like an artist, because I must, not to attain any particular goal, but because it is who I am.

THIS MEMOIR recounts six trips I took from my home in Melbourne, Australia, to the United States from September 2007 to December 2009 to train and to fight. It was during those two years and three months that everything changed for me. What I knew about boxing, what I could do as a boxer, and who I was in the world of women's boxing were all transformed. On my first trip in September 2007, nearly ten years after my first fight, I traveled to New York City to Gleason's Gym in Brooklyn, where many a female nose has been bloodied and broken, a place that loomed large in my mind as the home of some of the toughest, scariest women in the world. That first visit was the beginning of my reawakening. It led to a second visit a year later in September and October 2008. Then, finally, came the odyssey that was May to December 2009, when I traveled across America, from New York to Fort Lauderdale, Atlanta, Kansas City, Los Angeles, and Albuquerque, training and competing in Masters matches, there not to watch but to actually get into the ring myself and fight, something I had long thought was impossible.

I tell the story of the people I met and trained with and fought. On that journey, I met some of the trailblazers I had been following for so long. I encountered them less as a fan or journalist than as a fellow fighter, as one of them. By then we had ring stories to share, and their hard-won acceptance opened up a whole new world to me, one that I had once seen as a mere flicker of pixels, recurring names, and weight categories on YouTube. Now they were life size and, in many cases, larger than life size, and I was among them.

Less than a week after I returned home from my American boxing adventure in December 2009, the International Olympic Committee announced that female boxers would be included in the 2012 Olympic Games in London. The rise of women's boxing around the world, culminating in its inclusion in the Olympics, requires that women's bodies be reimagined. We can't keep convincing ourselves that they still reside inside a Victorian birdcage of benign fragility, cowering and frightened. We also can't keep imbuing them and their owners with moral purity. The increased acceptance of female athletes in many different sports has given women the freedom to be tough and mean and ruthless. And it is in the arena of women's boxing where this narrative is playing out most eloquently.

THE WOMEN I met in the United States were extraordinary one and all, from the incredible, freakish talents of Lucia Rijker and Alicia Ashley, to the edgy audacity of Melissa Hernandez; the dependable, unshakable resilience of Bonnie Canino and the frightening, thunderous power of Anne Wolf to the hilarious banter of the tiny, indomitable Terri Moss. These are characters in the true literary sense, as big and brave and as vivid as any of the greats of men's boxing have been. If they were all gathered together in the one room, the walls wouldn't be able to contain their energy and their unstoppable life force. And scattered and few in number though they may be relative to the men, they have pushed down the barriers once and for all so that no young girl will ever question her right to call herself a fighter. The first female Olympic boxing champion in 2012 should want to shake their hands for putting "their ass and their ego on the line," as Terri Moss would say. These amazing women should never be forgotten or allowed to slip under history's rug as the sport gathers pace and grows. I feel honored to have met them, to have been in the presence of their courage and their commitment.

Boxing cannot help but make you question who you really are. You cannot hide from yourself in a boxing ring. It might seem a crazy path to self-knowledge, but it is also a rich and rewarding one. My journey has revealed to me that I'm not the only one who thinks so. Women boxers are making a new discovery: we need each other to improve, just like the men do. Maybe that's what I like most about the culture of this particular sport. It *is* all about me, baby, that's for sure. But no one does it alone.

—Melbourne, July 2010

1 PILGRIMAGE TO NEW YORK

I WAS definitely out of condition when I made that initial pilgrimage to New York in September 2007. I no longer held any ambitions for my own boxing career. I'd slowly gained weight. I assumed it was middle age encroaching and that there was nothing I could do about it. Everyone I knew was thickening up, even the skinny ones. I was still training, even running, but in a plodding kind of way, with no zest, as if I were marking time. And since I no longer needed to make weight, I rarely stepped on the scales. It had been more than six years since I last fought, and my boxing obsession had slowed to a simmer. I imagined that I had reached the end of a particular phase in my relationship with the sport, as everyone must. I'd started looking at those old men who shuffle around boxing gyms trying to make themselves useful, occasionally hitting the bag stiffly, wondering if that too would be my fate—a kind of boxing granny figure exaggerating her glory days to the kids.

I'd had an exhausting year in which my mother had died after a prolonged illness. I was emotionally and physically drained, wrung

Gleason's Gym.

out from grief and resigned to the idea that visiting Gleason's, while certainly exciting, had probably come far too late in what had been a pretty late run at the sweet science anyway.

So when I climbed the stairs to Gleason's Gym on Front Street in Brooklyn for the first time, I didn't know what to expect.

I got chills up my spine because I knew I was walking into the heart of the world I'd always imagined. Gleason's was a piece of the sport's living history in a city that has now all but left that history behind. In 1925 there were 1,890 boxers registered in all of New York State, and in 2006 there were just 50. Gleason's is the city's oldest and, along with Stillman's near Madison Square Garden, among its most mythologized boxing gyms. People have written plenty about that climb—the noise, the pungent smells, the bell, the gritty floors, the bloody canvas, the sheen of sweat covering the bodies of the boxers. It's so cinematic and vivid for those making their first ever visit to a boxing gym that it can constitute a kind of sensory overload that makes every boxing writer's juices flow. But it was quite a different experience for me, so much of it cozily familiar rather than daunting and strange. The smells and the noise and the action were just bigger and louder and more vivid than at home in Australia.

I had been boxing long enough not to be intimidated by what outsiders often assume is a menacing environment. I'd learned by then that fighters are usually friendly. If some of them seem aloof, it's because they're trying to mask shyness rather than emit hostility. They tend to welcome curious visitors rather than shun them. Others are natural performers who, of course, need an audience. So I was expecting friendly faces at the top of the stairs and thought, maybe foolishly, since I am also somewhat of an attention seeker, that I wouldn't rule out a sparring session or two.

But I had heard some cautionary tales about sparring in America from Songul Oruc, one of the early pioneers of women's boxing in Australia. She'd spent a few hard years in the late 1990s fighting in the US and had warned me that sparring sessions were like territorial wars—harder than fights, in a way, because there was no referee to step in while the trainers' egos forced the pace. She had eventually wearied of the broken noses and the stress and returned home after three fights. I'd spent an afternoon with her in Melbourne and heard stories of gym wars that made my hair stand on end. So I promised my husband, Peter, who had watched my boxing obsession unfurl after innocently showing me how to throw a left jab all those years ago, that I would be careful.

The part of Brooklyn where Gleason's is located, known as DUMBO (Down Under the Manhattan Brooklyn Overpass), was once a treacherous industrial wasteland where drug dealers and murderers lurked. Now it has been almost completely gentrified. Across the street is an Apple store and next to that is the designer furniture store Bo Concept. Since Gleason's first opened its doors in 1937 it has been used as a location for twenty-nine movies, among them the Martin Scorsese classic *Raging Bull* as well as numerous mainstream features and offbeat art-house documentaries, including some notable films about women's boxing, like the award-winning 1999 Katya Bankowsky documentary *Shadow Boxers*. But its legendary status was forged by the men who trained there. Gleason's has been home, at various times, to more than 131 world champions including Muhammad Ali, Floyd Patterson, Jake La Motta, Mike Tyson, George Forman, Riddick Bowe, Virgil Hill, Larry Holmes, Thomas Hearns, James Toney, Marvin Hagler, Carlos Monzon, Emile Griffith, Ray Leonard, Julio Cesar Chavez, and many more. The list is wide and deep and comprehensive. Gleason's is the Harvard University of boxing. It hasn't always been in DUMBO. Its location has changed twice from its original home in the Bronx, first to Manhattan, then to Brooklyn.

The gym's owner for the past twenty-seven years, the urbane and soft spoken former Sears manager Bruce Silverglade has had the good sense to change with the times, holding art shows in the gym and staging events that combine boxing and chamber music. He also appeals to the alpha males and females of Wall Street by conducting annual boxing "fantasy camps." At the same time, Bruce has preserved something of the gym's grimy old-school boxing tradition, the chaos that is a feature of most gyms peopled by such a wide variety of passionate and driven individuals. Bruce's smooth but firm presence has a catalytic effect, bringing coherence to what could so easily disintegrate and fragment. While outside the gym loft apartments are selling to Manhattan yuppies for millions, inside a certain shabby charm has been preserved. Fight posters, photographs, and magazine clippings that tell the full story of Gleason's trajectory adorn the walls. But the electrifying energy of the place will keep you from looking at the walls long enough to piece together the story. The collage of peeling newspaper and magazine images blends into the living art of boxing unfolding in vivid color and clamor all around you, an art practiced at the highest level in a gym that feels like the sport's epicenter. One ring near the entrance is reserved for something described as "unpredictable wrestling," but the three other full-sized rings—constantly in use with people shadowboxing, sparring, and punching pads—are without question the main events.

That day in 2007 I was surprised and excited by the sheer number of women inside those rings and, indeed, on the posters too. And I mean women fighters, not just decorative side dishes to the main course, but genuine competitive athletes more skilled than most Australian male boxers. Once that would have sounded like an affirmative action overstatement. Now it's a simple fact. It was so striking to me that it made me wonder if perhaps boxing was more suited to women than men, despite decades of discourse to the contrary.

And here they were, neither subverting nor perverting masculinity or femininity, nor bringing the sport into disrepute. The women inhabited Gleason's as if they'd always been there. And any questions about their right to be there would be met with bewildered silence from the men I asked, as if the suggestion was weird, like asking if women should be allowed to wear trousers.

I'm accustomed to walking into a boxing gym and receiving a lot of sideways glances. I'd been to many gyms along Australia's eastern seaboard over the ten years prior to that day. I was always made acutely aware that as a female boxer I was an oddity, like a solar eclipse—something that does happen, but only rarely. At Gleason's I was noticed more for my peculiar accent than my gender, if I was noticed at all in the mad bustle of activity, in the shouting and clanging and *diggada-diggada-diggada* of the speed bag.

I knew that women's boxing was bigger in the US than in Australia, but I had no idea of the scale in real terms until I saw with my own eyes. Bruce, who sat at the top of the stairs at what looked like a prop desk from *Hill Street Blues*, told me the gym had three hundred female members and that thirty of them were active amateur and professional fighters. But it looked like more than that to me. It looked like women's boxing had reached critical mass and was now normal in America. No one turned a hair. Since Bruce sanctioned entry to women in 1983, Gleason's had become well known for its female champions. Some legends of the female franchise had long since dealt with the occasional hostile reaction to what many considered an intrusion into hallowed masculine territory. British journalist Kate Sekules chronicled those early years in her highly readable memoir *The Boxer's Heart*, which, along with *Shadow Boxers*, added to the canon of works about Gleason's and helped cement its place in my mind as the first port of call in any American boxing journey I might consider. The knowledge that many of the competitors in the first ever Golden Gloves contest for women, staged in 1995, hailed mostly from Front Street had penetrated my subconscious. Sekules' book now stands as an important document describing the genesis of a revolution that seemed to rock everyone's boxing world. Many of the women who trained there were college educated and middle class and able to communicate their experiences beyond the gym's walls into the realms of film, art, and literature.

The men and the women often came from quite different worlds. It couldn't have been easy for those men to share their hard-won territory with the women; nor could it have been easy for them to watch from the sidelines as all this attention was focused on a bunch of girls who looked for all the world like dilettantes who hadn't earned their place.

But those awkward and confrontational days I had read about were long gone by the time I arrived. The women had indeed earned their place.

In the lead-up to my first trip I had made e-mail contact with one of the pioneers, Alicia Ashley, a Jamaican-born bantamweight world champion who I had watched boxing on YouTube with giddy admiration. She was one of a group of five reigning female world champs in the gym at the time and had been training at Gleason's for close to twelve years. She later told me she didn't remember ever feeling intimidated at the gym. She came in as a fighter, already a kickboxer, and trained with her brother. She wasn't interested in anyone's opinion and just came, did her work, and left. Alicia has a smile that can illuminate midnight, but she can also put on a deadpan glare, warning that she won't suffer fools. Often it's a playful expression, but you can never be entirely sure.

Gleason's is also home to Maureen "Moe" Shea, famous for being Hilary Swank's sparring partner as she prepared, with Hector Roca's guidance, for *Million Dollar Baby*, a film credited, along with *Girl-fight*, with propelling many women through the doors of American boxing gyms. When I met Maureen on my second visit she talked a lot about the rhythm of boxing and the rhythm of New York City with her rapid fire Bronx Irish inflection. She had just knocked out

Alicia Ashley.

her opponent and said she regarded the ability to do that as "a spiritual thing." Most of my conversations with Maureen, the daughter of a cop, were conducted in a semiclothed state while she applied an array of girly unguents to various parts of her body, her hair wrapped in a turbanlike pink towel. It was like being backstage with a showgirl, not a fighter. In fact, the women's locker room at Gleason's was a patchwork of crazy juxtapositions: boxing boots stuffed in every spare bit of space, a mirror and bench designed for makeup application, pink bandanas drying off along with hand wraps, and exfoliating sponges and bottles of conditioner jostling for space. It was an object lesson in the human capacity to absorb many conflicting ideas into a single complex identity, something so easy to overlook when it comes to the female gender.

The first sparring session I witnessed between women at Gleason's was between two of the champs—a Puerto Rican veteran of fifty professional fights, Belinda "Brown Sugar" Laracuente, and a powerhouse from Westchester, Ann-Marie Saccurato. Saccurato had already overcome serious obstacles just to be walking, let alone fighting at this elite level. She'd nearly been killed in a car crash several years earlier and had been told that she would never play sports again. But she had proved the medical profession wrong and clawed her way back from multiple, horrific injuries. Belinda and Ann-Marie had once fought each other with the eight-round split decision going to Belinda. I stood in dumb awe as I watched Belinda goad and move with the kind of slippery evasion few fighters, male or female, can muster. Ann-Marie was more of a classic pressure fighter with an intimidating physical presence, her long, wiry torso taut with lean muscles. The hairs on the back of my neck stood up as I watched them. I felt a little shudder of vindication as I recalled how harshly female novice boxers had been judged when they had entered the ring unprepared in the old days, so poorly schooled that it was guts alone that got them through what were often flailing debacles. Most were

Melissa "The Hurricane" Hernandez.

trained by men who not only knew little about the science of boxing, but also seriously underestimated the female gender. I don't know how many times a male sparring partner had confidently told me that a woman would never hit me as hard as they did. I do remember the first time I discovered how wrong that assessment proved to be; the women I fought or sparred usually hit much harder than the men did.

Back then ringside and armchair experts would immediately jump to the conclusion that women had no skill, as if boxing skill was something you could inject, like a hormone. At Gleason's I was seeing for the first time how women looked when they had been given more than half a chance, some decent tuition, and the time in the sport that men take for granted. Not only that, the person who was doing most of the ringside coaching was a small, feisty Puerto Rican woman named Melissa Hernandez.

I turned to Alicia and asked, "Are all the women here this good?" She threw her head back and laughed. She reminded me that these were world champions—the best of the best. Banners in red and black lettering hung up high around the gym testified to the fact.

Gleason's is, ironically, the same gym where Joyce Carol Oates, an icon of American letters, researched her famous 1987 essay *On Boxing*. It was in this place twenty years earlier that she had concluded, "Boxing is a purely masculine activity and it inhabits a purely masculine world . . . Boxing is for men, and is about men, and *is* men." She added that, consequently, women boxers were "monstrous." With all due respect to Oates, who is one of my literary heroes, I couldn't help thinking how monumentally wrong she is. So many assumptions about gender that she made in what is otherwise an erudite, compelling piece of writing had been blown to dust over the course of the two decades following the publication of her essay. And in the very same place in which they had been formulated! It gave me a strange and eerie feeling. It demonstrated that so little is fixed in what we call culture. An idea that seems immutable and true in one era can sound laughable to the next generation. Maybe now the opposite could be true: boxing might be for women and about women. How else can people of small stature, who weigh no more than a jockey, exhibit their physical power? Most sports favor height and size. Boxers are matched by weight, and the smaller divisions— even among the men—have often been more exciting for their speed and dynamism.

Alicia weighs somewhere around 125 lb., and her style is unique and utterly compelling. Her toes, unlike most fighters', turn out, and her back is ramrod straight. I've heard her described as a "freak" and a "mystical animal." She moves with the seamless grace of a dancer and exemplifies all that is elegant about modern-day boxing. She had, in fact, been dancing on scholarships with Martha Graham and Alvin Ailey before injury propelled her into pugilism. Her brother and trainer Devon Cormack convinced her that her speed and flexibility would easily transfer to kickboxing and then boxing. Her fighting name is "Slick" for good reason. She is one of the finest female fighters, not just of the pioneering generation but the next one as well. I had already seen Alicia humiliate the German champion Alesia Graf in a clip of their title fight on YouTube and would go so far as to say that she is one of the best boxers I've ever seen of any gender. And I'm not alone in that opinion. It was a virtually uncontested view at Gleason's that Alicia was right up there.

"She's the best," said former Olympian John Douglas as we watched her spar one day. "She makes it look easy."

I had planned to train with her during my time in New York and hopefully learn a thing or two. We met almost every morning over the next two weeks, me riding the F train from Park Slope with a backpack full of gear, excitement and anticipation building on each journey. Alicia seemed to want to fine-tune my punching style, with an eye for detail that was impressive. She wasn't as concerned about my power as she was about my accuracy and what boxers call snap—landing punches with a clap, crisp and clear, against the pad. Sometimes we moved around the ring, and I tried to mimic her gliding, seamless style and obey her commands.

When she asked me if I ever sparred I hesitated for a second or two only because I had seen the standard and was a little worried about how I might fare. But on my last Saturday my fears were laid to rest. I had a great day sparring, among others, Camille Currie, who had that year contested the New York Golden Gloves and was Alicia's main fighter. She's a tall black girl, a little like Alicia herself, who was determined to make her mark in an increasingly competitive sport and in a weight class with genuine depth—132 lb.

And, as it happened, a whole new door opened for me, and out of shape and over the hill though I was, I got an inkling during the short time I spent working with Alicia of what might be possible if I could return in better physical condition and stay a little bit longer.

So I vowed to return a year later fit and ready for more. Alicia, somewhat used to such proclamations, took my words with a grain of salt. But I was already thinking about what lay ahead. More than an opportunity to improve, it was a chance to experience how it would be if women had a real place in boxing and to inhabit a world in which women's boxing was a tangible reality—not a theoretical proposition. I wanted to see exactly where I fit in among my own kind.

In the locker room before sparring. MONIKA MERVA.

2 BORN-AGAIN BOXER

DURING 2008, the year after my first visit to New York, I worked on getting myself into better shape back in Melbourne. In the US, meanwhile, it was all real-world action. Just a few weeks after I returned home, Ann-Marie Saccurato knocked out Jessica "Raging" Rakoczy in the final round of a spectacular upset to win the World Boxing Council (WBC) female lightweight title. Then it was Belinda "Brown Sugar" Laracuente's turn to fight Rakoczy, and while she impressed the purists with her skill as always, the cards didn't go her way. After that Belinda boxed Jaime Clampitt but again lost on the scorecards. I'd seen Belinda fight Myriam Lamare, the French 140-lb. champion and former amateur European and World champion on YouTube in an extraordinary display of skill from both fighters. I'd also watched Belinda spar and thought she must be the unluckiest woman in boxing since she was so clearly one of the most talented. She always fought the best in her division—Christy Martin, Holly Holm, Chevelle Hall-back, Myriam Lamare, Mary Jo Sanders. But Belinda needed more than talent to get her over the line. Half of her record of 331 rounds over 50 fights were recorded as losses. The odds were often stacked too heavily against her since she usually traveled away from home, sometimes at late notice, and was often the victim of hometown bias. But she was unconcerned with padding her record with easy wins.

By midyear Camille Currie, who had only just started training with Alicia when I was in New York, won the New York Golden Gloves, which was televised from Madison Square Garden. I had had the opportunity to spar with Camille during my visit. Maybe this would be as close as I would get, I thought, to that hallowed Manhattan ground—"She sparred a girl who fought at the Garden."

Melissa "The Hurricane" Hernandez, whose voice was probably the first thing I heard cutting through the cacophony that greeted me when I ascended Gleason's stairs, fought three times during my absence, once against the seasoned Chevelle Hallback to a draw on an all-female card in New Mexico, followed by two wins in what were, from all accounts, highly entertaining bouts against Melissa Fiorentino and Ela Nunez. In her mid-twenties, "The Hurricane" had turned pro after a short but impressive amateur career that started at a small Police Athletic League gym in the Bronx where she went initially to lose weight. She is one of a *new* new breed, the turbo tomboy, that likes to showboat. The first time I saw her she was wearing a wetsuit under her red satin shorts—a completely unsound method of weight loss I hasten to add—and a matching red bandana. Her tongue piercing winked in her constantly moving mouth, her husky voice honking out flat New York vowels like one of the city's notorious taxi cabs, mixed up with staccato outbursts of Spanish. Melissa is known across the country for being disqualified from the Women's Nationals in South Florida for taunting her opponent and hotdogging it around the ring like Cassius Clay after he had knocked out Sonny Liston. Floridians were still talking about it almost two years later. Even in California they know about "that Puerto Rican chick from New York."

Melissa spends as much time refining her strut as she does her punches. Her shameless showing off represents a whole new turn for women boxers, usually too concerned about boxing correctly to leave room for such behavior. Showing off is risky. The men who do it tread a tightrope between arrogance and embarrassment. Women have suffered enough embarrassment inside the boxing ring to not want to invite more. Certainly none I'd seen had the gall to stick out their tongues, shimmy their shoulders, and do a version of a Russian dance inside the ring like Melissa does. I find her completely irresistible, even when she doesn't quite pull it off and gets smacked in the face by an opponent for showboating instead of bobbing and weaving.

"Aren't you worried about losing your tongue when you stick it out like that?" I'd asked her between rounds with Tracy Hutt, a professional female boxer and gym teacher.

"I am, I am," she said. "But it hasn't happened yet."

"Is that because you have a fast tongue?" I persisted, and she doubled over laughing like we were in a bar and then resumed her eccentric dance of distraction while Tracy tagged her with a continuous stream of tidy, conventional jabs.

Melissa is saved by her disarming ability to laugh at herself, so it is pretty hard not to enjoy the show. She often stands with her arms resting on the top ropes outside the ring barking instructions to Belinda or any other boxer she trains, usually telling them to throw more punches—"*Siga! Siga! Siga!*" I really wanted to see Melissa fight one day because I had a feeling she was a sign of things to come.

Alicia, on the other hand, is serenity personified, gliding around the gym like she's on skates, perpetually cool and unhurried. She carries herself with the poise of aristocracy, and in a way she could lay claim to being boxing royalty. But the warmth of her personality is her most attractive quality, and it dissipates any diva tendencies she might have. Despite practicing a sport in which arrogance is an essential commodity and living in a country that cultivates it more than any other, Alicia is able to temper her abundant self-confidence with her humanity; she can as easily break out into gales of warm laughter as frown in serious concentration or mock disapproval.

I'd found it interesting to see how these very talented, extremely dangerous women wore their valor. Women are so often self-effacing even if, or maybe especially if, they are good at something. But it seemed to me at Gleason's that while these women knew exactly how good they were, there wasn't much haughtiness or false modesty. Usually matters were sorted out in the ring, and domination there could be capricious. I sensed a reasonable degree of respect among the women for each other's capabilities. The knowledge that success or failure could be one punch away for any of them created a natural equilibrium.

Alicia also fought three times during the twelve months I was in Melbourne. In her first outing of 2008 she easily defeated the plucky youngster Brooke Dierdorff who, in a nine-fight pro career, had taken on some of the toughest opponents in her division. Alicia showed again why her fighting name was Slick. Brooke was all heart, but Alicia's counter fighting made her look foolhardy. As Alicia waited for her next match, she entered and won a kickboxing tournament just to stay active. Then in June 2008 she lost the IFBA world bantamweight title in a split decision to another southpaw, Canadian Lisa Brown.

I kept track of these women's movements and managed to watch some of their fights on YouTube, increasingly my lifeline to the world outside Australia's tiny puddle of women's boxing. Now that Sharon Anyos had given birth to twin boys and didn't look like she would be resuming her boxing career any time soon, only two professional female fighters were currently active—a talented up-and-coming bantamweight, Susie Ramadan, and a former amateur champion, Erin McGowan. Most of their opponents were flown in from Thailand, there being literally no competition on home turf.

WHEN I climbed those famous stairs in DUMBO again in September 2008, this time fitter and lighter, I felt like I had come home. If anything was different, it was only that there were now even more women training at the gym than the year before. The bigger changes were occurring inside me. I had begun to see the sport in a new light, certainly when it came to my relationship with it. Over the years I'd gone from being so worried about my courage and character that I could hardly concentrate on my boxing to being more concerned about my punch rate and balance. I remembered how sparring once filled me with dread, and now it was so much a part of me that I could literally do it anywhere in the world. I marveled at the degree to which boxing had become an extension of myself, a means of expression, my art. I knew I still had a world of things to learn about boxing, but I felt I was finally ready. The painful and difficult rites of passage were well behind me, all the nuts and bolts that go into making a boxer: the awkward adjustments, the endlessly sore nose and jaw, the honing of counterintuitive responses until having a punch come flying at your face is as familiar to you as catching a ball.

At first I was attracted to the novelty of boxing, as well as my novelty status as a woman within this quintessentially male domain. I enjoyed the gasps of my middle-class friends and how being a boxer, even just wanting to be one, set me apart. It was fun to be the only woman in a gym full of blokes, the sole and solitary advocate for a different kind of womanhood, communicating with men in their own language instead of from the other side of some glib Mars vs. Venus divide. Reentering the world of Gleason's in September 2008 to a warm welcome from men and women alike, I realized how different this was from how it used to be for me. *What appealed to me here was not my separateness, but my connection.* I liked that I was no longer a novelty and that I could enjoy the sport with other women who, like me, had also at first questioned their courage and sought real answers, had similarly tested themselves against each other without the focus being on their appearance or their accommodating femininity or how appealing they might be to men. It was enjoyable for a change not to have people assume that this was a fraught world that you would only want to inhabit for a short time and then resume regular nurturing, girly activities. Or that boxing somehow negated any of those activities. Among the women around me at Gleason's, my future sparring partners, were mothers, hairdressers, beauticians, and architects. The sport bound us together. These were women who really understood boxing, who were as immersed in it as I was, and whose relationship with boxing was long term and profound. One of them, Keisha "Fire" McLeod-Wells, a New Yorker who wore a necklace with a cluster of golden gloves dangling from it, had even held her wedding ceremony in Gleason's, inside one of the rings. She'd worn gold hand wraps, and the bridal party, dressed like corner men, had carried belts into the ring. The groom entered in a hooded robe. They had a wedding cake shaped like a ring with little sugar-coated gloves decorating it. Keisha's obsession for the sport made mine look relatively tame by comparison.

These gals weren't going to look at me strangely if I got a black eye. They understood my shorthand, my need to shrug it off, because they were the same. Even better, the men in the gym seemed to accept, if not enjoy, having these tough, intense, young women around. The kiss-and-hug greetings melded with the stick-and-move protocol of the ring. A couple of men told me that day that the presence of the women had improved the atmosphere in the place for everyone.

Alicia greeted me with, of course, a hug, those long arms extending in an arabesque as she moved from the center of the ring where she was teaching someone on the mitts, to embrace me over the ropes, her big smile beaming as I stepped onto the ring apron.

Then she took a step back and looked me up and down.

"My God," Alicia said. "You've lost so much weight."

"I told you I was going to get in shape."

"Yeah, but . . ." Alicia said, looking me up and down. So I was serious, she could see now. The question was, how serious?

Between September 2007 and September 2008 I had actually dropped below my former fighting weight, much to my amazement, simply by eating less and training a little harder, increasing the intensity but not the duration. Because I had never really stopped boxing, I had never let myself go completely, and now that I was fit I was ready for action. I had spent the year practicing what Alicia had shown me: relaxing my shoulders and letting my hands go, turning my knuckles over and bringing my hands back faster, not pushing my punches.

"You're posing," she'd said back in 2007. "There's no camera. Who are you posing for?"

But she'd also told me on that last visit that I "moved great," which was like having Leonardo da Vinci say you'd built a nice house. It'd been all I had to keep me going for the next twelve months, and it had been enough.

Of everyone who has ever held the mitts for me, Alicia had been the least interested in my strength. In years of boxing I had acquired a reasonable left jab, I could move around a ring, and my overhand right usually hit its mark. I could slip, I could bob, I could block, and yes, I could take a punch. I had never been stopped in a fight, and in sparring my mishaps, although dramatic, had been few.

Now that I was fit again, what I wanted was to get some fluidity into my game, to use the slips to counter and make angles. To my own surprise, I had gotten through to the thinking part of boxing, to the very stuff that most people can't see or appreciate: the geometry, the ring-craft, the pacing. Getting as far as I had was its own reward for staying with it. But I was too easily impressed with myself when I made someone miss, so I wasted those opportunities instead of capitalizing on them. Now what I wanted was for all the parts to flow together into a seamless whole.

In New York everyone moved as if they had Herbie Hancock playing inside them. Everywhere I looked, from little kids to old men, there was a relaxed looseness. Shoulders were like well-oiled pistons. Punches came out seemingly naturally, without tension, without effort. In Australia, most boxers were stiff and tight, trying to make every punch count. But mostly the emphasis on strength robbed them of speed and made them appear robotic. In New York the approach was different and, I thought, more sophisticated. Flurries preceded the solid punch; people considered the geometry, the pace, the moves. The whole game was more refined.

My problem often arose when a pair of mitts or pads was held before me. Immediately I wanted to hit as hard as I could, even if consciously I knew that wasn't the object of the exercise. The problem might be, at least partly, gender related. I was used to the pads being held by men, and part of me was so accustomed to them exclaiming how hard I hit, that I'd grown to like the sound of that male praise. Part of me still wanted to astound men with my boxing, hear them ooh and aah. Most of all, I didn't want to hear them say I hit like a girl.

But you can't throw combinations when you're all tight. Alicia had set me on a new path. I had heard her voice in my head all year, saying, with that slight Jamaican inflection, "Relax it. You're pushing. Bring it back." When I got it wrong her lips would crease with a slightly sardonic curl as she shook her head.

So here I was one year later, as fit as I could get myself and ready to become a more refined boxer.

That first day back training in September 2008 I shared the changing room with a strong-looking blonde who, like a character from a 1970s sex romp, extended her hand to me and said, "Hello, I'm Anna from Sweden." At first I thought she was there for a workout. I'm not sure what made me think that. Her body was in good shape. Maybe it was the way she asked Belinda which locker she could use. She was so deferential that I assumed she was just beginning in the sport and thought that boxers were a bit scary.

Out on the vast gym floor Anna from Sweden let her blonde hair flop around her face in a sweaty mop while she hit the bags and shadowboxed. I was so distracted by these dancing locks that I didn't closely observe her technique. Her body language seemed too emphatic, like a kid playing air guitar to heavy metal music. Also, most of the women at Gleason's solved the hair issue with bandanas, making Anna's crazy locks seem so unnecessary. It harked back to the days when women fought without realizing how foolish they looked once their big nineties hairdos unraveled during a fight. By now braids and bandanas had supplanted that furious wild-woman look.

But it turned out that Anna Ingman was actually another one of the *new* new breed. Since she'd been just a kid when I started boxing in my early thirties, she was without the feminist baggage that had informed my youth and so was less inhibited about doing something that might not be seen as appropriately feminine. Anna's generation didn't have cartoon role models either, like Xena and Wonder Woman. Instead, Anna was looking at real fighters like Lucia Rijker. Rijker was a destroyer in the ring, hitting real people with real punches, not just feeling empowered by boxercise. Rijker is a self-contained warrior with intense big cat features and the caramel complexion of mixed-race parents. She is enigmatic and cool, methodically carving up every opponent put before her like a

Sunday roast. What self-respecting young woman boxer wouldn't want to be just like Lucia if she could?

Anna had had more amateur fights than most men I know in Australia. She was the first European Union amateur champion and since turning pro had won the WBC's junior middleweight international belt. She'd even spent some time training in Russia. She was preparing to fight at the Legendary Blue Horizon in Philadelphia. So much for first impressions. Hair, that great signifier of femininity, can be such a red herring. I should have known better after all these years.

"What weight do you fight at?" I asked her.

"Velterveight," she said.

"Will you be sparring while you're here?" I asked.

"I hope so, yes," she said and paused, looking me up and down. "What do you weigh, 140? Maybe we can schpar?"

"Sure," I said. "No problem." And she licked her big rosy lips before they spread into an eager smile. When I looked more carefully at her face, now that her hair was off it, I noticed that she had what looked to be a genuine, old-school boxer's nose. It had clearly been busted, possibly more than once. But Anna's flat, slightly bumpy nose made her look even more beautiful. Coupled with her blonde hair, blue eyes, high cheekbones, and full red lips, her eloquently crushed nose gave her a certain sculptural refinement, a compelling androgyny. The more I looked, the more noticeable was the tale her nose told, and I wondered how I'd managed to miss it the first time I'd seen her.

After my conversation with Anna, Bruce led me to his office so I could pay for the gloves I'd just bought from him. "You know," he said in his soft-spoken fatherly way, "if you spar her, you want to make sure she knows you don't have a fight coming up. I don't know Anna, she seems like a very nice person. But she's a fighter, and I know fighters. You don't want to get into a slugging match with her."

"So I should make sure Alicia's there to watch out for me?"

"And I'll be watching out for you too," he said.

The next morning I was completely knocked out by jetlag and had to skip training altogether. The following day, as I prepared to train with Alicia, she told me that the morning before she'd seen Belinda and Anna in the ring.

"How was it?" I asked.

She shook her head gravely. "It was rough."

"Yeah, they went hard?"

Alicia shook her head again. "She doesn't know how to relax. She was usin' her elbows and all kinds of stuff. And Belinda was doing it right back to her."

"She wanted to spar me."

Alicia laughed and shook her head. "Don't worry," she said. "There'll be plenty of people for you to spar."

On my way out of Alicia's office, I saw Belinda lacing up her boxing boots as she sat on one of the patched-together padded benches near her locker. I asked her how the spar went with Anna.

"It was good," said Belinda, her eyes widening, her honey skin shining. "She's a real go-getter."

"Did she catch you with anything?" I asked.

"Yeah," she said, still beaming, her hand going to her chin. "She caught me with some good shots. I thought whoa . . . fuck . . ."

The next Saturday was my first proper sparring day at Gleason's, and after getting changed in the crowded women's locker room, my first stop was Alicia's office. Her desk was cluttered with dusty trophies and the walls plastered with posters and photographs of her landing punches on her many opponents from an infinite array of angles. Piles of leather boxing gear lay like sleeping puppies on the floor, and there was a TV and VCR and a shelf full of tapes. On her desk was a black-and-white picture of her as a child with her choreographer father, a handsome man. And also, I was pleased to see, a laminated copy of a photo I had sent her of a group of us—myself, Alicia, Camille, and Melody—after my last weekend at the gym a year earlier.

Alicia was on the phone, and she pointed to my armor sitting on a chair. At home I would wear an open-faced head guard and twelve-ounce gloves with Velcro that I could remove myself if I needed to so that I could take a drink or more often retrieve one of my contact lenses without help. But at Gleason's it was customary for someone else to wrap your hands, lace you up, and strap you in. It was nice to have the attention, but it made me feel a little dependent, and I didn't like the paradox of having to go in there and fend for yourself, but not being able to even take a drink from a water bottle without help. But here I surrendered to local convention—a heavy pair of old-school sixteen-ounce sparring gloves, which had to be laced up; a closed-face head guard that covered my cheekbones and cut out a little peripheral vision; and for the first time ever, a body protector. When I remarked that I'd never worn one before, Devon, Alicia's brother, said from his desk in his heavy baritone, "Dat's because you ain't never been hit before, not like she gonna hit you to da bardy."

When I emerged from the office, feeling like I was in a deep-sea diving suit, Anna was there limbering up.

She brushed her hair from her face with her glove, looked me up and down, and giggled.

"You look like a little man," she said.

"Thanks," I said. "I think."

I sidled up to Camille, the tall rangy black girl with the great jab I had sparred a year earlier. We'd e-mailed each other from time to time during the year between that visit and this one, and I had seen her Golden Gloves win on YouTube.

"Hey," she said. "You're thinner."

"And fitter," I added. "But I'm not any younger."

When we'd sparred the year before, I'd made a lot of jokes about being old and unfit, needing rounds off to recover. I felt I'd done fairly well against Camille despite my poor condition. She had asked me to be aggressive, since she expected that from her next opponent, and I did my best to give her what I had. I was looking forward to working with her again as a measure for myself of my progress. DUMBO Fight Night at St. Anne's Warehouse around the corner from Gleason's was coming up in just days. After Camille's impressive Golden Gloves win, she was scheduled for a rematch with the same opponent on the Fight Night at St. Anne's. I couldn't wait to see her in action live.

THAT DAY we sparred a few rounds, but it was the feel of the ring under my feet that I enjoyed the most. It was so firm and smooth and spacious. It was as if I had stepped up a class just being in there. With my newfound fitness, it was so much easier to move around those big rings with plenty of gas in my lungs and without the extra twenty pounds weighing me down. But Camille and I sparred with extreme restraint. I'm not sure why. For my part I was concentrating on trying to throw more combinations. Neither of us seemed willing to push the other past a certain point. But, I thought, there were three more weekends to go. I would clearly be spoiled for choice when it came to sparring partners. I recognized faces from the year before and spotted several new ones.

During one of my breaks, I stood next to Alicia as we watched a minute or two of Swedish Anna in the ring with one of the tall amateur boys.

"I don't like the way she's pawing her jab," said Alicia.

"She doesn't seem to be going too hard with *him*," I said, still wondering if I should defy everyone and insist on doing some work with her.

"That's because she can't get in," said Alicia. "He's too tall."

As I watched her, I didn't think she was doing anything I couldn't handle. A short time later, while I was sparring, I saw in my peripheral vision that Alicia appeared to be getting into the ring with Swedish Anna. I apologized to my sparring partner, and I jumped out of the ring, making my way through the throng toward the ring Alicia and Anna were sparring in.

"That girl's trying to kill Alicia," said one of the trainers as he joined me to get a closer look at the action. And after watching for a while, I had to agree. Anna was intense.

"But Alicia's making her look bad," I said, and the trainer smiled.

Swedish Anna was living up to her brawler reputation. She was throwing everything she had at the 125-pound Alicia as if she were already fighting the main event at the Legendary Blue Horizon. She was still pawing her jab, but now she was also charging in, letting the occasional elbow precede her, and Alicia was countering with left crosses that looked like they had been fired from a crossbow. They hit the bull's-eye every time. I understood then why Anna had the kind of nose she did—Alicia's sharpshooting didn't stop Anna's attack and she took plenty of punches to deliver just one of her own. Alicia was trying not to get close enough to be shoved around and was using her skills to move around the ring and keep Anna off balance. Alicia had been right about Anna. She sure didn't know how to relax. As I watched, I speculated on how I would handle such an attack. I was about ten pounds lighter than Anna.

At the end of half a dozen rounds Anna got out of the ring looking weary, her nose bleeding, and glove marks peppering her fair Scandinavian skin. Alicia nodded to me to tell me to get in the ring with her. But first she held up her bright yellow gloves for Devon to wipe off Anna's blood. And there was plenty of it.

We touched gloves when the bell rang, and Alicia resumed her relaxed, Gleason's manner, hitting with precision but not malice. She created angles and surprises and capitalized on my errors without demoralizing me too much. And I snuck the odd one in here and there, too. When the bell sounded, and we took a short break, she told me that Anna had made her angry.

"I don't know why, I never get mad," she said. "But she was pushing and shoving me, and she has at least twenty pounds on me."

"But that left hand of yours landed every time you threw it."

"Yeah," she said. "But why did I get so mad?"

As the Saturday session was winding down, Hector Roca, who had trained me for one session the year before, came up and said, "You lookin' good."

"Thanks," I said. "I'm trying to be loose, throw more punches."

"Is hard with Alicia," he said. "She move too much."

Because Hector had been Hilary Swank's trainer for the film *Million Dollar Baby*, he had become almost as mythologized as Gleason's itself. He had some genuine fighters on his résumé, too, Buddy McGirt and Arturo Gatti being two notables. And in a way, his style was stamped on many of the boxers at Gleason's: busy hands, continuously flowing combinations, and pinpoint balance.

Hector's favorite words, of the ones I could understand through his thick Panamanian accent, were "Relax. Play with you hans. Move aroun'." But he was a quixotic man. "He can make you feel like the best boxer in the world, or the worst," Angela Querol, one of his former fighters, liked to say.

DUMBO FIGHT Night in early October 2008 had all the familiar elements of amateur boxing events everywhere: the graying officials in white polo shirts, fighters of all ages with headphone wires trailing from their ears, a crowd made up mostly of enthusiastic friends and family members come to cheer on the fighters. Alicia stayed close by Camille, and both of them looked so relaxed and content they could have been getting ready to go out shopping.

"How do you feel?" I asked Camille.

"I feel good," she said with a smile.

Around the time we'd sparred the year before she'd told me that she got so nervous even sparring that she would lose a few pounds in regular trips to the bathroom. Now she was calmly moving her head to the music on her iPod, which, she later revealed to me, held the entire *Rocky* soundtrack, Tupac, MOP, Young Jeezy, and a few reggae songs. Strange mix when you think about it. So much for Herbie Hancock. She handed me her iPod to take care of when it was time to glove up, which I did with a sense of honor. I wanted her to do well. It's always good for your sparring partners to do well. You can claim a little of the credit whether you deserve it or not.

CAMILLE'S FIGHT was against the girl she had beaten in the New York Golden Gloves match. It led to another win for her, a victory even more decisive than the first one.

Then, for the next fight, I saw two women step into the ring who, frankly, looked a little too old to be there. I'd seen them both at Gleason's and thought that maybe this was an exhibition bout, just for fun. But when the fight started, it looked serious. It looked like a standard novice fight with lots of pent-up nervous energy being unleashed in the opening seconds, both boxers coming out punching straightaway with not much lateral movement or defense. The woman in the blue corner was a southpaw. That made the fight slightly more untidy than most novice fights were, but with plenty of punches thrown, there was no lack of spirit or action. What I was witnessing without knowing it was a whole new turn in women's boxing. This was a Masters novice bout, a relatively recent addition to amateur boxing that allowed those older than the "open class" cut-off age of thirty-five to continue boxing under slightly modified rules while previously the only option was to retire or turn professional, where age limits are less strict. Two women over forty-five, biologically old enough to be grandmothers, were going at it, and for the first time they were doing so in an officially sanctioned Masters bout.

Maureen Reiniger, the southpaw from the blue corner, was a fifty-two-year-old manager with New York City Transit, where she had worked for more than twenty years. This was actually her second fight. Her opponent, Leila Ferioli, was a forty-six-year-old real estate agent. While I'd heard of the Masters, I'd assumed there were no women old enough willing to fight. But this was America, the land of opportunity.

Maureen had begun boxing only a few years earlier at the Boxing Academy for Women on Long Island before moving to Gleason's when her trainer was injured in a serious accident. She had a theory about Masters boxing, which was that as women age, their estrogen levels fall, and this gives testosterone a better chance of coming to the fore, thus making boxing a more appropriate sport for them. As a medical theory it might be completely unsound, but as a glass half-full philosophy it sounded all right to me.

Then it slowly dawned on me: if they can fight, then so can I.

A few days later I asked Belinda to film my final four-round session with a fighter named Sunshine who, when she wasn't punching me, was an affectionate, extremely cheerful person I liked a lot. Her real name was Amanda Beczner, a makeup artist who revealed to me later in e-mails that her womanizing father had given her and her sister each a pair of boxing gloves as children and showed them various choke holds and eye gouging techniques. Presumably, they could use these skills if they ever came across a man like himself. She had picked up the sport again in her twenties.

Later, when I watched the video, I heard Melissa, in the closing seconds of the fourth round, saying on the tape, "I like the way she boxes." And Belinda answers, "Meeesha?" Melissa replies in assent, "Ah-ha. She got a nice style. It very . . . it's clean."

Hearing their banter on the video almost made me weep with gratitude.

I returned to Australia a few days later in October 2008. Before I left, Angela—not only Hector's former fighter but also Gleason's matchmaker—assured me that if I found my way back the following spring, she could find a match for me, presumably one of the two I had seen fight, Leila or Maureen. And so I started to plot my comeback, setting my sights on a Gleason's show that was scheduled for May 16, 2009. I'd be back again—with my USA Boxing passbook in hand and registered with Gleason's—ready for a fight.

3 GIRLS' NIGHT

ON MY first Saturday night back in New York in May 2009, I was invited to a party with some of the women from Gleason's to watch the Ricky Hatton vs. Manny Pacquiao fight. It had been eight months since I'd seen everybody, and it would be the first time I'd see a big fight in real time with so many fellow travelers. Saturday night in Las Vegas falls on a Sunday afternoon in Melbourne, and so I usually watch alone or with one or two others, usually men. Now I was going to be in a house full of people, boxing fans and serious players, most of them women.

Hatton had been beaten the previous August by Floyd Mayweather Jr., a fighter who embodied, for me, American boxing at its finest. While Hatton's flat nose and unimaginative forward march appealed to many Australian fight fans, I enjoyed the slippery creativity of Li'l Floyd and had been happy to see him chalk up another win.

Alicia picked me up at Angela's place with Ruth O'Sullivan, a multiple Golden Gloves winner who trains at Gleason's, and Ruth's little boy Liam for the ride to Gerritsen Beach in Brooklyn. Ruth and Alicia share a condo in Brooklyn, Liam's father having left the scene. A redhead, Ruth is one of the skinniest women I have ever seen. The first time I'd seen her prepare for a sparring session at Gleason's, it looked like all the gear she wore weighed more than she did. And then I watched the way she moved in the ring, so continuously and effortlessly that not a single punch seemed to land on her.

Angela was going to join us later with her friend Ronica Jeffrey, another of the Gleason's Golden Gloves stars who had recently turned pro only to sit on her hands while waiting for matches to materialize. She had beaten Maureen Shea in the 2005 final the year Shea had her new pal, Hollywood star Hilary Swank, in her corner. It had been the upset of the tournament. Writing about the fight for WBAN (an online news source for women's boxing), Bernie McCoy reported:

> Ronica controlled the fight from the opening bell and won handily. Between rounds, Swank, giving it the "old Hollywood try," rushed along ringside to Shea's corner, encouraging her former sparring partner. If there was a moment for a come-from-behind finish, this is where the scriptwriters would have put it. But this was a boxing ring in Madison Square Garden, not a Hollywood sound stage, and there would be no "happy ending" . . . It was Jeffrey's night, it was Jeffrey's fight and Jeffrey's Golden Gloves championship. The 5-0 scoring told the story of the bout much more dramatically than any script could have.

I'd seen video of Ronnie's pro debut against Karin Dulin and admired her slip-and-hit rhythm and the way she got plenty of side-to-side leverage on her punches. I liked the way she leaned down to her left and popped out her right without warning. She was relaxed and fluid, a real cool customer.

THAT MORNING I had felt relatively normal despite having landed the night before after a twenty-hour flight. My body's clock was still set twelve hours ahead, but I felt rested enough to go to the gym and spar with Alicia and Camille, and it felt surprisingly good, as if I hadn't missed a beat. Only eight months had passed since my last trip, and I felt like I fit right back in. The only real difference this time was that my expectations were higher. This time I came to fight.

All I needed was a willing 138-pound woman who was over the age of thirty-five. How hard could it be to find one of those? Angela and Bruce had been confident a few months ago, but then, about two weeks before I left home, Angela sent me a message saying she hadn't been able to find anyone. I decided to come anyway, hoping my luck would change once I arrived. So in the gym that morning I told everyone I could that I needed someone to fight on May 16. Camille suggested that having my old fights up on YouTube might be deterring potential opponents.

"Especially that one where you bloody that girl's nose," Camille added, referring to my Australian title fight in 2001. "I felt sorry for her."

"But that was a long time ago," I said.

Camille was in the habit of doing online video searches of women she was going to fight. Alicia thought this habit of Camille's was slightly neurotic. But it seemed reasonable to me, and probably Camille wasn't the only one doing it. Alicia's attitude was most likely the exception. It takes a special kind of confidence to have no real concern about what might be coming at you in a boxing ring.

Even with the YouTube deterrent, I figured that in this city of nine million people there must be at least one medium-sized woman boxer over the age of thirty-five who would be willing to fight me. I was lucky enough to hear something that same morning: A fighter named Raul Frank told me his brother trained a woman who might be interested, and he would get back to me. I was hopeful that I'd find someone.

I was waiting to spar in the gym that morning when Bruce handed me the phone. It was Kate Sekules. I'd admired and enjoyed Kate's book *The Boxer's Heart*, which recounts women's first forays into Gleason's back in the early 1990s. So much was different now, and yet other things remained unchanged. It gave me a charge to be standing here in the very place she writes about, with some of the same characters milling about around me, alongside others she

Raul Frank.

hadn't mentioned, like the huge shirtless man with a head full of thick silver hair and a massive gut hanging over his satin shorts who would throw one punch at a time with a grunt and then look around to see who might be impressed. Or the man they called Pinky because, yes, he trains with a pink head guard and pink gloves and looks so feeble that I feared a breeze off the East River would knock him down.

Kate's still very English voice on the phone sounded enthusiastic but harried as we made our lunch date for the following week. Motherhood seemed to have replaced her former obsession with new concerns. Without the demands of parenthood to hold me back, I was becoming ever more entrenched in boxing, finding new points of entry and fresh ideas in it all the time. Boxing, like most arts, is nothing if not a selfish endeavor. "It's all about you, baby," was a phrase my husband, Peter, liked to taunt me with. I couldn't protest much because it was true. It *was* all about me. Why shouldn't it be?

AT GERRITSEN Beach we settled into the kitchen at our host's home. The house, which seemed to be frozen midway through a gut renovation, was owned by a heavily built but soft-spoken red-headed elevator technician Alicia called Shawno. Exposed plaster board and light switches hanging from naked wire were about all there was in the way of decor. But like any good bachelor Shawno did have all the necessary equipment for a fight night party—a huge TV, a couple of amorphous couches, and a grill on the back porch.

I quickly realized that nearly all of the women that were there had been, were, or were going to be fighters. Camille, Alicia, Angela, Ruth, and Ronica were each bona fide champions, while Jennifer Czirr, one of Alicia's aspiring boxers, was training to make her ring debut later in the year, and a tall, porcelain-complexioned girl I didn't know named Julie Anne Kelly had beaten cancer to win the Golden Gloves. There were also some women who dabbled in boxing but were primarily long-distance runners like the artist Grace Baley and another occasional boxer named Melody Yam, with whom I'd sparred.

The men were a different story, more like background characters in this drama, soft and indistinct creatures when compared to these women with their big, strong personalities and compact athletic bodies. I think it was the first time I had been at a gathering comprised mostly of women boxers and male nonboxers. None of the men, as far as I knew, had ever fought, although I couldn't be sure. The only possible fighter in the group was a longtime Gleason's regular, a guy in his fifties named Louie Shriffin.

"Did you ever fight?" I asked Louie.

"No," he replied. "I'm too scared. I don't want to be hit."

I turned to Alicia. "If you're smart, you don't get hit, right?" I said. She smiled and said, "Yeah, but he *is* a man."

I was just settling in when Melissa made her late and noisy entrance with her two barking dogs at her side, a pit bull she'd named Hagler and a little Yorkshire terrier she called Camacho, named after the two greatest welterweights of the modern era. Also in her entourage were two young girls who seemed as quiet as the dogs were loud. Melissa was in great shape, ready to fight and off the booze (she's known for her love of Coors Light), but wise cracking as much as ever. She told us Belinda was watching the fight at the Mendez gym, where she now worked, but would join us afterward.

These are my people, I thought as I looked around, each one more vivid than the next: blustery Melissa, elegant Alicia, mercurial Camille, cool and witty Ronica. They were performers, like actors, and perhaps with an extra intensity, bonded together by the transience, the uncertainty, and the physical danger. I felt that I was one of them now, an insider among the outsiders, each one of us a part of this new universe of women's boxing that had finally come into its own but wasn't yet fully recognized for what it was.

The fight was short, but still pretty remarkable and, I thought, prophetic and fitting. The underdog had won—Pacquiao, a modest Filipino who spoke broken English and who'd begun his career more than ten years earlier at a mere 107 lb. He'd beaten great fighters like Marco Antonio Barerra, Erik Morales, and Juan Marquez for the WBC title at 130 lb. He weighed in at 140 lb. for this fight. For the De La Hoya fight less than year earlier he had weighed 145 lb. Each time the pundits doubted Pacquiao would have the power to damage his naturally heavier opponents, and each time he'd proven them wrong.

Hall of Fame trainer Emanuel Steward, for example, had said, "Manny looked better than he is against Oscar and David Diaz. Oscar was dead at the weight, and Diaz is slower than most heavyweights. I think that Ricky will be too big and tough for him."

Hatton was also confident. "I'm bigger; I'm stronger . . . I'm undefeated at this weight in twelve years. At 140 pounds, I'm too strong and too big for anyone." But he was proven wrong within the first round when he went down face first from a Pacquiao right hook. Immediately, the girls at Gerritsen Beach whooped.

Close to the end of the next round, a straight left had Hatton out like a light. There was jubilation in the room all around me. Perhaps as women we'd all felt small and too weak and underestimated at one time or another, so a win for Pacquiao was a win for us too. Pacquiao winning proved that size bore little relationship to power.

ALICIA HAD almost predicted the very timing of the combination, the set-up for the left with all those vicious right hooks. It was as though she had seen it before it happened; she has this uncanny precognitive ability. It may have helped that she is also a southpaw. Whenever I sparred her I could tell she knew what I was going to do before I knew myself.

"That was beautiful," said Camille quietly as the slow-motion replay revealed Pacquiao's devastating accuracy.

"It was a knockout that will appear on highlight reels forever," wrote Thomas Hauser for Secondsout.com, "and a career-defining demolition. Hatton has a pretty good chin, and Pacquiao reduced it to English china."

I looked at my watch, concerned that it was nearly midnight. When Alicia emerged from the kitchen I was about to ask her when she was planning to leave, but she already had my bag with her and handed it to me as we made for the door.

4 THE SLICK CHICK

I was never really a patient person. Even instant gratification took too long. I had an aptitude for quite a few things in life, but I lacked the discipline needed to hone my raw talent in those things in order to become accomplished. Boxing was different, though. Aside from being physically stronger than many women, I had no obvious aptitude and was an extremely slow learner. Peter, who first introduced me to the sweet science, tells me I was hard not to hit in the beginning, so excruciatingly slow were my instincts and reflexes. I was often plagued by doubts at the worst possible times. I found it hard to think like an athlete. Talking myself into some improbable victory would have been unimaginable. The truth was I never expected to win. Just getting through a fight was enough for me. Matches were so few and far between, sometimes only two or three a year, that I never built up any momentum. Each time I fought felt like the first time, like breaking new ground all over again. Of course I see now that these mixed feelings were just symptoms of an overarching lack of confidence, a sense that as an athlete I wasn't the genuine article.

I feared that the truth would come out in devastating fashion and that I would be laughed at and humiliated. When people claimed they "couldn't wait" to get in the ring I was bewildered. I could always wait.

I wanted to look good, move well. I'd rather lose a fight looking right than win it looking clumsy or desperate. Losing the aesthetic felt like the greatest danger, a danger even greater than losing a fight—and yet losing was depressing. Losing control *and* the fight made for utter misery. It took me a while to learn that the fear of looking bad plagues most boxers, not just me. People assume that pain is what a fighter fears most. But actually it isn't. Pain is familiar and tolerable. Humiliation lurks like a hidden phantom, it can tower over you, it is mysterious and confusing. Very few fighters are willing to sacrifice their trademark style for victory.

But by May 2009 something important had changed inside me. After all the years of practice I had become a reasonably competent, if fairly dull and conventional, boxer. I knew what I was doing, and I understood the sport in a deeper way than before. I didn't feel like an interloper anymore. I'd been in the game long enough to look back and contemplate my performances. I'd concluded that I usually looked better in the gym than I did in my fights. Sparring also has its own aesthetic, just as fighting does. A fight isn't just an athletic contest, it's also a demonstration of will. You need to show how much you want to win and how hard you are willing to work. If it looks like you don't care, you can inadvertently prejudice the judges against you by giving them the impression that you don't want it badly enough. These were all things I had been oblivious to, but that had now arrived front and center in my consciousness.

I wanted the chance to redeem myself, to see if I could stand up under pressure. I wanted to see if I could fight with a level of confidence I'd never known before. I wanted to see what all the years, and particularly the nearly two years since I first came to Gleason's, amounted to. Would the technique I had been polishing in the gym desert me when I tried to concentrate on winning? The idea of fighting felt completely different to me now than it had in those early days. I trusted my body. I was less anxious. I knew exactly what was going to happen once I stepped inside the ring. Someone my weight, gender, and age was going to try to hit me in the head. Unless they pulled out an Uzi, there would be no surprises.

Being hit in the face is, at first, a terrible affront, a violation, an intrusion into personal space, an action loaded with emotional implications that go back to childhood. It's impossible at first to be detached about it. That takes practice. People don't hit you unless they are angry with you. Nor do you hit anyone else other than as a last resort. As a form of expression, hitting and being hit is about as primitive as you can get, one that's been superseded by a whole array of more rational ways of expressing your feelings. Removing all the conventional codes from the act of punching is one of the biggest breakthroughs you must make in the journey to becoming a boxer. Eventually you understand that the physical impact of being hit isn't so disturbing when there is no emotion connected to it, when it's no longer personal. That's when you can start to think like a fighter.

Now I was eager in a way I never used to be. I no longer wanted to wait. I hoped that Leila Ferioli's opponent would get sick and I would have to step in. I had been expecting to fight either Leila or Maureen, as these were the two women I'd seen fight at St. Anne's Warehouse the previous October. I visualized either a fifty-two-year-old southpaw or a slightly younger novice in orthodox stance whenever I shadowboxed back home. But it looked like neither of them was willing to fight me, and there was no one else at Gleason's who was 138 lb. and over thirty-five. In an attempt to cast the net a little wider, I found out who Maureen's last opponent had been—a fifty-three-year-old art school professor from Minnesota named Alexis Kuhr—and sent her a Facebook message.

"Honestly? I think you'd cream me," she wrote back in response to my offer. "I need a couple of more fights at least in order not to make some very stupid beginner mistakes. You have a much stronger notion of how to control the ring . . . I need at least a few more fights before I would feel I could be a good opponent for you."

She'd seen me on YouTube and, just as Camille had predicted, was deterred. A couple days later, I arrived at the gym as Leila was leaving.

"Please fight me," I blurted out.

"I don't think I have enough experience," she said.

"But I haven't fought in seven years," I said.

"But I'm forty-six," she said.

"But I'm forty-four," I said.

"Really? Oh, well then we should spar," she said.

"Yes," I said. "I'll come in any time you like."

"You'll have to check with my trainer, though," she said.

Her trainer, Stu Bakal, was a surly-looking guy who made me think of Harvey Keitel playing a New York trainer. He wore a black bandana and a muscle shirt and stood watching with his arms folded across his chest as his fighters worked the bags. He regarded me with a strained but polite smile, pretending he had no clue I might want to take on his protégée, which can't have been the case since I was sure Angela had asked him if Leila would fight me. I decided to leave it to Leila and Stu to sort out between them. I wasn't really sure of the protocol.

Despite my newfound confidence and eager anticipation, my first training session with Alicia after the weekend felt exhausting, and I wasn't sure why. Maybe she'd cast a spell on me. We began with a few rounds of jabbing and slipping. Slipping is when you move your head—and that includes your torso—to the side of a punch as it comes to you. You can slip either inside a jab and risk getting hit with your opponent's right hand if you don't move again or throw a counter punch, or you can slip to the outside, which is safer, since your opponent would have to shift position and readjust to throw more punches at you. When I started, slipping looked like an act of genius or telepathy, and I doubted I'd ever be able to do it. The boxer doing the slipping must have uncanny foresight and amazing reflexes, I thought. But then I learned that this slipping movement was all part of the dance. Boxers move anyway, punch or no punch, and so slipping is more arbitrary than it looks. I remember the day I realized this. I was sparring with an Australian bantamweight champion, a man with quick hands and good skills. When I moved my head, he missed. If he missed, I reasoned, then so might everyone else. That's when I started to fall in love with the sensation of punches gliding past me. Hearing the rush of air in their wake, I almost forgot about punching. I could spend whole rounds simply not getting hit. What I didn't do enough of was countering. When you make someone miss you are supposed to "make them pay." That means catching them open while they are throwing punches. A fighter is most vulnerable when on the attack, and slipping creates opportunities. I knew I was letting many opportunities go to waste.

After our slipping and countering drill we did three of what Alicia calls "proper rounds," which are just general sparring sessions. This essentially means Alicia performed a freeform dance in which she played the part of a black female D'Artagnan, easily anticipating my slow and feeble attempts to hit her gorgeous face and treating me like a weak but earnest child. Who could blame her? I struggled, and I was surprised to find that I was huffing and puffing to keep up. I'd been sparring a lot of active rounds at home with people like Susie

Ramadan, an up-and-coming professional bantamweight; Sarah Howett, a gifted actor, kickboxer, and boxer; and other young women, many half my age and younger. And I'd been holding my own pretty well on my good days. I hadn't needed to take rounds off to recover. But with Alicia, who was closer to my own age than anyone I sparred in Melbourne, I was feeling tired. Was it me or was it her? She seemed to be giving me no breathing space. She frustrated me with slips and counters and didn't ever give me a chance to gather myself and regain my balance before she resumed. I felt like I was plodding heavily around the ring taking slow, ineffective swipes at her. Maybe it was jetlag, a weird affliction that, nearly a week later, was still doing strange things to me. Maybe it was the six sprints I'd done up the hill to Columbia Heights the night before in the rain. Maybe it was the rain. It had been coming down in a steady stream ever since I arrived, blotting my memories of the city in the fall when clear, crisp days followed one after the other.

Alicia explained how to use tempo. She was showing me how a slow move followed by a quick punch or series of punches could catch people by surprise and put them off their game. She'd made her point in the middle of a round when she leaned slowly toward me, like she was about to say something, and then popped me with a jab. It worked beautifully, her movement acting like a decoy.

She also told me it was important to make an opponent worry about one side and then change sides. Like Pacquiao had made Hatton worry about his right hook and then knocked him out with a straight left. I liked it when Alicia talked tactics. That added a whole new layer to the game. I'd never considered using tempo as a decoy before. After the session we stood and watched as two welterweights climbed into one of the rings. Alicia was one of the best people to watch sparring with because she could unpack the action with her learned observations.

"I like this kid," she said. "He sometimes seems slow, but he's very accurate and then he can speed up." Then she added, more quietly, "But he takes too many punches." The boxer she referred to was landing quick and accurate left jabs on his more aggressive opponent.

"This kid," Alicia said of his opponent, "holds his left too low. That's why he's got a black eye."

I thought about my own lazy left and wondered if I would ever get it back in time to block the counter. Or was I like the black-eyed boy, unable to think of more than one thing at a time?

Her favorite was proving her right, throwing slow curved rights and then shooting out one-two combinations that were straight and true and hit the mark.

It did seem to me that the boys sparred harder in this gym than the women did, most of the boys anyway. Or was it just that men really do hit harder after all?

Maureen Shea usually sparred a small black man called Sugar who hardly touched her. But I had also seen Belinda and Melissa slug it out mercilessly, two women battling in the trenches without giving up an inch, the men who were watching shaking their heads in dismay. As we turned, I noticed Melissa in one of the other rings doing some rounds with Sugar.

It looked a little unbalanced. "He doesn't put you under any pressure," Alicia said quietly.

Sparring with men, whatever people say, can never be a genuine test. Early on, I sparred with men because it was the only option. Now I did so only as a last resort. I couldn't understand why any woman would do it unless there was no other choice, which was certainly not the case at Gleason's, a gym full of such talented women. Notions that it would make you tougher or better prepared didn't wash with me. You either get a merciless beating from an overpowering foe or no punch lands on you. Sparring with a man brings you physically closer to him than you would normally get other than in intimate situations, but it really only mimics the action of a fight in a very diluted way. You feel each other's breath and hear each other's involuntary animal sounds. It can seem like an odd simulation of incongruous, intimate activities—violence, dancing, sex—without really resembling any of them. That can make it interesting, but not necessarily useful.

As the week marched along and I tried to get my body clock calibrated, I asked Raul Frank each day, "Have you heard anything yet?" He had offered to talk to his brother, who trained a woman who might be willing to fight me.

And every day he'd say, "I'll know more tomorrow."

I liked Raul. Originally from Guyana, he had coincidentally been the first person I ever sparred at Gleason's. The only man, as it turned out, once I saw for the first time with my own amazed eyes how good the women really were.

I had been training alone one afternoon when he made the offer. Raul was a top-ten rated International Boxing Federation (IBF) light middleweight, and he hit the bags hard. But I knew it would be safer for me to spar with him than with another woman, even if he had twice gone twelve rounds with Vernon Forrest for a world title. I'd seen Belinda and Ann-Marie go at it, and I was more worried about how I'd fare with either of them than with Raul. Belinda seemed to have an infinite variety of moves and was capable of doing what seemed like endless rounds. I'd counted close to twenty one morning. Ann-Marie was built like a man or at least, as Alicia described her, a cute boy. She had been getting ready for a major fight and was as lean as a lioness with the strongest, longest-looking torso I'd ever seen on a woman.

As I'd anticipated, Raul wasn't about to buck convention and try to knock my head off. After three or four tippy-tap rounds he said to me, "You should fight. You've got the talent. You just need some conditioning."

Flattered, but panting hard, I thanked him but declined the invitation to run with him around Prospect Park. I knew how slow I was, and he was clearly in top shape. He had stepped into the ring thirty-eight times and had won twenty-eight of those encounters, putting fourteen opponents to the ground in the process.

He had never won a world title, but in 1997 he gained a split-decision victory over Purcell Miller for the United States Boxing Association (USBA) welterweight title, and then in 2004 he won the IBF welter- and middleweight Latino titles.

The next time I saw Alicia she said, "I hear you sparred Raul."

"Oh," I said sheepishly. "He was just playing with me."

She smiled her signature sunbeam smile and said, "That's what we would all do." I didn't know whether to be reassured or insulted. Not only was I going to be babied by a man, the women were going to baby me as well?

NOW, NEARLY two years after that first visit, fight night was fast approaching, and still no one had come out of the woodwork for me to fight. I'd gone from one extreme to the other, from not being taken seriously to being taken more seriously than was perhaps warranted. As my eyes searched for Raul, who was always in a hurry, carrying arms full of equipment here and there, New York began to feel like a very small place. The endless moving carpet of people on the streets and the subways felt like an illusion, like some kind of rent-a-crowd. The only people who mattered to me were women over the age of thirty-five who weighed 138 lb. and were willing to step into a boxing ring. But there seemed to be none. If I wanted to, I could have started constructing my delusions of grandeur right there.

"They're all running scared," said Peter when I described the situation to him. I couldn't quite believe that, but maybe they were.

One night, on a Masters website, I found a female boxing page under construction, with only one woman who had a picture to go with her profile listed, but she was too light for me and too far away, in Colorado Springs. I found another profile with at least a name, a weight, and a location: Sarah Gregory from New York at 132 lb. She was nearby and not too far off in terms of weight. Then I logged on to the message board and found this:

> I'm also looking for an opponent for Ringside
> this year. I'd hate to travel so far and not get the
> opportunity to compete. Still no fights. Where
> are the female masters these days?
> Age: 48 years, Weight: 145, Bouts: 0

The message was from "JackieNJ."

Where are they all? Jackie, they're right here!

I skipped into Gleason's the next day with hope in my heart and excitedly told Bruce and Angela about Sarah and JackieNJ.

"That would be Jackie Atkins from New Jersey," said Bruce.

How small was this world? I wondered.

"She's in tremendous shape," he said. "She has the most incredible physique."

"How many bouts has she had?" I asked.

"None," said Bruce.

"It says she weighs 145 pounds."

"And she's one of the nicest people you'll ever meet."

Angela sent both Jackie and Sarah e-mails regarding the show. I headed out onto the gym floor where Alicia was straddling one of the sit-up contraptions that no one used, next to one of the rubbermen torsos that also seemed neglected. She was reading the paper.

"I think I found someone to fight," I said. "Jackie from New Jersey."

Alicia put down her newspaper and looked up at me.

"Jackie Atkins?" she said. "Oh, she's very strong. She's one of those big girls that comes right at you. Every time we have a clinic Bruce gets me to spar her."

"Maybe she's too heavy then," I said.

Alicia shook her head. "I wouldn't recommend Jackie," she said.

"Hmm," I said, feeling my spirits deflate. "Alright then, forget Jackie."

That night, still unwilling to accept that I had come all this way for nothing, I sent a message to Bonnie Canino in Florida telling her of my problem. I told her I was even willing to pay part of the airfare if she could find someone I could fight.

Bonnie "The Cobra" Canino had been one of the names I'd read about on the WBAN website all those years ago, when I started investigating the possibility that there were other women boxers in the world. I'd looked at pictures of her in the 1990s with her mop of brown curls and chiseled washboard stomach. I finally met her in 2008, when I flew down from New York to Florida to spend a few days working with her. She'd run the National Women's Golden Gloves tournament in Florida for the previous five years and was well connected with fighters and trainers all over the country. At one stage she and Alicia had fought each other. She'd also fought Lucia "The Striker" Rijker, and there was footage on YouTube of her sparring Christy Martin. Bonnie had fought the best and was a world champion, and today she is recognized as a pioneer and a crucial player in the continued growth of the sport.

Bonnie responded saying she knew a woman who was ready to fight since she was already training for the Golden Gloves in July. She would get back to me.

By now I had moved from a slicker converted warehouse about half a mile away with a nice young man called Evan to a sixth floor walk-up on Plymouth Street in DUMBO. It was closer to the gym but also perhaps too close to the Manhattan Bridge. It was almost possible to reach out and touch it from the window. I loved the view across to the city and the slightly grungy entrance that still retained some of the area's industrial past. The nearby trains went clattering through my sleep like a herd of stampeding elephants.

I paced around my loft, stopping to shadowbox in front of the full-length mirror, the reflection of the East River glittering like a lamé cloth behind me.

"I'LL ASk him again and let you know tomorrow," said Raul the next day as he rushed out the door with an armful of leather punch pads, belts, and head guards piled so high I almost couldn't see his face. Was it me or did Raul seem to be looking a little bit stooped all of a sudden?

I poked my head in the door of the office and asked Bruce when Angela would be in. "Lemme see," he said, looking at the schedule pinned to the wall. "She's supposed to start work at two, so I would expect to see her maybe around four."

Although Bruce dressed mostly in shades of beige and had the low-key demeanor of a conventional businessman, he also had an appreciation for the more colorful and less conventional traits of

Angela's dog Brooklyn wearing a Gleason's t-shirt.

others. He'd been in the boxing world for a long time and had at one stage been a USA Boxing official. Angela was his right-hand woman. He described her in his e-mails as "New York's Finest Matchmaker." She was a former salsa dancer, with a great mane of wavy auburn hair and large expressive eyes. For a long time I had trouble connecting the woman who sat at the computer wearing glasses during the week with the woman who sparred with such idiosyncratic flair on Saturday mornings. The year before, I had changed my flight and was without accommodations for a couple of days. Angela generously offered me her bed while she and her beloved black-and-white pit bull named Brooklyn slept on the couch. Brooklyn would often trail her around the gym. If she lost sight of her owner, she would wear a bereft expression until she had Angela back in her sights and would then trot gaily toward her. I once saw Angela sitting on the ring apron with Brooklyn's front paws on her shoulders; they were quietly gazing at each other with unqualified love while all around them people were shouting, sweating, and hitting each other.

There were already more than twenty bouts on the card, and Angela was telling everyone that the show was full. My unbending optimism was being tested. Back home Peter had cautioned me against this very scenario. "Don't be such a naysayer," I'd said. After all, until I actually turned up everyone had seemed so sure of getting me a match. I'd already seen two potential opponents with my own eyes so I knew they existed. But my frustration was starting to ratchet up a level each day. I was trying to keep training as if I were going to fight, but something wasn't feeling quite right. On my previous visit to Gleason's everything had felt perfectly synchronized—my skills improved just from being there and women my weight appeared from nowhere to spar. It was as though someone had orchestrated it all so that I would be lulled into believing it would be a simple matter to pair up for a fight when it wasn't.

"Americans are all 'can do' until it comes to the crunch," I moaned to Peter. "And now they're all 'can't do.'"

I went back to the gym in the afternoon to see if Angela had heard anything. I was starting to feel like her stalker. I lived so close by that it now took me longer to climb the six flights of stairs to my apartment than it did to walk from Plymouth to Front Street. The stair climb could only do me good since my gym time was dribbling away trying to get my knuckles turned over exactly right. That was another problem. I felt like I was training for an Origami contest and wasn't getting enough of a physical workout.

Could I be going backward? Alicia seemed more pedantic than ever. It was as if only one punch in ten was meeting her approval. If I wasn't pulling my punch back too soon, I was pushing it. If I wasn't winding it up before I threw it, I was failing to turn the knuckle over sufficiently. I was beginning to wonder how much this minutiae was going to matter when I was in the ring with some crazy woman trying to knock my head off, when the cool choreography of padwork was replaced by the anarchy of a fight.

Then Alicia's brother Devon had a go at adjusting the trajectory of my punch. If I'd thought Alicia was fussy, Devon raised pedantry to a whole new level. It obviously ran in the family. This small, heavily dreadlocked Jamaican man with a deep baritone voice could certainly hit hard, but I was starting to believe the adage about not being able to teach old dogs new tricks. Surely, after all these years, what I was doing wasn't so wrong? Why not cut me a little slack?

At least both Devon and Alicia knew exactly when to dispel my rising aggravation with a joke. Or the simple word, "right," would quickly dissipate my murderous thoughts. I was pretty easy to placate, really.

A group of Norwegians had arrived at the same time as me, and Alicia was telling me we all had similar technical problems, which ultimately amounted to too much forward movement. But then Alicia is not a come-forward fighter. She glides smoothly on her nimble dancer's legs and hits her opponents as she changes direction, before they even realize they have fallen for a trap. She had been teaching herself to fight inside, forcing herself to stay in range, and from what I saw, was doing a good job of it. But her natural inclination is to be slippery and elusive. Finishing people off seems a little undignified to her. It is better to slice away at their confidence bit by bit, like pulling the wings off a fly.

Alicia's other brother, Maurice Ashley, is a chess grandmaster, the first black American to earn this title. She once invited me to an event at the Malcolm X & Dr. Betty Shabazz Memorial and Education Center, the place where Malcolm X had been shot, for an afternoon honoring young chess players. All of a sudden I was given the chance to sidestep through a little window into a world of black pride and civil rights history. I was grateful for my boxing connections because without them, whatever windows there might be into the lives of others in New York or anywhere else, I would never get a chance to step through them. I've never been a very good tourist. The whole idea of tourism depresses me. Every time I saw a sightseeing bus drive through the streets of New York I felt relieved not to be on it. The closest I ever got to the Statue of Liberty was seeing it from the Brooklyn Heights Promenade during the sprinting and jogging parts of my workout. I was much more interested in seeing things I hadn't seen before, like twenty chess-obsessed black kids receiving encouragement from adult civil rights warriors. I was reminded of Barack Obama and of the view his rise to prominence provided of a black America that was refined, intellectual, and gracious—one that would at last blow the tiresome, insulting clichés away. Maurice and his wife, Michele, a public-school principal in Bedford Stuyvesant, appeared cut from the same cloth as the Obamas; they are well educated, civic minded, and warm.

Alicia's boxing style is a unique blend of her astonishing physical talent and her rare innate intelligence. Only an extremely smart person is able to think so many moves ahead in a boxing ring. In

Maurice's arena of chess, that sort of approach is an obvious prerequisite, but in boxing it is what elevates some fighters above the pack, and it makes Alicia very special. Devon, a world kickboxing champion known for his ring-craft as well as his power, is just as gifted. Each of these three siblings clearly possesses a special physical and mental synergy that sets them apart. Nevertheless, I was starting to crave a mindless punch pad workout just the same, just to get my heart rate up a little.

KATE SEKULES eventually came to the gym in the middle of a training session one morning. She said she was too rushed to have lunch but thought she'd come to the gym while she had a moment. I stopped so we could sit down on one of the benches and talk. We'd led parallel lives in many ways, although in opposite hemispheres, and I was keen to swap notes. Quite a bit of time had passed, probably fifteen years, since she had first set foot in Gleason's as a young and single career journalist. Although she'd lived in New York all that time, her English accent was still strong and clipped.

"We were really seeing history!" she said, speaking of those years a decade and a half ago. And it was true. No one at the time could have anticipated where women's boxing would go. It could have just as easily faded away as it had so many times before.

Sekules' book, *The Boxer's Heart*, was probably one of the main reasons I'd chosen to come to Gleason's in the first place. It was my favorite out of a spate of female boxing memoirs that had been published roughly at the same time, including the more earnest *Kill the Body, the Head Will Fall* by Rene Denfeld, which examined broader cultural ideas about women and violence and exposed the hypocrisy and contradictions of 1980s feminism. There was also a rather ghastly, almost vindictive book, *Looking for a Fight* by Lynn Snowden Picket, that painted a grim picture of Gleason's and cast Hector Roca as a sleazy sadist. But in Kate's book the characters were rendered lovingly in vivid and often hilarious portraits. The gym in the 1990s was frequented by only a small group of women very uncertain of their own and each other's physical limitations. I still open the book at random pages to find myself absorbed anew. Each time I discover some detail that has since become a familiar part of my own experience of Gleason's, except that, unlike the old days, the women—young, old, and in between—are everywhere now. They're the trainers as well as the fighters, the amateurs, and the pros. And there are teenage girls at Gleason's who have never for one second questioned their right to be there.

As a fighter, Kate herself had taken it all the way to the Legendary Blue Horizon in Philadelphia as a pro. Fifteen years later, she seemed to have shed her boxer's skin and frankly looked a little out of place in what had once been her second home. She spoke enthusiastically of her time at Gleason's and had even returned in recent months for some training sessions. But, a bit like a recovering alcoholic returning to a bar where she had once spent many long nights, she looked like she didn't want to want it.

I suggested she train with Alicia, but she seemed hesitant. I thought it might be because the dynamics of a woman training with another woman didn't seem right to her. Part of what initially makes boxing so compelling to some women, myself included, is its status as a masculine stronghold. You get a little rush from having made your way inside, and participating in the rites of passage required to stay there can be glorious (the broken nose, the black eye, the creaking jaw). Being taught and guided by a man can seem almost romantic, with all that attention focused on you. But while that's all very seductive in the beginning, something else eventually takes its place.

I had always imagined a time when boxing could genuinely be a women's sport and not just an occasional macho sidetrack for adventurous tomboys. And I'd always imagined as part of that fantasy that the trainers would be women, not men. Although it was a man who

Yuko Yamamoto.

spent the most time with me initially, I sometimes doubted how good men in general would allow you to be and how many of them would see only your feminine limitations. I felt I could learn more from watching another woman box, particularly if she boxed well. Boxers like Lucia Rijker, with her explosive power, and Alicia, with her speed and creativity, had already shown me the standard to reach for. Things had definitely changed since Kate's time when Jill "The Zion Lion" Matthews, who described boxing as "the punk rock of sports," had declared that as soon as it was normal for women, "I'm outta here." And the feisty flyweight was indeed long gone. While I identified with her and with Kate as well, that beginner boxer part of me was gone. Like any long-term relationship, things had shifted and changed as the years had gone by.

Slick was starting to test my happy little fantasy of a women's boxing utopia, however. I was beginning to think she was the toughest, most demanding trainer I'd ever encountered. She was just so damn hard to please. "Don't push it, flick it. Don't pull it back before it lands. No, you didn't turn it over. Don't lean. Where's your other hand?" (Slap.) "Now relax it." Between her and the empty space where my opponent's name would be, I was getting more and more dispirited. As Saturday approached I consoled myself with the hope that at the very least I would be able to vent some of my frustration with a good, hard sparring session. Past Saturdays had offered many different sparring partners and a decent workout.

Instead I found myself in the ring with Devon, who far from using his obvious power and refined technique, spent his time throwing an irritating barrage of unorthodox and frankly wrong punches, designed only to aggravate. He didn't look very tidy and didn't seem to even notice the punches hitting him. He just kept tossing them like we were having a snowball fight. It made me even more confused about how I would fare the following weekend. You could almost guarantee that there was no woman on earth who would fight me the same way that Devon sparred. In fact, there were probably few men who would either. All I really wanted was to jump in the ring with some approximation of what I was likely to encounter and have a decent, realistic dress rehearsal for May 16. But it wasn't proving easy to get what I wanted.

Later that day I received a sliver of hope from Yuko Yamamoto. I'd seen her around the gym before, but we'd never spoken. Her smiling face was on one of the many photos I admired lining the locker room walls. She was grinning ear to ear with a medal around her neck. It looked like a candid shot taken moments after she had stepped from the ring. Yuko told me she had a friend who weighed 132–35 lb. and had been ready to fight but her opponent had dropped out. She had reached the semifinals of the Golden Gloves and had fought in about ten matches but was too old now and didn't want to go pro. It sounded like a pretty fair match—competitive but not too daunting.

I told Alicia about it and said, "Now I'm starting to feel nervous."

"About what?" she asked.

"Fighting."

"Why? I thought that's what you came here to do."

5 BIG HAT, NO CATTLE

DAYS PASSED, and Yuko's friend, a woman named Kaori, still hadn't confirmed. I hadn't heard any news from Angela about Sarah Gregory either. And not a peep from Raul. I was also still waiting for some word from Bonnie in Florida about a woman named Michelle Straka, whose trainer claimed she wasn't fit to fight. Straka, however, contradicted her trainer and told Bonnie that she was indeed in shape and ready. I felt like I was in some kind of twisted dating game.

I still nursed the hope that everyone would say "yes" all at the same time, and then I could take my pick.

In the meantime, though, I felt like a wallflower watching everyone else get to dance while I sat hopefully on the sidelines. It reminded me of the years I'd spent in one of Melbourne's roughest, blood-house gyms where the trainer, Keith Ellis, the brother of the former IBF junior lightweight champ Lester Ellis, sometimes appeared to run the place for his own sadistic entertainment. I had watched as men and boys staggered out of the ring, their T-shirts stained pink with blood, while I wondered when it would be my turn to also get the living crap beaten out of me. It was in that gym, known as The Champ Camp, that I had my nose broken when I walked into a punch thrown almost reluctantly by a bantamweight named Nathan Sting who notoriously "couldn't crack an egg." I nearly fainted when I realized that my nose had slid across my face to where my cheekbone was. The trainer, who himself had a nose that seemed to fold over, pressed his thumb against the cartilage of my nose to force it back into place. I remember hearing a creaking sound and being surprised at how little it actually hurt.

"We're teaching her to sniff around corners," he'd announced to the cackling group.

Unlike the old days, by the summer of 2009 I knew what another female could do in the ring. Sparring with women fighters was no longer merely an abstract idea—a pastiche of film noir, my own imagination, and clips of Mike Tyson felling the bum of the month. Sparring is important preparation for a fight. You need it to learn how to time your defensive moves, to push your aerobic conditioning, to reassure yourself on all kinds of levels, and to adapt to whatever someone else brings into play. Boxing can sometimes feel like an obsessive-compulsive disorder in that you go over the same old ground over and over and over again. As Gerald Early writes in *The Culture of Bruising*, scratch the surface of any athlete and you'll find a potential obsessive. A professional athlete can be as boring, he says, as the single-minded stockbroker, "burrowing with all the grace and tenacious Faustian drive of a mad squirrel towards the epiphany of some truly profound irrelevancy."

Because of that, microcosms of unrelenting simplicity, places like boxing gyms, can seem like oases. Indeed, time spent in boxing gyms has often helped me clear my mind or distract me from difficult problems. It can be a very effective way to recalibrate your priorities. Boxing can present you with an immediacy that supplants everything else in your life, sweeping it off the table. In *On Boxing* Joyce Carol Oates reflects that to write about boxing is to write not just about oneself, but to contemplate "the perimeters of civilization—what it is, or should be, to be 'human.'" The experience is quite different from inside the ropes. There, boxing has a reductive effect. Once you step through those ropes, civilization as you know it recedes. What goes on in the ring isn't even a metaphor. It is exactly what it is.

Oates says, "the writer contemplates his opposite in the boxer, who is all public display, all risk and, ideally, improvisation: he will know his limit in a way that the writer, like all artists, never quite knows his limit—for we who write live in a kaleidoscopic world of ever-shifting assessments and judgments, unable to determine whether it is revelation or supreme self-delusion that fuels our most crucial efforts."

Elsewhere in her now-classic essay Oates speculates that the appeal of boxing for the writer comes also from the desire to offer a place on the page to the fighters themselves, who are, she says, often "characters in the literary sense of the word. Extravagant fictions without a structure to contain them." This idea was hitting home right now.

Although I didn't want to be outside the ropes, I was comforted that at least as a writer I had so many "extravagant fictions" before me. But when I thought about it, I realized that in the well-known works of such authors as William Hazlitt, A. J. Liebling, and Norman Mailer, these characters have always been male. The flamboyant literary types that peopled the pages of Liebling's *The Sweet Science*, Pierce Egan's *Boxiana*, and Mailer's *The Fight* came from only one side of the gender divide. Even contemporary boxing writers like Thomas Hauser never mention the women, and they're missing a great story. What I noticed more and more was that the women in the sport are just as vivid and just as worthy of being provided with some literary structure to contain them. If the men can be credited with carrying so much that is fundamental to the human condition, why should the women be any different? Maybe their presence would help expand our understanding.

And these were female characters who, at last, didn't depend on their sexuality or their position in relation to male characters to define them as people. They weren't competing for male attention or for accolades for their beauty or subservience. They weren't being valued for their support or their assistance. They stood alone, and they were strong, self-contained, and utterly unapologetic.

On Saturday, a week before Gleason's fight night, I watched Keisha "Fire" McLeod-Wells—the woman who had held her wedding ceremony in the gym—spar Dominga Olivo.

I'd first met Fire when I visited the gym in 2007. Bruce had introduced her as "one of our fighters." I had looked her up and down in disbelief. She was a sassy twig of a black girl, carrying a clipboard, strutting along in high heels, made up, hair done, fingernails manicured and color coordinated in pink and lavender, jewelry clinking, and smiling a hostess smile.

"I fight with Team Freeform," she had told me on that visit. "I'm one of the elite fighters."

Fire had recently turned pro, after winning every conceivable medal and belt and trophy available to her as an amateur, and was preparing for her second fight in Panama at the end of the month. I'd never had more than short conversations with her, mostly related to banal practical matters, like buying gloves and paying gym dues. Her corner locker in the changing room was the most girled-up of all the lockers, festooned with the kind of decorations you'd see in a teenage girl's bedroom—magnetized letters, a purple loofah, a picture of herself with the words "Bad News" written on it wearing a hot pink shirt and pink hand wraps and holding up her fists. Somehow she had made boxing seem like the very pinnacle of fem-

ininity, as if it were a sport all little girls naturally dreamed of
excelling at one day.

The year before I'd seen her call a halt to an unofficial Mixed Martial Arts show that had occurred when some college kids invaded the
gym one Saturday afternoon. The gang had exploited the ten dollar
spectator charge at Gleason's to stage their own show. But the com-
batants were an ill-matched ragtag bunch, and although their antics
had the boxers laughing and gawking, things began to get a little wild.
Some of them had dispensed with head guards and were wearing
small MMA-style gloves, laying into one another on the ground like
they were in a street fight. Eventually Fire decided she'd seen enough.

Standing up to their pleas and threats, Fire stopped the show.

"That's it," she'd said and hustled about fifty of them out of the
gym, all 110 lb. of her.

Dominga Olivo, a former amateur star and veteran of twelve pro
bouts, was training to fight the Canadian Jeannine Garside at 126 lb.
Dominga, the mother of two, is originally from the Dominican
Republic. Her boxing style, like her English, is basic and without a
lot of range. She wore black leggings and a T-shirt featuring Barack
Obama framed by an American flag, in stark contrast to Fire's all-
red getup. From what I saw, Dominga sparred to kill, as if anything
less were grounds for getting fired. Her trainer, a stout, gray-haired
man with a beard and cap, was shouting to her in Spanish. She blew
my theory about restrained skill being the primary aesthetic at
Gleason's. She grunted like a woodchopper wielding an ax, each
punch landing with an emphatic thud.

I'd already seen Dominga in a documentary on her Golden
Gloves showdown with Melissa Hernandez in which she first
appears with her long black hair tied back tight, sitting demurely in
her lounge room sorting through her golden glove necklaces,
awarded for each of the tournaments she had won. "Two tousand
two, two tousand tree, two tousand four."

But the fight footage doesn't really convey her heavy-handed intensity in the ring.

This was the first time I had seen Fire, whose best weapon was a long chopstick of a jab, under such pressure. And I was impressed by how she took Dominga's punches. She stood up to the barrage with an unflappable stoicism, which was remarkable given that she was the lighter of the two. She also looked much better than she had in the past, despite taking some hits. I knew about her impressive record, but she had struck me, when I'd watched her spar, as a little untidy, even a little bit stiff. One of Gleason's male fighters suggested to me that Team Freeform's style was weird or unorthodox, and so their unsuspecting opponents were often thrown. This was their secret weapon. But Fire was beginning to look less weird since she had begun training with Mark Breland, the former Olympian, and developing a more pleasing style of boxing. She had certainly developed her image to perfection anyway. Each sparring session was also a kind of fashion parade. She usually color coordinated the whole shebang, right down to her socks. And more often than not she would spar in a skirt rather than shorts and would never wear the same costume twice.

Fire's former teammate Emily Kramer speculated on her blog about the contradictions and difficulties of maintaining a feminine aura in such a male space.

"It takes gall to express unapologetic femininity in the city center of machismo," Emily wrote. "The pink gloves worn in the tough-girl charade are no less flippant than my 'pretty face' under the raggedy headgear—simply a true expression of what is. A former teammate, Cara, lost her false eyelash during sparring in one of my favorite spectator moments. She simply flicked it off into the spit bucket alongside the snot, the blood. Kept on trucking."

This is exactly what Fire did when the big-punching Dominga was coming at her. She kept on trucking and showed herself to be a genuine survivor.

Later that day I watched Ronica Jeffrey spar a tall blonde novice who was matched for May 16 in my weight class in what was to be her first fight. I guessed she was probably less than half my age, maybe around eighteen. When I saw Ronica spar her it confirmed all my suspicions that Ronica was one talented customer. She was good at getting inside the reach of the tall, blonde girl. She did it in smooth increments with no extraneous movements. She boxed just how I wanted to box, in fact, as if it were all just a walk in the park. She had excellent balance, a great hook, and a really quick, effective jab. She moved her body and could feint and then move her body again and let the punch pop out, her intentions always well concealed. And no punches were wasted. She was energy efficient, accurate, and appeared totally relaxed.

The following Monday, I did finally manage to spar some rounds with Sunshine at Mendez Gym on Fifth Avenue, but it was what happened later that I found more interesting. After Sunshine left I watched two fourteen-year-olds, Michelle and Kristina, get ready to spar. Michelle was wearing a pink T-shirt and Kristina was in black. I had chatted with them both in the changing room. I remembered them from the night of the Hatton vs. Pacquiao fight at Shawn's place in Gerritsen Beach when they had been among Melissa's crew. I also remembered Michelle from my first visit in 2007 as a slightly surly looking girl with long straight hair that framed her face with sharp bangs. I'd watched her in the ring in what could well have been her first sparring session.

Now Michelle was moving like a cool veteran, slipping and popping out the jab against her less experienced opponent, who was coming straight for her, stalking her, but with low hands and not much head movement, her face a wide open target for Michelle's jabs. Kristina was getting a little demoralized but kept on trying. Eventually she went down from a good, accurate, and straight right hand from Michelle, who swaggered to the neutral corner with such cool nonchalance that Belinda threw her head back and laughed.

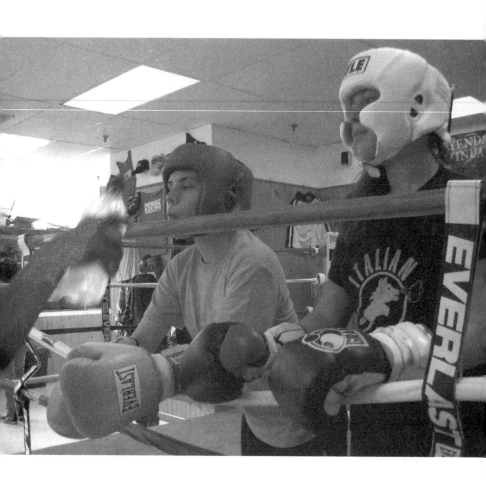

Michelle and Kristina.

When Kristina hit the deck it reminded me of the embryonic phase of my life as a boxer. I had ventured with my trainer for the first time to another gym to spar strangers, a bunch of women who had traveled there from a rural town. Within about thirty seconds of the start of my first round I was on the canvas, caught by an overhand right that had capitalized on my perpetually low left hand. Although I was completely rattled by the incident, I bounced back onto my feet almost immediately. It had all happened so fast that I wasn't sure if I'd missed a chunk of time and had, in fact, been lying there unconscious for a while, twitching and punching the air as so many boxers continue to do even when they're out cold, knocked off their feet like wind-up dolls, engines still whirring. When I think back on it now, I can see I had been felled by my performance anxiety more than by my opponent. I'd left the ring feeling a bit traumatized, and someone else took my place while I recovered. It took me days, if not weeks to process what had happened. Actually, it probably took me years. The experience had been *the* pivotal moment for me, the point at which I came to understand at my very core what was truly at stake. The turmoil within comprised a potent mix of distress, humiliation, and many different and disorienting facets of existential pain, but no actual physical pain. I wailed in the car on the way home and moaned and snuffled through the evening, cursing my feeble character, my lack of genuine toughness and courage. Almost every encounter in the ring that followed was an attempt to atone for that lack. Perhaps I am *still* looking to atone for it every time I am given an opportunity to prove that I am calm under fire, that I am brave and able to remain composed.

I could see tears trying to push their way out of Kristina, but she wasn't ready to quit. After the spar she went through some drills on the pads with the trainer Leon "The Cat" Taylor, but she had trouble looking him in the face. I could see the battle raging within her. It was a whole new fight for her now, the one against her own emotions. She had to hold off on the tears to keep going. She had to fight to stop herself from running out into the Manhattan streets, far away from the unbearable rawness of boxing.

"No," implored Leon. "Why you standing there? Move your head. If you don't move your head, I'm going to rip it right off."

He was hard on her, but in a kind way, as if he knew she was working through complex feelings. She was processing it all at about ten times the pace I'd managed when I was twice her age. Belinda shrugged. "It's the only way to learn," she said.

As I watched I wondered if I would have been as up to it as a fourteen-year-old. I doubt it. I often lament my late start, but maybe I wouldn't have been capable of dealing with all that boxing tossed in my direction any sooner, maybe my late start was the earliest I could have started.

"You've got a big heart," I said to Kristina, and for a second there she almost cracked a smile. Then her eyes darted to the window, still searching for some kind of escape. I really hoped I would see her inside the ring again one day.

The next day I'd had lunch with WBAN writer Bernie McCoy, a large, ruddy-faced man with snow-white hair who carried a battered bag and still seemed like the native Brooklynite he was although he'd moved to White Plains. He'd been a sports reporter, and when he retired he'd looked around for a niche and decided on women's boxing, which was woefully underreported. Very quickly he'd come to appreciate the sport and to know it and all the players inside out. It was strange listening to this septuagenarian old-school male sports scribe who you expect would regard women's boxing as an abomination. Instead he had nothing but the highest regard for the athletes and an intimate knowledge of their various abilities as well as a lot of strong opinions about how the sport was run. He also had an endless collection of colorful one-liners for any occasion.

When I told him of my frustrations he'd said, "Well, ya know they've got a saying in Texas, 'Big hat, no cattle.'"

In the next twenty-four hours I learned that Sarah Gregory "wasn't ready" and that neither was Yuko's friend, who said she would be ready for the next show, by which time I would be back in Australia. Raul's brother's boxer had said that she "wasn't in the right frame of mind," or something like that.

I was going through the list with Angela in the office when Gleason's fight manager Damon de Barry said, "Oh, no, she doesn't want to fight."

"Who?" I asked.

"That woman that Raul's brother trains. She hassled me for a fight on Fire's undercard, and then I got her a match and she said she didn't want it."

Big hat, no cattle.

That night, on Bonnie Canino's advice, I rang a few South Florida gyms looking for Michelle Straka's trainer, a guy called Dave Marks, to try to persuade him to let her fight me.

A woman at one gym said that she saw Michelle sometimes. I told her my problem and that I was even willing to help pay for her airfare to New York.

"Dave's the one to talk to," she said. "But he probably thinks she's gonna get beat up."

When I finally got Dave on the phone, he said, "Oh no, Michelle's been very, very sick for some time and won't be competing at all."

This sounded to me like all the other excuses I'd been hearing. They were all beginning to sound feeble and faint and tinny in just about the same way. Hadn't it occurred to any of these fighters and trainers that I'd traveled ten thousand miles alone and plunged myself into completely unknown territory among strangers and mere acquaintances, not to mention a time zone that reversed my circadian rhythms and made getting proper rest almost impossible?

Who was the one taking the risks here? Why did people say they wanted to fight when actually they didn't?

"Oh, I have a good friend who wants to fight in the Masters," said Liz O'Donovan, an Irish nurse who trains with Devon.

"Really?" I said. "Will she be ready by the sixteenth?"

"I think so," she answered. "Her name's Jackie."

"Jackie?" I said, my heart sinking. "Is she from New Jersey?"

"Yeah, that's right," said Liz.

Now I was going around in circles—and finally becoming resigned to the possibility that I might not be fighting after all.

A couple of days later at the gym I noticed Alicia talking to a vivacious black woman in a baseball cap. I remembered seeing her the week before, and in fact, I also remembered her from the year before. Back then I was talking with Alicia when I got scooped up in a squealing group hug with the vivacious black woman, the trainer Don Saxby, Alicia, and myself.

"Hey, Mischa," said Alicia. "You've met Jackie, haven't you?"

Suddenly, the penny dropped.

"You're Jackie from New Jersey?" I said. "Of course, yes, we've met before."

She smiled a huge, sunny smile. And I stood smiling back.

So *this* was Jackie. Why had I thought she was white? As I stood with her and Alicia chatting, I noticed Alicia sizing us up, her eyes making a discreet assessment of us both. Jackie was built like a sprinter and looked to be in tremendous physical shape. I couldn't imagine Alicia putting me in the same class physically.

Jackie walked away to continue training, and Alicia said, "You know, I think if you really want to fight on Saturday, then you should fight her. She's strong, but your movement is good. Your jab is good. I think it'll be all right. So why not?"

It wasn't exactly a ringing endorsement but was enough for me. Alicia must have reconsidered her opinion of me based on what she had seen over the previous ten days. And that was ironic because I felt that I had been gradually sliding into some kind of torpor. My aerobic fitness had deteriorated, my movements were sluggish, and my snap and stamina had worsened.

But despite Jackie's imposing physical presence, I did have more experience and that was worth a lot.

And if I was to lose, so what? The odds were stacked against me anyway.

When Alicia asked Jackie, she agreed, the only qualifier being that she would be a little late for the weigh-in.

"That's OK, just tell Angela," Alicia said.

"Wow," I said to Alicia as Jackie walked off to the locker room. "She didn't even hesitate, did she? She didn't even look at me twice. She didn't ask me anything about my history or my weight or anything."

"I'm going to AC on Friday night, though," said Jackie on her way out of Gleason's. "I got ringside tickets. I thought I wasn't fighting so I could relax."

"You party hard then," I said to her.

"I'm takin' you with me, girl," she replied with a shriek and was gone. AC was Atlantic City, of course, and Friday night was the night before our upcoming fight at Gleason's. Bruce had been right. Jackie seemed like a really likeable person.

At night, Gleason's was a different world. In the morning, when most fighters trained, it was intimate enough to be the setting for a sitcom like *Cheers*: banter and repartee ricocheting; the recurring visual themes like the Guyanan John Douglas in his bandana and baseball cap (which he always wore backward) smiling at every woman with a pulse, a couple of guys playing dominoes, Hector tying someone's gloves, Maureen Shea shadowboxing, a delivery of water bottles arriving for Willie at the snack bar. At night it was as if the walls had closed in. The wrestlers were constantly slamming each other onto the floor. You could have up to six people shadow-boxing in one ring. You had to shout to make yourself heard over the clamor. There were people all over the place. And I was there to do a few rounds with Yuko.

I couldn't have asked for a better sparring partner in the days leading up to the fight. Yuko was ideal in that she was aggressive, wild, and somewhat unorthodox. I don't know why, but I'd expected something neater from a Japanese woman.

She later told me that she thought of herself as an optimistic underdog figure. Well, that made two of us.

Sonya Lamonakis, Gleason's superheavyweight female champion, came up to me after the spar and said, "You've got some skills there."

I really liked Sonya. Everything about her was big-boned and big-hearted, from how much she adored her job as a primary school teacher to how much she put into her much-loved boxing. She was passionate and popular and from what I could see, dangerous.

The next morning, my final training session before the fight, I did three rounds with Camille. But I still felt like I was struggling too much, gasping for air and feeling heavy and slow. And Alicia's comments from the sidelines seemed only to highlight my inade-quacies: "Work your combinations, Mischa. I'm seeing one and one. Double the jab, Mischa. Drop, Mischa. Nice move, Mischa. Don't pull back, Mischa."

My confidence was draining away. I'd assumed I'd be fighting Leila or Maureen Reiniger. But I was fighting Jackie the Amazon instead, a much tougher task. At least I was going to be fighting, I told myself. I let my tiny circle of New York friends and acquaintances know that it was on. Saturday night at 7:00 p.m. Fight night at Gleason's Gym.

6 SOMETHING IN THE AIR

I COULDN'T ignore it any longer. I'd felt its insidious tentacles around my throat that morning when I was sparring Camille. I was coming down with a cold. It could have been one of those second-rate New York sniffles, a harmless twenty-four-hour impostor that is sent packing after a good night's sleep. But I feared it might be something worse. It felt more like an approaching storm than a passing drizzle. There was a raspy scratch in the back of my throat, a claggy sensation when I swallowed.

I retraced my steps, past all the infected people I'd had contact with since I'd arrived. There was a panhandler called Jeremiah who had pestered me and hugged me as I walked back to DUMBO from Williamsburg. He didn't leave me alone until I gave him an Australian note, and then he wouldn't stop kissing and hugging me.

I thought of all the swine flu warnings and the Mexicans wearing face masks when I'd arrived in Los Angeles a week and a half earlier, and the millions of hands that had slid along all the subway railings I had touched.

And I thought of the number one suspect, Alicia Ashley herself, with whom I had shared the air at close quarters all week and who just the day before had complained about getting a cold.

The next day I had brunch with a group of my brother's friends, and they came upstairs to the gym when they dropped me off to check it out. They all had that look of trepidation that people tend to have the first time they enter a boxing gym, as they tried to absorb all the noise and chaos, which in this case was further amplified by the presence of a French tour group. Bruce had organized a boxing exhibition for them, and we'd just missed a couple of guys sparring but managed to catch a few rounds of Fire and Angela. During my hunt for an opponent Sonya had suggested I fight Angela if I couldn't find anyone else. I'd thought it wasn't a bad idea. We'd sparred already, and it would at least give me a chance to get in the ring in public. But she wasn't registered to fight, and since she was the person who would be running the show on Saturday night, asking her to switch roles and fight in the middle of it seemed too much to ask.

Angela had been one of the models for a book Bruce and Hector co-authored entitled *The Gleason's Gym Total Body Boxing Workout for Women*, which had ridden on the success of *Million Dollar Baby* and was aimed at all the Hilary Swank wannabes who came to the gym after the film won an Oscar. Angela had also trained with Hector and had about the same number of fights as I had. Although she wasn't fight fit, she was showing some fancy moves in the ring with Fire. Alicia had a high regard for her ability to move and punch from any angle. A contest between us might have been interesting.

I asked Alicia how her cold was.

"Better," she said.

"That's good," I said. "Because I've got it now."

She told me to take Nyquil and Theraflu and knock myself out so I could sleep a solid eight hours. She seemed so certain this would cure me that I believed her.

Suddenly it looked like Melissa and Dominga were going to spar so I told my brother's friends—Jeffrey, Mark, Steve, and Lorelei—to stick around. And it was worth staying because the eight rounds we watched were just like a fight, or so it seemed. Neither one of them held back a single punch. Melissa was doing her crazy shtick—the Russian-dancer squats, the tongue wagging with its stud glistening, the whoop-whoop-whoop sounds, switching her stance. Dominga stayed true to her usual ax-swinging style—100 percent effort, stepping with the jab, keeping extraneous movements to a minimum.

The more I watched, though, the more I realized that Melissa was playing with Dominga. Knowing Dominga's patterns so well enabled Melissa to spin her web of movements off them. I suddenly saw that facing an aggressive boxer can be a kind of gift if you know what to do with all that advancing energy. At first it looked pretty even, but I understood after a while that Melissa had reached a whole new level with her boxing and was cruising through the rounds.

The two of them had fought three times when they were amateurs so they were used to each other by now, like a couple of regular dance partners. But Melissa capitalized more on that familiarity than Dominga, who didn't seem to be able to adapt or adjust.

"Everyone feared Dominga because she was undefeated," Melissa explained to me later. "The first time I fought her I was 0-2, I was a bum. And she beat me. The third time I whooped her. I nearly stopped her. That was when Belinda saw me and said, 'You're turning pro.' Now I set traps for her. You know exactly what she's going to do. She always tries to knock you out."

Their Golden Gloves showdown was captured in Leyla Leidecker's film *The Life of Million Dollar Babies*. One of the more amusing scenes has Dominga wheeling one of her children out of the changing room in a pram, and Melissa jumping up to hold the door open for her. After Dominga leaves, Melissa's face takes on an evil smirk. In the next scene she is complaining to one of the other fighters that Dominga uses the pram as an intimidation-resistance tool. "You can't talk trash to her with her baby there," she says.

Leyla captures Melissa's every shimmy and shake in the film: doing a cut-throat gesture before the fight, flexing up on the ropes after the win, screaming out Puerrrrto Rrrrrico as she walks, victorious, back to the changing room. You simply cannot fail to notice this little woman. She was "on" all the time.

Melissa, it seems to me, is the standard bearer for a different kind of womanhood emerging from the foundations of this sport.

Dominga is something else altogether. She is uncomplicated and kind of rough. Her English is so limited it makes her seem more cut and dry. It is impossible for her to compete with Melissa's fluid and entertaining monologue, and she doesn't even try. She sticks with what she knows best, being a hard-ass. It's like Sonny Liston snarling while Cassius Clay babbled. To Dominga professional boxing is work—not fun, not an art, not an exploration of the self or even a performance. It is hard labor, and she does it for money. But it is more than that for Melissa, for whom boxing is also an affirmation of her hardy, tough, electric self, that hypercharged thing for which boxing is the only available outlet. Melissa, for example, can gush over animals like Angela's dog, Brooklyn, who frequents the gym, and even pictures of my cats, while Dominga, I suspect, would break the neck of a chicken without flinching.

As I wandered around the gym talking to people, those who had seen me spar assured me I had the skills to win the fight with Jackie. Whenever I visualized the fight I saw myself moving a lot and going to the body. But my sinuses were under pressure. My throat was sore.

My brother's friends were very impressed with Melissa. "I want to see *you* fight, though, Mischa," said Lorelei.

"Oh," I said. "I'm not going to be as exciting as this."

Despite her interest in watching me fight, Lorelei didn't look too keen on being at the gym; the men, on the other hand, were captivated. Eventually, however, they buckled to pressure from her and left. Soon after, I also left the gym and headed back to my cozy loft. I was feeling a little light headed and looked through the full supply of pharmaceuticals I had bought to help fight off the cold: Sinex nasal spray, amoxycillin, NyQuil, Contac, and Cold-EEZE lozenges. I wondered if the pending contest was just making me hypersensitive to every subtle physical symptom.

I was asleep by ten.

I woke up groggy. Had I recovered? I couldn't really tell. I ventured out cautiously to get coffee and take a short walk around the park under the Brooklyn Bridge, trying to wake myself up and get my blood circulating. I felt as if I were holding back the flood gates. I wasn't sick. Yet. But I wasn't very well either.

So I tried to rest. I spent the day watching clips of myself sparring just to reassure myself that I could indeed fight, that this was what I did all the time, every week, in fact, and had been doing since the late 1990s, so what was the big deal? Cold or no cold, it was like a reflex for me by now. But how many comeback attempts had I seen after long layoffs in which fighters were so creaky and rusty they looked almost atrophied? Sparring wasn't the same as fighting.

Then, for the umpteenth time, I watched Lucia Rijker teeing off on the unbelievably tough and resilient Jane Couch. The decision had gone to Rijker. I read on the WBAN site that Rijker had great respect for Couch's toughness because she went the distance.

"I tried to knock her out the whole time," Rijker said. "I hit her with some great shots. I absolutely was trying to finish her the whole time."

Then I got up and shadowboxed around the loft under the skylight. Checking myself in the mirror, dropping down and bobbing up, rehearsing my moves.

I was reassured by my last conversation with Devon. "I have fought people younger than me, bigger than me, faster than me, and stronger than me," he said. "But I had experience over them. That experience counts for a lot."

As I cleared my throat and blew my nose, I hoped the cold wouldn't rob me of the advantages I might have.

I went and got a final coffee and headed over to Gleason's for the weigh-in at about 5:45 p.m. The place was packed with people and chairs arranged around the ring closest to the office. I'd been warned that the climate turned tropical on nights when Gleason's held club shows, and it was certainly more muggy than usual. I saw people lined up to be checked by the doctor. I saw the young blonde girl who had sparred Ronica standing in front of a man with a stethoscope with her arms outstretched.

I wandered over to what I guessed was the weigh-in line and saw two small girls, not much more than 100 lb., chatting with each other. I recognized them from the previous October when they'd tried to kill each other at St. Anne's Warehouse on DUMBO Fight Night.

"Hey," I said. "Didn't you two fight each other?"

They smiled and nodded.

"That was a war," I said. And they giggled.

Theirs had been a truly crazy fight. At one point the two of them had stood swinging in front of each other in what looked like a comic parody of what people think boxing is. Melissa and Belinda, who had cornered one of them, screamed instructions all the way through the fight, and the other girl, who also had female trainers, got the same deal from her corner. It seemed to be a battle for which of the female trainers could shout the loudest.

Between rounds Alicia had turned to look at me with one of her deadpan expressions.

"This is just like an Australian fight," I had said.

I'd seen one of the girls sparring with Tracy Hutt, a skillful professional, and was expecting to see some good boxing when she fought. But she lost it all in the ring.

"I was so mad that night," she explained now, assuring me that she planned to keep her cool this time.

Then, much sooner than I expected, I saw Jackie walking toward me. She was wearing a bright orange halter-neck top that showed off her magnificent shoulders and arms. She was wearing a black pencil skirt and high heels and carrying a gym bag.

"Did you think you were going to fight me?" she squealed.

"Yes, of course," I said.

"But I didn't bring my book."

All amateur boxers are required to carry a small book that shows they are registered with USA boxing and have been cleared by a doctor. Fights and results are also recorded in the book. I treated mine as though it was more valuable than my passport.

"No," I said. "You *have* to."

"I don't think they'll let me without my book," she said.

"You have to get in the ring with me," I said, thinking of the people I had told to come and how I'd have to now call them all and tell them not to come. "Even if it's just an exhibition."

"I don't think I can even do that without the book," she said.

"Can you go and get it?"

"It's a three-hour round-trip," she said.

"Why didn't you bring it?" I asked.

"I didn't think it was on because we weren't on the list."

The list was the running order that Angela had e-mailed to all the competitors. Then she held my gaze for a second and said, "You sure you wanna fight me?" as if such a proposal were suicidal.

"Yes," I said. "I am sure. That's why I'm here."

How could she possibly not have realized that?

I went into the office to talk with Angela, who was there with

Me and Jackie.

Bruce. They appeared to be combing the rule book for something, but I don't think it had anything to do with me.

"I don't know how this happened," I announced. "She says she didn't bring her book."

They both stopped what they were doing and looked up at me with blank faces.

"I don't know how she could possibly have thought that we weren't going to fight when she said she would be here Saturday. I mean, she said she was going to be here late, but that she would be here to fight."

Neither of them said anything. Some other drama was sapping their energy.

"I'm flabbergasted," I said, "that anyone could interpret the conversation we had in any other way."

Bruce shrugged and looked sympathetic. "You can use some Australian curse words if you'd like."

Angela flipped through the pages of the rule book.

Jackie was behaving as if our conversation had never taken place, making me feel like a crazy person who'd imagined it all. I left the office to look for Alicia.

A few minutes later, I turned around and saw that Jackie was now in the office having a huddled conversation with Bruce and Angela. Every now and then she looked at me with a slightly guilty expression.

I saw Louis Shiffrin in the milling crowd.

"Hey, are you fighting?" he asked.

I updated him on what had just happened.

"Boxing is full of liars," he said.

In fairness to Jackie, I assumed Angela would at least have called her to confirm, and maybe Jackie had been expecting that call since she'd said the running order didn't have our fight on the list. Except that it did. Someone had just shown it to me minutes earlier.

Also in fairness to Jackie, it was short notice. But she had been trying to get on the show, or so she said, so she'd been training for something. But for what? Training to make her arms look impressive in a bright orange top, perhaps.

In fairness to me, she was nearly ten pounds heavier, several inches taller, and reputed to be a hard puncher. Looking at the two of us standing side by side, her in her heels, it looked like it would be an easy win for her. It looked like she'd wipe the floor with my little white ass.

Maybe Alicia's confidence in me threw her.

Once it became clear that we weren't going to fight, Jackie and I joined Leila Ferioli, who was waiting to fight by the ring. She told us about Maureen's second fight, which she hadn't trained for and which she had assumed she'd win because she had won the first one.

"She was stopped in the first round," said Leila. "It was humiliating. But she was too arrogant."

"Sometimes it's better to lose a few fights to make you reflect on your mistakes," I said.

"No way," said Jackie. "Uh, uh. I'm not training as hard as I do to lose. That's what I tell all of my kids"—meaning the kids she trained.

Maybe that was it. She was guaranteed not to lose if she didn't fight.

All I could do was point her out as the woman who was supposed to fight me. It was awkward. I just didn't want people to think I had reneged.

Alicia, whom I had messaged earlier, finally appeared, shrugged, and said, "It happens."

She was wearing a black cap, black polo neck top, and gray flared slacks. As usual she looked super cool and stylish.

She was right. It happens. It had happened to me before—my opponent for the state championship one year simply didn't show up—and it will no doubt happen again. Maybe my fight with Jackie just wasn't meant to be. My cold was already feeling worse.

I told Jackie my next stop would be the Golden Gloves in

Florida, and she said she'd be ready for me in July, but I was thinking, "Fuck her. She's had her chance to fight me, and it's gone. I'm not giving away weight and size again." Jackie was heavier than me, which gave her an advantage.

"Maybe," I said. "But at 138 pounds."

"But as Masters we have a ten-pound differential."

Big hat, no cattle.

I walked off and complained to all and sundry.

"She scare of you. She scare of you. She scare of you," chanted Hector Roca when I saw him.

Yuko shook her head and said, "She's not 145 pounds. No way."

What an anticlimax!

I didn't really want to stick around, but my friend Sally was on her way to DUMBO. So I missed a big chunk of the card while I ate dinner with her at Rice, a restaurant around the corner on Washington Street.

We returned to the gym just in time to see Leila Ferioli's hand raised in victory. Then she went back to the corner to embrace a smiling Stu, who now looked less like a menacing Harvey Keitel and more like a genial Tom Hanks.

"What was it like?" I asked Louie.

"Oh, it was a real slug fest," he said. "Leila was down in the first round. And they just stood toe to toe most of it."

I laughed to myself that she probably would have had a much easier time fighting me.

Then it was time for the young blonde girl. I watched the fight standing next to Alicia on the apron of the wrestling ring. Her much shorter opponent came out guns blazing, throwing not just one of the stiffest, fastest jabs I'd ever seen, but also managing to weave under-the-counter punches like a total pro.

"Wow," said Alicia. "I like her confidence. I think she's had more than one fight, though."

She stepped in and out it popped, her left arm like it was on steel springs. She demolished the taller blonde girl whose sparring sessions with the cool Ronica had been no preparation for this force of nature.

Afterward the winning girl was walking around glowing, still clutching her trophy. She said she was from a new gym in Queens and she was their first and only fighter.

"It was so stressful," she said, smiling from ear to ear.

The next day I saw her victim, sporting a big black eye, sitting with her friends in a café in Williamsburg. They were all sitting quietly, not speaking. I quickly learned that was because they were all too hoarse from screaming the night before.

"I was really upset last night, but now I feel fine," she said. "I just need to go back to the gym and work harder."

Me, too, I thought. Me, too.

On Monday morning, before I left to go back to Australia, I had one last sparring session with Slick.

This time Melissa held the camera.

At one point I can hear Melissa saying in a soft, pleading voice, "C'mon, Mischa, c'mon."

But by then it was too late. The cold had taken hold. My chest was congested. I was all out of steam. There was no pop.

By the time I walked through customs back in Australia I was so sick I thought I was going to be quarantined. I was in bed for two weeks before I recovered enough, only to have to begin training and preparing to fight all over again. My May 2009 trip to New York hadn't lived up to the expectations I had built up for it. Now I wouldn't have much time to get my feet back under me and get ready for the Golden Gloves in Fort Lauderdale, Florida, which was coming up in July.

7 LEAVING THE COMFORT ZONE

AS LUC SANTE writes in his book *Low Life*, New York "is a city and it is also a creature, a mentality, a disease, a threat, an electromagnet, a cheap stage set, an accident corridor. It is an implausible character, a monstrous vortex of contradictions, an attraction-repulsion mechanism so extreme no one could have made it up."

You could say the same about boxing. Boxing, too, is a densely packed percolator of creativity, a fascinating bundle of contradictions, and a magnet for eccentricity. It operates on multiple layers that remain hidden to the untrained eye and can easily be misunderstood. I enjoy being a boxing insider now in the home of modern boxing, and I am even happier that the sport has also given me an inside take on New York City, so I don't see it the way everyone else does. The city and the sport have become enmeshed for me.

I worked out a loose five-week plan for my return to the US in July and August 2009 that began with one week of training in New York before heading down to Florida for the Golden Gloves. I'd stay there to train with Bonnie before heading back to New York for a week to fight in Gleason's August 1 show, which was going to be held outdoors under the Brooklyn Bridge, and then travel to Kansas City for the Ringside World Championships. In the meantime I would be on the lookout for other tournaments I might be able to add to my already pretty full schedule.

It had been six weeks since I'd left New York, and I felt as if I had just jetted home for the weekend. At Gleason's someone asked me if I had been "out of town." Others greeted me as if I had never left. The only difference I noticed in the routine clank and chaos was that Delon Parsley, who everyone called Blimp—and for good reason—had visibly shrunk, although he was still massive. And the trainer Jihad Abdul-Aziz, who had lost weight on my previous visit, had put weight back on, as if the two had made a quiet exchange in a back alley.

I'd gone with both of them to the professional fights in Long Island the year before, with the more regular-sized trainer Don Saxby in the backseat with me while the two giants weighed down the front of the car. Jihad, dressed in Muslim garb, had been the driver. Despite his imposing size and untrimmed beard, he has a very sweet nature and speaks in a soft and gentle voice. Being in the car with them was like being in an episode of *The Wire*. I had no clue what any of them were saying because I was unfamiliar with the slang. Then, when we got to the Hilton in Melville, it felt as if we had stepped out of *The Wire* and into the *Sopranos* as I watched a group of predominantly Italian officials standing in a group talking loudly. I was constantly worried that Blimp and his friends would forget I was there and leave without me. I was always scanning the room for the giant black men I had come with, easy to confuse with the numerous other giant-sized black men in the crowd. I had no clue how to get back to Brooklyn.

Back home in Australia, after my second trip to New York, I had decided that since I'd only have a little over a month of training before heading back to New York, I needed to almost overwork my fitness regimen to compensate for losing condition through jetlag and the horrible cold I had had. So I had ramped up my routine, adding two mornings a week with a running coach who took me through a fifty-minute sprint routine that included stairs, hills, and plyometrics. I also spent one day a week in a fitness class doing punch drills, shuttle runs, and strength work followed by sparring teenage boys. I continued my regular sparring, training, and running routine on other days. Six weeks later I had left home feeling that I couldn't possibly be any fitter. I also made sure to get flu shots.

One morning during my first week back in New York, I ran across the Brooklyn Bridge and back and felt better than ever. The bridge had become my key fitness marker. And I enjoyed the journey, dodging the meandering tourists like Rocky, taking in the incredible view.

I'd passed Jennifer Czirr, a fighter I knew from the gym, traveling in the opposite direction, and we had waved to each other. I thought, "New York is my alter ego's hometown. No doubt about it." In another life I'd have ended up here.

When I got back to the gym Jennifer exclaimed how fast I'd been running, although even at my best I'm a pretty slow runner. She said she had worried I was going to overtake her.

"But I was going in the opposite direction," I said.

"That's what I mean. I thought you would get to the end and come back and overtake me before I finished."

I really liked Jennifer. She had been one of the women watching the Hatton-Pacquiao fight at Gerritson Beach in May. She appeared to be utterly devoted to Alicia, was warm-hearted and generous, and had self-deprecating humor about the battles she fought with her own weight.

I met up with Yuko, whose friend I nearly fought in May and who I had sparred with in the lead-up to the non-event with Jackie, to spar again. Alicia turned up right on time, acting like she expected us to get started immediately, although all the foot tapping was probably just an act. I'd noticed that she enjoyed making other people rush and panic by saying, "I haven't got all day." She'd rush you, but she wouldn't rush herself if she could help it.

Alicia was in her city clothes—a jaunty cap like something the Supremes would have worn at the height of their fame, a tight-fitting miniskirt, and high heels. She looked liked one smooth sister, appearing out of place in Gleason's grubby, dank interior. Whenever I saw Alicia, I was bowled over by her beauty. Out in the world, people would have no idea that this elegant woman actually punched people for a living.

She'd made the trip back to the gym just for me, after having battled with a stream of sparring partners earlier in the day, culminating in a memorable session with Melissa. Now it was early evening. I was at the front talking to Sunshine about how the Mendez gym was so dull compared to Gleason's.

But Gleason's was also time consuming because if you spent an hour training, you could spend another two hours talking, being fascinated by sparring, talking some more, watching more sparring, then start to leave just as someone arrived and then talking more at the threshold of the front door.

"I've been here since three," Sunshine exclaimed from her position next to the front desk.

"I was here this morning for two hours," I said, "and I didn't even train." Much of that time had been spent loitering around as I waited for Alicia and Melissa to spar. But it had been worth the wait. I'd dropped in on my way back from a run and heard Melissa shout across the gym, "Hey, Alicia, ya wanna spar?"

And Alicia shot back, "When?"

Melissa said, "Soon."

And I said, "What's soon?" and Melissa said, "Twenty minutes."

I could have gone home for a shower and lunch by the time they actually got in the ring. It seemed that there was real time, and then there was Gleason's time. Gleason's time had its own rhythm. "Soon" could mean anything from right now to some time before dark. But because styles make fights, the spar promised to be a good one. I was interested to see how effective the little power ball would be against Alicia's slippery fluidity.

Some hours later, after Alicia had unloaded a continuous stream of catlike taps on Liz, after she'd squeezed in a few rounds with rock climber and amateur boxer Alexis Asher (who would be joining us in Florida), after waiting for the "crazy new girlfriend" to arrive with Melissa's wetsuit—she couldn't possibly spar without it—the sweat had already dried on my shirt and my skin had started to feel a little clammy when they finally got underway.

A crowd had quickly gathered. Devon was calling his instructions to Alicia and addressing her as "Ashley."

Blimp was telling Melissa to turn when she got inside instead of standing right in front of Alicia.

"I don't wanna turn," she shouted back at him.

Whenever I was in the ring with Alicia I was almost paralyzed by inhibitions, worried that whatever I did she would see coming. I didn't want to be any more telegraphic or predictable than I had to be. My feeling was that the harder I tried, the better it would be for her: my efforts would only make me easier to read. But Melissa wasn't put off by Alicia's mercurial qualities. All the usual elements of her ring repertoire were in play again, the whoop-whoop war cry, the bouncing squats, the tongue wagging, the wisecracking.

"Don't hit me there," she said at one point, a comment that had Jennifer in fits of laughter.

Then suddenly, after the second or third round, it got more serious. Alicia seemed to wake up and accelerate the pace. The

Blimp and Melissa.

competitor in her was finally on the job, and she was throwing more meaningful punches.

It appeared to me that when she sparred with us mere mortals she worked like a choreographer, not just blocking her moves but also roughing in a pace. Her slips and counters reminded me of scatting, with their own unique rhythm—fast, slow, slow-fast—and slightly off-balance tempo. Sometimes her head would move the exact distance her opponent's glove moved, and she would be in place to answer with a flurry. It was mesmerizing to watch, her head shimmering like a snake's, the yellow gloves, the out-turned toes, her body covered head to toe in red sweat pants and a long-sleeved shirt. Then, when she put her pedal to the metal, like she was doing now against Melissa, it was really quite spectacular. The opposing styles and the high level of athleticism brought something special to the encounter. Melissa's stomping and swaggering, her strut and shimmy seemed to have a point to them now. The whole gym was spellbound.

The two sparred about eight rounds, and it was clear that Alicia was forcing herself into the target zone, staying closer to Melissa than she wanted to and perhaps getting hit more than she usually did. But it was difficult to say who was ahead. Alicia had told me when she came to get me from the airport that her previous spar with Melissa had left her with sore shoulders and an aching neck, and one time she had e-mailed me that Melissa had dropped to one knee after receiving a body punch from her. The intensity seemed to enliven her, and it was clear this time too that getting out of cruise control was something she relished. Being challenged was an opportunity to improve.

Now Alicia was pointing impatiently at Yuko on the stationary bike. "She's already warmed up," she told me, "and you haven't even changed."

So I winked at Sunshine and jumped to it.

After the third round with Yuko I was wrecked. But I'd recovered reasonably well between rounds and had worked hard during them. My jab especially felt busy and smooth and hard and fast. And I was pleased with a nice right-left combination I had used and so was Miss Ashley, who asked for more of them. But the next time I threw my right hand, I dropped my left, and Kamikaze Yuko whacked me with one of her wild right hooks.

After the spar Yuko's trainer Grant said to Alicia about me, "She can box better than a lot of people here, don't you think?"

And Miss Ashley put on her most heart-melting smile and nodded yes with sincerity.

"Stop," I said. "You'll make me cry."

After my cold had cleared up back in Australia, I felt more robust and up for a challenge. Bonnie had assured me that there would be at least two 138-lb. Masters at the Golden Gloves, including the elusive Michelle Straka. So maybe I could be picky.

Back in New York, on my first morning at the gym, I had been surprised to see Jackie and that she appeared to have lost weight. She looked almost gaunt, but still superbly muscled and still a shining example of how to age with grace and vigor. I watched her, while trying not to appear to be watching her, as she sparred Sugar, the small black southpaw who moved a lot but didn't hit anyone. I could see Jackie's side-to-side head movement and her sleek black arms and long jabs. I couldn't help but admire her magnificent, athletic body. But I also saw that Jackie couldn't really put her punches together on the move. She needed to be planted. I saw a very low left hand, hanging down like Mayweather liked to have his. And in that, I saw an opportunity for myself.

When I finally began my session with Alicia she revealed that she was getting a shot at the WBC super bantamweight championship. Argentina's Marcela Acuña had offered to fight her in a title defense. It was a surprise offer since Alicia had already beaten her twice. The fight was scheduled for late August.

The session with Alicia on the mitts felt pretty good. Was it me or was it her? Was I imagining it, or had something or someone made

Alicia less demanding and more mellow? Was it the Acuña fight? Or had I improved? I was hearing the word "right" more often now, and there seemed to be less nit-picking, although she still complained that I was pushing my punches.

That day I had to spar not just Alicia but Devon as well—double trouble. But I was determined not to get frustrated and just do my best rather than let them put me off. With Alicia I tried a new approach. I tried to stay in close so at least she couldn't pick me off. And I would try to use my nearly twenty extra pounds to shove her around. But she still managed to pick me off from close range, and my extra weight felt like a liability that slowed me down. And yet this was the lightest weight I had ever boxed.

Afterward she said, "What did you expect?"

"I had to try something!"

With Devon I tried instead to stay on the move and do what I seemed to do best—neutralize the attack with movement. And it worked up to a point. All and all, I could have felt worse at the end of it.

Then Alicia told me to go a couple of rounds with Grace Baley. I wandered over to the elevated ring where she was waiting. I'd never seen Grace in headgear before. She looked so much smaller and more vulnerable than usual. Grace was a mosaic artist and mother of two with a studio nearby, and she trained with Alicia a few mornings a week. She had run in the New York Marathon with Alicia the year before and was part of a group that was connected through Gleason's and included Camille, Angela, Jennifer, and Melody. I'd been to Grace's birthday dinner at the Cowgirl Hall of Fame before I'd left town in May, and I liked her a lot. In fact, I liked the whole group, although they were kind of loud. I'd once called home, and Peter said, "Why are you shouting?" And I yelled down into the phone, "I'm not shouting!" It was contagious in New York. I blamed the trains, the sirens, the clanging city sounds, the fact that everyone everywhere seemed to be talking at once. The streets of Melbourne were muffled and subdued by comparison.

Now, not only was Grace's wavy black hair tucked into her head-gear and her sharp-witted words dulled by a mouth guard, but her expression was a little uncharacteristically anxious.

Within about five seconds she shouted at me, "Lighten up!"

"What?" I said. "Lighten up? Oh. Sorry."

It was strange to hear those words when I was convinced that I wasn't threatening or dangerous enough. Grace could hit hard, but her defense wasn't developed. She wasn't a fighter yet. I didn't think my punches were heavy, but they must have felt so to her. At the same time, she couldn't really know how hard she was hitting me. After all my soul searching about how ineffective my punches were, now all of a sudden I seemed to be hurting someone without even trying. What I had been striving for—being dangerous—appeared to be coming a little too easily.

The bell sounded, and I apologized again, maybe too much. I was very fond of Grace and loved her work and her sharp, dry sense of humor. I really didn't want to upset her.

"It's OK," she said. "I just don't want to . . ."

"I know, go home with a headache," I said.

Still, the next time I landed a punch, I instantly apologized. Now I was being patronizing. Oh dear. All of a sudden what had been simple became complex again, with Grace bringing real world responses into the ring where matters had, for me, been pretty simple for a long time.

After sparring we all went and had lunch at Bubby's around the corner, Camille, Grace and her two daughters, Devon, Alicia, Jennifer, Melody, and Angela. No one would have guessed that we had spent most of the morning hitting each other.

Over coffee Camille told us how that week she'd seen a man in his sixties wearing nothing but Speedos and a cowboy hat in the middle of Manhattan pushing a baby carriage with a dog in it wearing a tutu around its neck. "No one even looked twice at him, not a smirk or a snigger," she said. "I thought 'Are they seeing what I'm seeing?'" I was going to miss the place.

When I arrived at Newark's Liberty Airport to head down to Florida, I felt a little sad and apprehensive about leaving the city so soon. I was also a little worried about letting go of my New York life rafts. I would miss the proximity of art and literature and my favorite coffee shops. I would also miss being able to walk everywhere I needed to go. I had been staying in a nice quiet apartment in Brooklyn Heights where I could sleep through the night not too far from the clatter of DUMBO. I could walk to the gym in five minutes. When I was done I could walk to the Foragers Market on Front Street for a vegetable salad, the kind of simple nutritious food I liked and was, frankly, a little obsessed about procuring.

It wasn't what I was leaving New York to do, which was to fight, that made me nervous. It was the idea that I would be plunging into a different side of America, the one that is easy to ignore in New York City, where you can almost believe the rest of America doesn't exist. I had some idea what to expect *out there* from my three-day training trip to Fort Lauderdale a year earlier, a place I imagined as a heavy, stodgy, overly patriotic, God-fearing, right-wing, car-dependent, and most alarming of all to me, vegetable-free zone.

It was this anticipated challenge to my diet that was especially troubling to me. I'd lost twenty pounds since my first visit to Gleason's and had dropped below my former fighting weight by several pounds. I've always been a healthy eater, though. My mother had been an early health-food fanatic and vitamin advocate when such people were considered crazy, and in my middle years I'm an echo of her. I had gained weight as, with age, my metabolism had slowed to a crawl. On the advice of a dietician, I simply cut my portions in half—a ridiculously easy strategy. The content remained the same, however: healthy, fresh vegetables and only a little red meat and fish. I was worried that out there in America my sources would dry up.

The people gathering at the gate lounge to board the morning Continental flight to Fort Lauderdale were already looking different to me: slightly overfed, a bit soft around the edges. Once on the plane, crammed together in the economy seats, people looked bloated, the excess flesh spilling into each other's spaces, making the plane's seats look like children's furniture. People had to fold their arms so as not to touch each other. I also noticed some pretty weird faces with cat-woman eyebrows and trout pouts. A few women had fake boobs. There was one man wearing a white tank top, white shorts, and white shoes, with very white teeth and dyed auburn hair. He had a tan the color of roasted pumpkin flesh. The fake look is completely fine, apparently, while naturally old is completely unacceptable.

8 COBRA COUNTRY

THE YEAR before, I had sampled the thick Florida air training for three days with Bonnie Canino at her Dania Beach gym. Until then most of my impressions of Florida had been gleaned from Susan Orlean's 1998 book *The Orchid Thief*, a portrait of an odd character called John Laroche. It made south Florida seem full of intrigue and swampy strangeness. "Florida is a wet, warm, tropical place, essentially featureless and infinitely transformable," Orlean writes. "It is as suggestible as someone under hypnosis."

A place that was such a blank canvas was the perfect setting for restarting my dormant boxing career.

On that first visit to Florida I stayed at the rather ordinary Comfort Inn on Stirling Road in Fort Lauderdale. Its most interesting feature was that it was staffed almost entirely by Jamaicans who were friendly, but whose English was completely incomprehensible to me—as was my Australian accent to them. Most of our attempts at communication involved us smiling at each other saying, "What?"

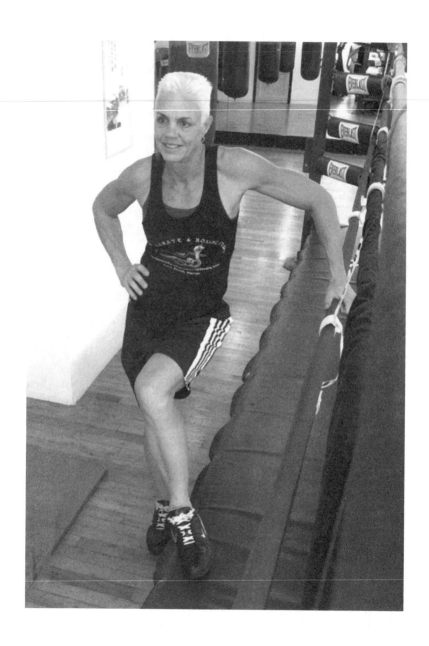

Bonnie Canino.

There seemed to be a fast food joint on every corner, and a nearby fluorescent pink and black billboard sign told me the Fort Lauderdale Gun Show was coming soon. Up the road, past a McDonald's and a Taco Bell, was a featureless shopping center that, thankfully, included a Barnes & Noble with a Starbucks where I could get almost passable coffee. The store was staffed mostly by white people over seventy. It was no more than five hundred yards away but felt like an impossibly long trudge through a parking lot in the thick air. I was, aside from various lone, down-at-the-heel figures, the only person walking. It sure wasn't anything like New York.

When Bonnie came to get me from the airport I was unable to take my eyes off her. She had striking, androgynous, white Annie Lennox hair and the kind of cool equilibrium you might expect from an old cowboy who has broken every bone in his body and is afraid of nothing. Her quiet, unflappable quality, not to mention her big hands, made quite the impression on me as her long, muscular arm retrieved my backpack from the luggage carrousel.

I'd been in awe of Bonnie for ten years, and it was almost surreal to be sitting in a car next to her while she spoke in her steady, low voice about her life of fighting and her ideas about training. I thought of her as a female version of Freddy Roach, the world famous West Coast trainer who is in the gym twelve hours a day.

Roach had once told an interviewer: "People say, 'How can you stay in the gym all day?' and I say, 'It's what I do, it's what I like.' They say, 'Don't you have any hobbies?' And I say, 'Yeah, boxing.'"

Bonnie had twenty years of fighting behind her both as a kick-boxer and boxer and several now as a coach. She'd been one of the first to march forward with a steely look in her eye, ready to show the skeptics how much heart and power women really had. And that look wasn't entirely gone now; her attention had merely turned to coming generations.

"I stopped fighting because I don't have that bite any more, that hunger," was how she put it to me that first day.

But actually I found that she did still have that hunger and she certainly did have some bite, which she unleashed in the gym every Saturday when she and her fighters did track work and then sparred. She was in tremendous physical shape for a woman of any age, let alone one who was about to turn forty-seven. I'd never seen arms on a woman like the ones hanging lithely from Bonnie's wiry torso with its washboard stomach and taut skin. Her shoulders were angular and square, and veins wrapped around her arms like vines. Most women in their midforties were generally brandishing bat wings and love handles. Few were as lean as Bonnie. But I was finding more and more in boxing that the sport has an age-defying effect. Women in their forties looked amazing; they were agile and bright eyed.

Bonnie told me if anyone pissed her off in the gym, she made a mental note to take it out on them on Saturday. She told me casually that she had broken noses and fixed them as well for "plenty of girls" and brought both men and women to tears. She told me this in an off-handed way, as if she were giving me directions to the store. So I thought I'd ask her, while we were on the subject, if she could possibly avoid breaking my nose this time, only because I planned to spend the next three weeks sparring back in New York.

She shrugged and said, "OK."

I'd been a little concerned about my nose because Bonnie and half the gym it seemed were southpaws, and it was a southpaw who'd broken my nose once, so I've never felt comfortable with them. Because they lead with the right hand instead of the left, the dynamics of the fight change. An orthodox boxer leads with the left hand and uses the right hand for power shots. Boxing a left-hander can feel awkward because your left jab isn't so effective against them. You need to move differently and deal with more surprises. Some people handle them better than others and there is a perennial joke in boxing that even southpaws hate fighting southpaws.

While I sensed Bonnie was potentially dangerous in a quiet, simmering way, Yvonne Reis, Bonnie's partner and boxing protégée was more forthright. She liked to give blow-by-blow accounts of every encounter. These stories of ass-whoopings and butt-kickings dished out inside the sunny confines of Canino's Boxing and Karate Studio left my head spinning. Yvonne would get so excited in the telling it was slightly unsettling.

A tall, strong woman, Yvonne had a haircut identical to Bonnie's. The women, I learned, had actually cut each other's hair. Bonnie had once been a hairdresser, so she'd cut Yvonne's hair first and then guided Yvonne as she did the same for her. The two of them then spent the afternoon sitting around with bleach in their hair to get the full effect.

Yvonne had conscientiously trumpeted all that Bonnie had achieved in the sport, saying that she was too modest and too reserved to do it herself. Modesty and reserve were not words you'd use to describe Yvonne, who was ferociously and unashamedly competitive. The louder her voice was, the higher the pitch, and it didn't take much to get her charged up. Originally from Boston and once married, Yvonne had competed in almost every fighting form, starting with karate, then kickboxing, and later boxing. Now she was doing mixed martial arts.

"What? I'm gonna quit now that I'm just starting to get good at it?"

She was also in her forties, also lean and youthful, with a statuesque beauty that she seemed almost entirely unaware of.

"I used to be the fat girl," she'd explained. "And I still feel that way."

Within five minutes of meeting her I'd decided that if we sparred, all I was going to do was stay out of trouble, and I didn't care how much of a coward I might appear to be. And that was exactly what I did.

Barbara Buttrick.

"I ran around the ring like a chicken," I told Peter, who couldn't have been more pleased.

In my few days with her, Bonnie made sure I had everything I needed, shuttling me to and from the Comfort Inn and her gym, feeding me, training me, and much to my delight, introducing me to Barbara Buttrick—the only living link with the past of women's boxing, back before Christy Martin got herself on the cover of *Sports Illustrated* in 1996.

I'd first heard about Barbara when I was preparing for my ring debut in 1998. I'd found a black-and-white photograph of her in a magazine and became intrigued by the story behind it. The accompanying text told me that this little angel-faced woman had "pulverized" many women and men as she'd punched her way through more than a decade of carnivals and ring contests; there was scant detail about her otherwise. I didn't even know if she was still alive or where she lived. I was curious about how, in the 1940s, a woman had come to take up the manly art.

What struck me most about the photograph was her clear-eyed confidence as she looked up at the camera, the shot taken by someone much taller than her tiny four-foot-eleven, ninety-five-pound self. There was not a smidgeon of seduction or beguilement in her eyes. Her confident, self-contained gaze must have been quite unusual for a girl of her times, especially one so slight and, dare I say it, pretty. She was wearing a black ballet leotard cut to the thigh showing off her shapely, athletic legs, which ended in a pair of black, ankle-high boxing boots, white socks folded neatly at the top. She was holding her bandaged fists low in front of her, and her angelic, heart-shaped face was framed by her hair, which had sensibly been cut short.

Thanks to Bonnie, I had finally come face to face with the Tiny Atom of the Ring, as she was sometimes known in her heyday. And for a woman on the brink of her eightieth birthday, she still looked fit enough to do a few rounds although a recent knee operation had slowed her down somewhat. She said she attended a small rehabilitation gym near where she lived in Miami Beach and that that was about all she did these days aside from walking. But it hadn't been that long ago that she'd still jumped rope and hit the bag.

No one would pick out this retired bookkeeper as a fist-fighting legend, though. Who would guess that this little old lady, who easily blended in with the elderly population, had had a stiff left jab, with which she'd broken at least three noses and scored twelve knockouts?

"I was small," she'd told me in her Yorkshire accent, fresh from a recent visit home. "But I was mean."

She hadn't actually headed south to Florida to retire. Instead, while she was still a young woman in the 1950s, she had crossed the Atlantic to train at the famous Fifth Street Gym in Miami Beach where a young fighter called Cassius Clay was also cutting his pugilistic teeth.

"I knew him," she said. "But we weren't friends or anything. He was just another young fighter in the gym."

How extraordinary, I thought. Ali was breaking ground for black American men while this fearless, utterly original little woman was in the same gym, and yet history has never properly celebrated the subversive role she played. Back then, it really was all about the men. And in the 1960s it became about men and power, men and race, men and class. All eyes were focused on Ali, who embodied each of these concerns. Black power was ahead in the queue for minority rights, and Barbara Buttrick was too far ahead of her time to be a catalyst for a women's movement that hadn't even gotten off the ground yet.

Like "The Greatest," plenty of Barbara's contemporaries have since been etched deeply into the history of boxing, including Ali's first major scalp, Sonny Liston, the multiple world champion Emile Griffith, and old-school trainers and managers like Angelo Dundee. But Barbara is really only known among insiders.

"We usually see each other at funerals these days," she said of her old pals, her gold boxing glove earrings catching the morning sun.

When I asked Barbara how she got into boxing, she said, "Let me tell you the story," and pulled out a well-kept scrapbook as if she were about to read me a nursery rhyme.

"When I was maybe fifteen or something like that I was playing soccer with a girl, my friend, kicking a ball in a field that was muddy," she said. "We went back to her house, and her mother said, 'You can't come in with shoes like that!' and she threw a newspaper down for me to clean them. And in the newspaper was this article, and I said, 'Oh, oh, oh, wait a minute, I can't clean my shoes on this. Give it to me.'"

The article, which is now on the first page of her scrapbook, was about another woman boxer, Polly Burns, who had fought in London from 1914 to 1918.

"I thought, 'I don't need eleven people to box like I do to try and get a soccer team together.' So I cut the article out, and I started to learn to box.

"I used to just box in the backyard with the boys. I bought a set of boxing gloves and a book called *The Noble Art of Self-Defense.*"

Eventually, she found a trainer in London and worked as a typist by day while every night she went to the gym for three hours of bag-punching, rope-skipping, and sparring with her coach, Len Smith, whom she eventually married.

She then began her career fighting in boxing booths at carnivals, and if there were no female takers, she'd spar with men.

"There was a lot of publicity, and of course everyone was against it. The other boxers didn't mind. But basically the writers used to blast me in the press, 'Women doing this, blah blah, disgusting' . . . You know, that kind of stuff."

In 1952, Barbara and her husband headed for America, where she won eight bouts in a row and knocked out the US female bantamweight champion.

In 1957, she moved to Dallas. She and opponent Phyllis Kugler won the state's first boxing licenses for women, and a world title bout was held in San Antonio. Barbara won a unanimous decision, making her the first women's world boxing champion. By then, she had fought in one thousand exhibitions with men and eighteen professional women's fights, only one of which she lost—outweighed by more than twenty pounds.

Barbara and Smith finally settled down in Miami Beach in 1959. She continued to fight until 1962 when she retired to raise her daughters.

Nearly thirty years later, in 1990, she was elected to the International Boxing and Wrestling Hall of Fame. Then, during the new era of women's boxing, she reconnected with her old world. Today, Barbara is president of the Women's International Boxing Federation, the sanctioning body she'd established in the mid-1990s. The recently retired German fighter Regina Hamlich had been their highest profile champion, the Germans paying her well and giving her main-event status. Bonnie also ranks among their champions as one of the first to win a WIBF belt.

Hearing these ring stories come from the mouth of a grandmother was a bizarre experience, but I took it as a sign of things to come. Forty years from now there will be plenty such elderly women, probably including myself, who will be talking about their stiff jabs and nose-breaking good ol' days. Who knows, some of them might still be swinging at each other. I hope so.

9 GLOVE UP

I WAS probably the first boxer to arrive in Fort Lauderdale for the 2009 Women's National Golden Gloves tournament. I got there on Tuesday afternoon, and registration wasn't due to begin until Wednesday. So I had a strange and isolated twenty-four hours floating around the bland microclimate of the Hilton Hotel waiting for the circus to arrive. I'd catch little snippets of Michael Jackson's memorial service at the Staples Center, which only seemed to add to the feeling that I had entered a parallel universe.

The temperature inside was a comfortable sixty-eight degrees, but outside was a different story. As soon as you moved past the reach of the cool air blowing out of the air-conditioning vents at the front doors, you were hit by a wall of air so hot and so thick and so still you could almost grab it with your hand.

Once again I was thrown into uncertainty about the state of my fitness. Listen to your body, they say, but I didn't know what my body was telling me. I went for a run out in the choking air, up the highway, under an overpass, alongside a canal, and through a vast car park. I had no idea what kind of distance I had covered, but I suspected it wasn't very far. I felt like I had dengue fever. If my body was saying anything at all, it was saying, "Get me the fuck out of this heat!" The only upside was that if I needed to make weight by sweating, it would be easy.

Alicia and Jennifer were already in Florida but were staying at Alicia's aunt's place near the beach until it was time to register. They sent me a message to say they would see me the next day. Camille was arriving Wednesday evening. Alexis, Sonya, and Emily were also due in from New York sometime the next day.

On Wednesday morning, when I went in search of the registration room, I noticed some new arrivals in the lobby and around the grounds, and they were in substantially better physical shape than your standard hotel guest. Hungry for some company, I wandered toward a small group I saw—a white man, a young black woman, and an older white female. A couple of them were wearing polo shirts that said "Old School Boxing."

The man, Craig, and his fighter, Tori, were from Washington, DC. The older white woman, Jean, was an official from USA Boxing.

Craig asked, "Are you fighting?" But before I could answer, he said, "Of course you are, you're in great shape."

"Masters, 140 pounds." I felt obliged to qualify my division; I suppose I didn't want people to think I looked old for my age. I'd rather they think I looked young for forty-five.

"There are two more Masters at 140, I believe," said Jean. "So you *will* be fighting."

Tori, who was almost excruciatingly polite, said she was in the 165-lb. division and was 5-0.

"I'm hoping to go home 8-0," she said.

"Watch out for her when you fight," said Craig. "She'll be screaming."

"Yes, ma'am," said Tori. "I can't help it. That's just how I am. I vocalize."

I wandered outside, where I saw a young woman with long black wavy hair in a bikini and with a baby on her hip. No normal American would have such an impressively flat stomach *and* a baby so I pegged her as a boxer as well. Thinking of Dominga, I knew the baby certainly didn't rule her out. I went back inside for a while to take a break from the heat.

Two young women in matching team track suits were now where Tori, Craig, and Jean had been. They said they were from Maine. One, the heavier of the two, a tall blonde, had fought in the Women's World Amateur Championships in China the year before. They had each fought an extraordinary number of fights and looked like they could be in any sport from track and field to hockey. They appeared quietly confident.

Then I was greeted by two friends from Gleason's: Jackie Atkins and her Irish sidekick, Liz, who were making their way through the lobby. Wheeling their suitcases behind them, they both looked as if they were attending a business convention. Jackie's hair was freshly curled into ringlets, and she looked as fit as a racehorse.

She squealed hello, and we embraced like long-lost friends.

Registration began at 2:00 p.m. Not only would there be sixty women and girls coming to fight, but many of the trainers and officials were also female, as were the ring doctor and the paramedics. Gradually a picture was forming of what the world of women's boxing might really look like, and it was more varied than I had anticipated.

The woman with the baby I'd seen outside was now lined up behind me, still with her baby on her hip. When she saw the championship belt on display, she said, "Oh, you're giving me my belt already? That's so nice of you." There was something familiar about her, but I couldn't place her.

On my way back to my room I met up with Terri Moss for the first time. She'd brought two of her fighters, Krichele Featherston and Crystal Bush, and another woman she introduced as Lisa. Terri and I had sent each other messages via Facebook so I had been expecting to see her.

"Hey, chick," she said. "Good to meet you. Hey, do you know anything about a Masters boxer from Tennessee called Susan Dunn? She said she was going to be here, but I haven't seen her. She's a comedian."

"Really? I'd love to fight a comedian," I said. "It could be funny."

I quickly realized, however, that if anyone was going to be funny, it was going to be Terri Moss. In my exchanges with her over the preceding months, I'd discovered several things about her I like: she favors fresh food and is a Michael Pollan fan; also, she is in the *Guinness Book of World Records* as the oldest female professional world champion boxer; and not least of all, she has James Brown's "The Boss" playing on her website. She is, after all, Terri "The Boss" Moss, also known as "Li'l Hands of Stone." The WIBF minimum weight champion—that's the 103-lb. division—she is barely more than a few pounds heavier than her fighting weight. What she lacks in size she makes up for with the force of her bright, vivacious personality.

Terri launched into a story prompted by my mention of Barbara Buttrick.

"Hey," she said, flicking me on the arm. "Did ya ever hear of Silvia Torres?"

I shook my head, although the name did ring a bell.

Torres, she told me, had been in Barbara Buttrick's weight class. She was tiny, like Terri, and had always wanted to fight her back in their heyday. She claimed Barbara had ducked her.

"But I think she's dead now," said Terri with a shrug, as if the fight might otherwise have still been in the works. "I met her when she was doing a documentary on the Fifth Street Gym in Miami, where Muhammad Ali used to train, because she spent time training there too. She was in her workout gear walking around like this." She did an impersonation of an old woman shuffling and pulling her sweat pants up to her waist, which made us all laugh.

"She said Barbara never wanted to fight her. And then I met Barbara here at the tournament and mentioned Silvia to her, and she said, 'Oh yeah, I never heard of her until later. Apparently she wanted to fight me, but I never knew about that.'"

Then she walked around again, shuffling, doing a reprise of her Silvia Torres walk, and she got another wave of laughs.

Later I had a look at the WBAN website, and sure enough Torres was there. Born in Cuba and orphaned at the age of six, she started boxing a year later, appearing on shows in Cuba in the 1930s. Then, when the Castro regime banned the shows, she moved to Florida, where she claimed to have had five hundred fights and thirty knockouts. As the home of more than one aging female pugilist shuffling around Miami Beach looking as harmless as all the other liver-spotted retirees, Florida started to look like the most suitable place to hold the Golden Gloves.

Terri's impersonation might have been a glimpse of her own future because by all accounts she was still up to her neck in the sport despite having retired in 2007 when she beat Stephanie Dobbs for the title. She runs the Decatur Boxing Gym in Atlanta with Xavier Biggs, the brother of 1984 Olympic Gold Medalist heavyweight Tyrell Biggs. Straightaway she handed me an invitation to a dinner and boxing show that would reunite the 1984 team, the greatest American Olympic boxing team ever, which included Mark Breland and Evander Holyfield among others. Unfortunately, it was taking place a week after I was due to fly home.

Terri introduced me to Kevin Franklin, the head of officials for USA Boxing, who was also from Georgia. His wife Angel would be the timekeeper and his daughter Kevina would be one of the referees.

As I was talking to Terri, I caught a glimpse of Anne Wolf, whose daughter Jennifer Wolf Fenn was competing at my weight but in the novice class.

"I think I've watched that clip of Anne knocking out Vonda Ward about five hundred times," I confessed to Terri and Bonnie. The YouTube clip of the knockout has clocked up more than three hundred thousand hits and is one of the most spectacular finishes in women's boxing. Wolf's wild dance of victory around the ring is also noteworthy for its pelvic thrusting, her leap onto the turnbuckle, her breast beating, and ecstatic, unapologetic jubilation as Ward lies in a supine heap.

Bonnie and Terri both launched into critiques of Ward's poor defense, her low hands and high chin style that was just waiting for someone like Anne to come marching in with an overhand right to clock her. Ward was out cold before she hit the canvas, her long limbs buckling like twigs as the commentator shouted, "Tim-ber!"

"They practically had to pick up her head and put it back on," said Terri with her southern drawl.

The far distant world I'd seen through a computer screen was coming to life right before my eyes. Tiny six-inch-high figures had grown and become life size. Facebook profile pictures had acquired legs and were walking around. It was a strange feeling. Like Alice walking through the looking glass, I was now moving around in a world that had been my dream world for so many years.

Soon after that, Alicia arrived in a canary yellow dress with Jennifer by her side. It was so nice to see their familiar faces. I joined them in their room for a while, and although the temperature felt comfortable, Alicia turned it up. It was never too hot for her; in fact, her Jamaican genes reveled in the sweltering heat. She told me that in her ideal world she would live on a Caribbean island, with satellite TV, and no one else around. For someone with hermit aspirations, she was very sociable. I left them to settle in.

Our next date was 9:00 p.m. poolside for the draw.

I went in search of more female boxers. It was still feeling a little unbelievable to me to see so many. Outside I saw Wolf and her daughter again. I approached them cautiously, as you would a wild horse and its foal. There was something intimidating about Wolf, and it wasn't necessarily her imposing physical presence. She was tall, thickset, and broad; it was as if she were more densely packed than your average woman, even your average woman boxer. She wore a peaked, military-style cap, and shoulder-length dreadlocks framed her face. Her Cherokee ancestry was visible in her high cheekbones and deep-set, serious eyes. Her feet and hands were huge.

As I approached, the woman I had seen wearing a bikini and carrying a baby on her hip started talking to Wolf about some girl called Queen, whom she had fought when she was a novice. I gathered that she, against expectations, had won the fight. It sounded like the girl with the baby was now somewhat of a veteran. They were discussing the transition from novice to open, after you have clocked up more than ten fights.

"My baby's just turned eighteen," said Wolf. "But she can bang, let me tell you, she'll stand there and bang with you all night long." Jennifer smiled coyly behind her mother. This surely was a whole new way for a woman to boast about her daughter. I didn't think I'd heard anything like it before.

The bikini-clad woman spoke at length about the various stages of her boxing career, and I watched her, wondering where I had seen her before. Then I remembered.

"Hey," I said. "Do you train at Mendez?"

"I used to," she said. "But now I'm in the Marine Corps. I didn't want to be working in no McDonald's crying every night. I'm listed as nondeployable, though, because of the boxing. And with the Olympics coming up, maybe . . ."

"You're a southpaw, right?" I said.

"Uh huh."

I'd seen her when I visited the Mendez gym in Manhattan, and one of the trainers there had pointed her out to me as being particularly talented. I'd taken some shots of her hitting the bag. Her name is Melissa Roberts. Her baby, Mahlia, was born with a congenital hernia and had spent her first year fighting for her life in hospital. Melissa had suspended her career for three years and resumed it in 2007. And by the sounds of it, she had been making a strong impression wherever she fought. She and Anne Wolf had clearly crossed paths many times before.

Melissa wandered off to be with her partner, and the trio looked like a nice normal young family vacationing together.

I spent the next hour or so being mesmerized by Wolf, who was sitting on the edge of a hammock by the pool.

"I can hit," she told me in a low rumbling voice. "I can hit hard. I hit like a man, and I'm gonna hurt you. When you get in that ring with me you better have your soul right because I'm gonna *destroy* you. I have no conscience about what I'll do to you when I'm in the ring. I'm trying to survive, and I'll destroy anything I come in contact with before it destroys me. I'm a natural killer. I will kill with no regrets."

"I don't doubt that for a moment," I said.

"I'm just a natural warrior, I'm gonna go down swinging."

I told her that I'd watched the Ward knockout a number of times.

"People say that was a lucky punch," she said. "But uh-uh, that wasn't no lucky punch. I tried it three times and got her shoulder. She went to throw a right at me, and I decided I had to step around and go between her gloves. And that takes balls because I coulda got caught with her right, too. But I timed it good.

"I was mad at her because she said to me at the weigh-in when we posed for a picture and I was looking up at her, she says to me she's going to be signing autographs outside in the hotel lobby after the fight.

I said to her, 'You think you're gonna beat me? Tomorrow we're going to do battle, and I'm gonna *destroy* you,' and I looked straight at her chest, and she was—what do ya call it?—hyperventilating. She was already scared. I said to her, 'When you go to bed tonight, you think about that.' I hear that she didn't sleep that night. She was scared."

"I'm sure she was," I said.

"I went to see her in hospital after the fight, but they said she was too sick. She was there for two days."

Wolf was on a roll now.

"When I fought Marsha Valley she said she was going to bully the bully. I said, 'You gonna bully me? My parents died when I was a kid. I lived on the streets eating out of trash cans. I lived with killers. How you gonna bully me in a boxing ring?'"

"Are you angry when you fight?" I asked, a little intrigued by what gave some boxers that murderous impulse that I seemed to lack.

"No," she said.

"So where does that come from, the need to destroy? Is it just the sport?"

She looked at me, a little annoyed. "No!" she said sharply.

"Does it come from emotion?" I asked her.

"Yes, it does. It comes from emotion."

"From hurt?"

"No," she said, this time more reflectively.

But I suspected otherwise. I'd seen a documentary on Wolf when I was back in New York. My roommate in DUMBO, Evan, had kindly taped it for me. I learned what a difficult life she'd had and was chilled by her intimidating persona.

"Wow, she's scary," I'd said to Evan then, as we watched together.

"Yeah, she is," he'd replied, biting his thumbnail, his knees drawn to his chest.

So it wasn't a complete shock to see her in what looked to be continuous stare-down mode.

Wolf has had a tough life by any measure, the kind of life that prepares you well for the professional prizefighting ring, regardless of your gender. She was orphaned at eighteen when her mother died of cancer, and her father, a drug dealer, was shot and killed soon after. Her brother was also shot dead while he was robbing an IHOP in Texas. She was homeless and destitute at twenty-four with two kids in tow.

"I didn't sulk about it," she said. "I felt, 'That's life.' That's one thing that makes me a natural killer when I'm in the ring—I had a hard life."

She had also been sexually abused and had done some jail time. When she found boxing she was angry and in pain, and she says it saved her life.

Maybe Wolf had what I lacked most, with my kind and tolerant parents; my expensive private school education; my early exposure to intellectuals, artists, and poets; and the many choices I had had in life. Boxing was not the end of an already hard road for me—it was the beginning of a new one. But the soft and comfortable ride I'd had before I began to box had ensured that I harbored no rage to tap into when I fought. For some people the rage was barely a pinprick away. It seemed to me that for them the path to winning was much simpler.

Like Alicia, I'd never really wanted to kill. I liked the feeling of knowing someone was trying—and hopefully failing—to kill *me* rather than the other way round.

I wondered if it was possible to change that without necessarily becoming demented. Many fighters could and did win without rage, and a lot of them told me that anger merely fogged their judgment or made them reckless, and they were better off without it.

But I didn't think Wolf was one of them. I think that, like some of the most devastating fighters—both male and female—she was thankful for the opportunity the sport gave her to unleash her fury without risking incarceration.

As we were talking, I noticed Jackie and Liz jogging past the pool. Jackie was clad head to toe in a dark track suit. The weight limit for my division was 141 lb., and try as I might, I couldn't get below 138 lb. and into the next lowest category, which was 132 lb. With no opponents at that weight, however, there wasn't much of point to shedding the pounds. So with Jackie jogging in the heat it looked like we might finally meet in the ring over the next couple of days, if I agreed. There were two other 140-lb. Masters and none at 152 lb. as far as anyone knew.

Wolf watched them as if they were a herd of deer on the horizon and said, "They must be Masters."

I told her the story of what had happened with Jackie in New York, and she said, "You should tell her there's no way you gonna fight her ass after she did that, and you come all the way from Australia."

She lifted herself up out of the hammock a little stiffly.

"You look so strong," I said.

"Still?" she said, smiling, the shark mask suddenly falling away.

"Oh yeah," I said. "You look like you can do some damage, that's for sure. I wouldn't want to fight you."

Then she broke into a warm, white-toothed smile and limped off in search of her baby.

By dusk the hotel was swarming with toned, fit-looking young women of all sizes heading toward the pool for the draw. Ordinary Americans vacationing at the hotel looked like a different species; they were flaccid and soft. Even the healthy young ones looked weak in comparison.

Alicia and I went to get Camille from the airport and rushed back to the hotel so she could register with only minutes to spare. Emily, Alexis, and Sonya had all settled into their room. Sonya had a barking bronchitis that sounded dreadful.

"Maybe you shouldn't fight," I said.

She dismissed my remark as if it were the most preposterous idea she'd ever heard.

"I'd fucking fight with one arm," she said, her curly black hair looking slightly frizzy in the humidity.

It was almost dark, and there was a big crowd of athletes and trainers, so we all pushed in close together. Names in each weight category were drawn from a hat, and the matches were made at random. If there were an odd number of fighters, like the three 140-lb. Masters, then one would get the bye. This meant that two of the women would fight and the winner would fight the third woman—the one who had gotten the bye.

Camille, at 132 lb., was in the most populated weight class and was likely to fight on all three nights. Her nemesis was Patricia Manuel, a boyish-looking girl with a Mohawk and glasses who had beaten her at the Nationals. Alicia had told me that Camille could have won but had let herself get psyched out by what she thought was Patricia's power.

Bonnie had given everyone the option of fighting in a matched bout, win or lose, so we could all get some experience. If I got the bye, I could fight twice, maybe even three times if I fought Jackie. But I was playing my cards close on that one.

I'd joined Jackie and Liz for a salad soon after my chat with Anne Wolf and began to debrief them about our conversation. I asked Jackie if she ever had the desire to kill or if it was more of a sporting competition for her. She didn't strike me as the kind of person who harbored a lot of bitterness or rage. She was too cheerful and open. She said she didn't see herself as a killer. "But if I get hit, I get mad," she said. I took note.

Back by the pool there was an undercurrent of tension in the air, but the tension was one of anticipation rather than menace. It was amazing to see, even in the dim light, so many different types of females gathered. It was impossible to say what kind of woman took up boxing and pursued it to this level, so far beyond the fitness class where it had, for many, begun. Still, I couldn't help categorizing them into subgroups. There were none that fit the stereotype of what some people must imagine when they think of female boxers. There were plenty of slouchy tomboys with their jeans slung low and bravado oozing from their every pore. But then there were the tall, straight-haired white girls who embodied the word "Amazon" and who did their own posturing. These were counterbalanced by the petite, pink-wearing girls and yet others who were sporty or reedy. Other women and girls looked like they could be your insurance agent, your lawyer, or your next door neighbor. There were also a few sassy, slightly snooty types. The crowd was peppered with mostly male trainers, but there was no doubt that the men were the supporting act and that the women were the main show.

Camille drew a stocky little freckle-faced redhead named Amber from Kansas City.

"She looks like she's made for you," I whispered in Camille's ear.

"Fuck her," said Camille, while managing to keep her best smile fixed on her face.

The Masters' names—the once-elusive Michelle Straka, another boxer named Kim Hicks, and me—were called, and we all gathered next to Yvonne as if we were about to play a party game. Straka was taller than me but a little droopy looking, with a few tattoos on her arms. Hicks, incredibly, was a good deal shorter than me. I'd never fought anyone shorter than me. Both of them were biting their lips.

I got the bye, which meant I would be able to see them in action, and if I wanted to, I could fight the loser as well, or Jackie, on Saturday night.

Jackie nudged me. "They looked scared of you," she said.

"No," I said. "Did they?"

"Hell yes," she said. "C'mon, you know people, you can read body language. They looked scared." And then she laughed. "They saw your guns," she said.

"*My* guns, what about *your* guns?"

Just then a girl with long dark hair and a goofy grin came bounding up to Jackie and said, "Do you want to fight me?"

"Well, sure," she said. "But I'm a Master."

The girl shrugged and bounced around. "That's OK," she said. "Why not?"

"Well, how are old are you?" said Jackie.

"Thirty," said the girl excitedly before getting distracted by something.

Jackie looked at me. "I don't think she's all there," she said.

Camille had told us in the car when we collected her from the airport that the previous year there had been a slightly crazy girl at the tournament who looked like Dennis Rodman. She was unrepresented, and when she and Alicia had given her a ride somewhere, she told them that she had lost deliberately.

"There's always one," she'd said.

When the girl walked away I caught Camille's eye. "Dennis Rodman?" I said, and she nodded.

10 SHOWTIME

ON THE first night of the competition, the New York group set up near the red corner in the Hilton ballroom after posing for photos in our Gleason's T-shirts. The hotel's thermostat must have been set particularly low that night because it was freezing. People actually had to put on jackets and coats, which seemed crazy at the height of a tropical summer.

The evening began with a performance of the national anthem, which Kevin Franklin's wife Angel and their daughter Kevina sang together. They did some nice harmonizing, and Kevina's high notes were almost out of range for human hearing. Angel had asked that caps be removed before the anthem was sung, and one old black guy refused and left the room rather than take his off. A little act of defiance in the patriotic melting pot. It's a beautiful song, "The Star-Spangled Banner," better than most anthems no doubt. And the phrase "home of the brave" always goes over well at boxing venues. Still, patriotism always unnerves me a little. I can't help thinking of the Nuremberg rallies.

The first to fight were the novices. The more boyish of Terri Moss's two tomboys—Krichele, who had a couple of fights behind her—was up against Heather Whiteley, a girl with a massive shiner and a smile to go with it, who Bonnie was coaching. Heather had been walking around showing off that florid purple and yellow bruise all day as though it were a diamond wedding ring. Once she started boxing you could see how she got it.

Bonnie was calling out to her, "Keep those hands nice and high, Heather." But she was getting hit with straight shots that came between her gloves and snapped her head back. One shot in the second round sent it back so far that it looked like her head was going to come off. I turned around and saw Alicia wincing.

Hearing the higher pitch of mostly female voices shouting from the crowd and from the corners was a quite a change from most boxing events.

Gleason's team.

"That's it, don't wait for her!" and "Be first!" were among the phrases being called out from the crowd.

Jackie was a committed red-corner girl regardless of who was in it.

"You jab, red, you use that reach, girl. There you go, that's what I'm talking 'bout baby."

Winners came out of the ring and seemed to head straight for Jackie to get a hug. "I'm so proud of you, girl," she'd say as if they'd trained together for years.

"You know her?" I asked after it had happened a few times.

"She was at Bonnie's gym today, and I helped her on the pads," she said.

Then the Masters' bout started, and I sat ringside on the edge of my seat with my camera set to movie mode. Jackie sat right beside me. The shorter of the two, Kim, was actually the better boxer and knew how to move her head, while Michelle Straka, the taller one, was uncoordinated, her feet staggering as if she were on a listing ship. She had no clue how to use her reach, and I even saw her lift her back foot when she threw a sloppy jab, something usually only a raw beginner would do and any decent trainer would have corrected long ago. From the opening seconds I knew I could beat either of them, even on a bad day, and so I didn't really care who won. The rounds seemed short, although the gloves were smaller than I expected at twelve ounces.

The USA Boxing rule book stipulates sixteen-ounce gloves for Masters and two-minute rounds. So I'd been wearing sixteen-ounce gloves all the time in training. But it seemed that the rule book was open to interpretation, as if it were some holy scripture written in an obscure language that only a select few could read.

The upcoming Ringside tournament in August was going to try to enforce a different head guard for Masters, one that, coincidentally, only Ringside sold. I had read somewhere that they were also going to make Masters wear eighteen-ounce gloves over one-and-a-half-minute rounds, as opposed to two minutes for everyone else and three minutes for the men. That was beginning to sound not just ridiculous but almost dangerous. I'd never even worn a pair of eighteen-ounce gloves. Why not just strap pillows to our hands?

That day I'd spoken to my Ringside contact, Dave Lubs, who said the Ringside-made head guard was going to be mandatory, even though there was no mention of it in the online version of the rule book.

"The book is wrong," said Lubs.

I was thinking of ditching Ringside. It sounded like the whole massive show was just a ruse to sell stuff to a captive customer base of fighters.

Kim Hicks ducked and weaved her way to a win over a stumbling and flailing Michelle Straka. I was hoping Straka would stick around despite the loss to fight either me or Jackie on Saturday night. Without her I would be backed into a corner and have no choice but to get in the ring with Jackie. After everything that had happened, how could I possibly refuse?

After the fight I saw Straka being led through the crowd by the hand as if something had gone seriously wrong with her.

I reached out and tapped her on the arm. "Are you all right?" I asked.

And she squinted in my direction and said, "Oh yeah, I just can't see, I don't have my contact lenses in."

No wonder she could hardly land a punch.

Camille fought a great fight against Amber from Kansas City. Although she had a tendency to get stuck on the ropes at times, Camille's work rate was high, and her punches were flowing and scoring cleanly. Amber responded with great tenacity. It made for an exciting encounter.

Camille was the victor and would be fighting again the following evening.

Some of the fights that night were very tough, and heart often beat skill. For example, the tall woman from Maine was outdone by a shorter, less skillful black girl, which was unexpected and somewhat of an upset. Overall, I thought the women fought more like professionals than amateurs. The style is very different from the Australian and European style where body punches hardly count and the work rate is higher, lighter, and generally cleaner. But I like the US down-and-dirty style better; it has more soul to it and more of a gutsy rhythm. I knew that it didn't work well internationally, but there was no career path for Masters anyway, so what did I care about international standards?

When I borrowed Camille's portable scales the next morning they read 138 lb., so I went down to the weigh-in feeling confident. Everyone looked a bit dour and weary with the exception of Jackie who was bright eyed and shiny in her designer gym gear. Even though she had no one to fight she was weighing in to get the walk over—namely, to win by default. Maybe that explained why she was so chipper.

The weigh-in line moved reasonably quickly, Jackie brightening the mood by saying, "Us Masters should go first cause we're so old we need to go back to bed and get our rest."

"You can't say that with those guns, girl," someone said.

I hit the mark at 138 lb.

After the weigh-in I caught up with Terri Moss and her girls again, and they insisted I come with them to have a "breakfast of champions" at IHOP. I'd never been to an IHOP before so I couldn't resist.

"Oh, you'll love it," said Terri. "It's real American food, all sugar and fat."

While we were waiting to be seated, I took in a lungful of the air and said, "You know, America smells like sugar to me or corn syrup or whatever it is. You know, that sweet smell."

"Hey," she said to the girls. "Did y'all hear that? You know how different countries have different smells? She says America smells like sugar. How 'bout that?"

This wasn't the kind of restaurant I would normally eat at. But pancakes were carbohydrate bombs so it probably wasn't a bad idea. The IHOP was packed. We had to wait a while for a table.

Our waitress was a fat middle-aged woman with long gray hair and a slightly bossy manner.

"She's gotta be from New York," said Terri. "Everyone in Florida is from somewhere else. Mostly it's New York."

Terri and her girls ordered tomato on the side with their pancakes, bananas, eggs, grits, and French toast. I had pancakes and jam.

"You don't mind if we say a quick prayer?" asked Terri. "We're from the Bible Belt." And they all put their heads down while Terri rushed through grace. This was an odd thing for an Australian to witness. I'd never seen people say grace in public before.

"This looks like it's just a regular breakfast in America," I said, looking around at the crowd. "We eat pancakes only on special occasions, you know, like birthdays."

My observations about food appeared to be of special interest to Terri, who was keen to hear what I thought and what I ate.

"I don't eat much meat," I said. "Kangaroo mostly."

She raised her eyebrows.

"You know," she said, "it would be great if you could fight that Susan Dunn at the Georgia Games next weekend. I think it would be a good opportunity for you. I really thought she'd be here. She said she was coming."

"Maybe," I said as my pancakes arrived. "I'll see how things go."

"Yeah, right now what you need to do is rest. You know what a fighter's best weapon is?" she asked. "It's not roadwork or padwork or sparring, it's rest. You need to be well rested before you get in that ring tonight. You need to feel like a racehorse, chomping at the bit."

Much to everyone's amusement, I took snapshots of everyone's food as if each dish were a point of interest on a sightseeing tour. With a belly full of corn starch and sugar I went back to my room to nap. Later in the afternoon, as I started to get ready to go downstairs, it occurred to me that I had never felt so good before a fight, so calm and confident and clearheaded. It was such a contrast to how I'd felt in New York in May. It helped that I'd been able to get a good look at my opponent the night before, that I had nothing much to do but lounge around, and that I didn't have any injuries or oncoming colds. It also helped that I had been boxing for so long. In fact, my time in the sport was probably my best weapon.

The only niggling worry I had was that something entirely untoward would go wrong, and for some reason I would lose to Hicks. But I couldn't imagine what that thing might be. I knew I'd never forgive myself if I got beaten by that garden gnome, so I was careful not to get too cocky.

Camille was also fighting again, but she was closer to the end of the schedule while I was at the front, listed as fight three. This time Camille would be up against a quiet girl with long wavy hair. "She looks like a dude," said Camille. "I always get the ones who look like dudes."

Alexis was fighting Christina Cruz, Emily would be right after me, then Camille, and then Sonya, being a super heavyweight, would be the last fight.

Once the fighting started, despite her bronchitis, Sonya's voice was projecting well across the ballroom. "You girls have got bodies too you know!" she bellowed when boxers were head hunting. "Punch, punch, punch."

"You've got a good voice," I said to her.

"Yeah," she laughed. "A schoolteacher's voice."

Jackie followed me to the glove table after Alicia had bandaged my hands. "I'll be the tall skinny one for the first time ever," I said.

Once I was gloved up, Alicia took me through some punches. She wasn't happy with the way I was dropping down.

"Have you seen her?" I said. "She's about four feet tall."

"Oh, well, forget about it then."

Before I knew it we were in the ring.

The first round felt like I was gliding around, and every jab seemed to land. They came out smoothly and hit the target. Pop, pop, pop. A few missed when she bobbed her head, but it didn't feel like she even touched me. Well, maybe once. Her trainer was hysterical in the corner, shrieking like a demented race caller: "Use your legs! Use your legs! Do it again! There you go! There you go!" It was quite distracting. In the past I had usually managed to zone out any noise, but this guy had a piercing voice, and the room was only about half full. It seemed that he was saying "There you go" every time *I* hit *her*.

I came back to the corner, and Alicia told me to relax and throw straight rights instead of curling them like I would to hit a taller person. In the next round I tried to throw more combinations when I heard the New Yorkers shouting, "Combinations Mischa, combinations!" These people were obsessed with combinations. And they usually worked. Punches in bunches, as the adage goes, the idea being that if you throw three or four punches in quick succession, at least one of them will land, maybe more. Throw one at a time, and it's easier for the other person to defend themselves. But my jab was having a 90 per cent strike rate.

"Let your hands go, Meeesha!" shouted Sonya.

In the third round I was a little more tired and thought that I could win the fight if I just stayed on the move, but there was that pressure to throw combinations, and so that's what I tried to do. However, I found I was right in front of her too much and that she could hit me. Her punches felt like wet rags and had no impact at all, but still, I could have avoided them altogether. I didn't need to lose that contact lens in the final seconds.

These were two-minute rounds thanks to some negotiating by Bonnie. The first Masters bout had been one-minute rounds, barely long enough to get warmed up.

When the fight was over one of the female judges looked up at me and said, "You need to work on that last round. You need to get more condition." I'd never gotten feedback from a judge like that before, so it startled me. Usually they are stony-faced figures who don't even look at you after the fight. Some of them, I suspect, don't see much even during the fight.

"You're very good, though," she said. "You box well."

I tried to look over the referee's shoulder at the scorecards as he collected them from the judges. Alicia thought that was hilarious.

"Are you sure I won?" I asked her, and she nodded, smiling that million-dollar movie-star smile.

I'd been stiffed a few times in Australia and gone back to the corner laughing and joking only to see the other side get their hand raised. But this time it was mine that went up.

As I stepped out of the ring people said, "Good job," and patted me on the back.

Sonya told me I should have thrown more punches.

"But I was landing my jab," I said.

"But you want to do more than land. You want to stop them," she said.

But did I? Even if in theory I wanted to win by stoppage—namely, when the referee steps in, the corner surrenders, and the fighter can't continue or is knocked out—the idea seemed to leave my head once I was in the ring. Was there something wrong with that or something right?

Afterward, when I was roaming the room I came across Bonnie.

"Hey," she said, "you looked like a pro in there. You haven't lost anything. You're in shape, too. Are you gonna fight that New York girl?"

"I dunno," I said. "I might have a fight next week in Atlanta."

"But you're here now, and it's an opportunity. You should take it, you know." Then she paused and said, "I would."

That did it for me.

"OK," I said. "I'll talk to Alicia and see what she says."

I found Alicia delighting in the 132-lb. semifinal match between the aggressive Patricia Moreno, who had beaten Camille in Denver, and a black southpaw from California called Yolanda Ezell, who could have been a replica of Alicia herself.

Alicia was squealing with delight as she watched the fight. Camille was taping the bout on her digital camera with her eyes wide and unblinking.

"She has that girl so confused," said Alicia.

"Tell me," I said when the fight had finished, "do you think I should fight Jackie tomorrow?"

"If you want to," she said.

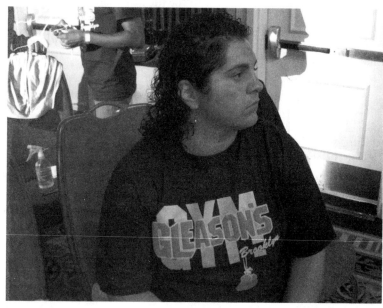

Sonya Lamonakis.

I messaged Peter that I would probably fight her, and he expressed reservations again because of her size. I'd e-mailed him the group photos from the day before, and they made Jackie look so much bigger than me because she was at the edge of the shot and I was closer in.

"Peter's worried about my fighting Jackie," I said to Jennifer.

"Why?" she asked. I thought she meant, "Why are you fighting Jackie?" so I explained, "Well, because she has no one in her weight class, and she came all this way . . ."

"No," she said. "Why is he worried? I've seen Jackie box, and you're a way better boxer than her."

Terri Moss messaged me soon after: "By the way, we all think you won because of the pancakes."

I tracked her down in the audience.

"Shit, that was so easy. It was like a cakewalk for you. You're jabbing, moving, looking relaxed, pah, pah, pah, like get me a coffee, will ya . . . I like the way you box, you got a nice style."

"Really?"

"Yeah, you know what? You've got rhythm. You could have done nothing but jab your way through that fight and you would have still won it."

"Well, my corner told me to throw more combinations."

"Well, me, I woulda just told you to keep doing what you were doing."

In my euphoria after the bout I missed Emily's fight. It sounded like the decision wasn't right, and she may have been robbed. I did manage to catch Alexis's fight, though. She chased Cruz around the ring relentlessly but had trouble trapping her long enough to land anything.

"C'mon, beast out, Lexie!" yelled Sonya.

Alexis looked demoralized after being defeated for a third time by Cruz, whose hair, after the bout, came miraculously out of her helmet in a clean, fresh cascade.

Sonya's was the last bout. She was up against a fairly massive woman, and it was a slug fest in the great heavyweight tradition, the two of them standing toe to toe pretty much the whole time. Sonya's work rate was tremendous, considering the size of the woman leaning on her and the fact that her lungs were still not clear from infection. I could see why she thought I could have done more, because she didn't leave anything in the tank. She knew what she was saying when she told people to beast out. Sonya wasn't known as "Amtrak" for nothing. She not only won, but she left behind a train wreck as well, breaking her opponent's nose.

The next morning as I was waiting on the weigh-in line I ran into Patricia Alcivar.

I'd known about Patricia for years and knew that she was one of the first women to fight in the New York Golden Gloves back in the mid-1990s. But she had been a teenager then and so was still only in her early thirties despite being what could only be considered a boxing veteran and technically part of the pioneering generation.

Her Facebook status updates were ridiculous, hypercharged posts positive beyond all reason, rain, hail, or shine. She'd already run something like ten full marathons and was up each day at 4:30 a.m. reporting on the miles ahead of her and the fitness challenges she vowed to undertake that day. In one update she reported that she'd held the plank position (a yoga pose) for twenty minutes. She could pump out eighty push-ups in a minute.

As we waited in line together, sitting on the floor, she told me that although she'd been boxing for a long time she was forced to take three years off due to an illness and had resumed training only in the past year. Her plan was to turn pro soon. She was a 119-lb. Colombian woman with a dimply smile and long, dark ringlets. She was originally from Queens and had moved with her husband to North Carolina. I'd read somewhere that she'd left home at fifteen and supported herself through school living alone in New York. She'd lost the night before but was weighing in to get a matched bout that night with Alexis, who had to fly back to New York immediately after the bout to take an exam the next day.

Jackie was her usual cheerful self at the weigh-in line, a poster girl for those over forty. This time she was weighing in to fight, and her opponent was me. But her demeanor toward me didn't change. She was still oozing her charismatic charm. I was struggling to get my head around the idea that in a few hours we'd be hitting each other.

I thought it would probably be best for me if I tried to steer clear of her for the rest of the day.

That night when I went down to the ballroom, I ran into Anne Wolf again.

"Did you fight last night?" she asked.

"Yes," I said.

"D'ya win?"

"Yes."

"That's right, I seen you." She gave me a smile of recognition. "You got a good-ass jab on you."

"I'm fighting Jackie tonight."

"I like Jackie. She's nice."

"She's very nice. Very likable."

"You jab and move, girl, and you jab high and low and move to your right, away from her right hand. Good luck, anyway."

By now I'd seen Jennifer Wolf Fenn (Anne's "baby") bang her way through her fight in such a crowd-pleasing manner she could have been at the MGM Grand in Las Vegas. She was a great proponent of that solid American amateur style. As I prepared to fight Jackie, I felt a tingle of nerves, but at the same time I was less concerned about the possibility of losing than usual. I knew that I couldn't get hurt, and something told me luck was on my side. During my first career in Australia, I had felt decidedly unlucky. If a fight was close, I'd lose. I tended to need stoppages or shut-outs to win. Sometimes it made me a little paranoid.

But according to Terri Moss there was no such thing as luck, good or bad. "It's 90 percent mental," she told me. "You have to think like a champion. I've been in the corner with opponents, and I've said, 'Are you gonna win tonight?' and they say, 'I don't know—maybe I will, maybe I won't,' and I feel like saying, 'Buddy, I *know* you ain't gonna win.' I always wanted to be 100 percent in the ring myself, but I never was. The best I managed was about 85 percent. But you're fighting, so you know there's always someone else in there with you, so, what can you do? Anyway, so you've got to not let yourself think about it. That's what makes a champion. Have you seen that Mike Tyson documentary? He talks to himself, I mean he's crazy, but it worked for him. He'd say, 'I'm the heavyweight champion of the world. No one can beat me, no one can beat me. I can't lose.'"

She started shadowboxing around, all 105 lb. and five-foot-nothing of her.

"I'm always gonna be the heavyweight champion," she said, her voice getting louder. "No one can beat me." She gave my shoulder a little flick. "I do that kind of thing too, even now I do it."

That was just the kind of talk I struggled with. I still thought it was better to be realistic than to talk myself into thinking I was Mike Tyson.

I knew I could lose, but I wasn't planning on it. I was definitely going to try to avoid it. I would do my best. What more could I do?

I joined Alicia and the others inside the ballroom. "So, what am I gonna do?" I asked Alicia.

"With Jackie?"

"Yes."

"You're gonna move and move," she said.

"And jab?"

"And jab and throw a bunch of punches and then move."

"OK, that's what I thought I'd do, but I just wanted to check with you."

"I will slap you if you don't listen to me," she said.

"OK," I said. "I can take it."

When I first met Terri Moss and told her Alicia was my coach, she seemed surprised. "I saw her slap her fighter last year," she said.

"Really?" I said. "Oh, well, she's already hit me so many times, what's one more?"

"She's slapped me, too," Camille said.

"So I heard," I said. "Did it help?"

"I think it did," said Camille.

There's a minute in the corner between rounds, but it feels like about ten seconds. It's hard to take everything in. If you're a trainer wanting to get a point across in that minute, a slap is probably the most succinct way to make your point.

Alicia had bandaged one of my hands when it was time to corner Alexis to fight both Patricia Alcivar and the clock.

She had to check in at 8:00 p.m. for a flight back to New York, and although the fight was due to start at 7:00 p.m., things were, of course, running behind. Sonya had Alexis's luggage ready to take downstairs and had booked a cab to take her to the airport.

"She should forget about the fight and just go and take the test. It's more important than this," said Alicia, shaking her head. "This isn't important."

Alicia had to wrap three pairs of hands before the open bouts started. Camille was bout sixteen and Sonya, of course, was at the end.

This time one of the fighters sang "The Star-Spangled Banner" more beautifully even than the harmonizing Franklins. Then Arturo Gatti, who had died under mysterious circumstances in Brazil that day, was honored with a ten-bell salute, rung whenever a boxer dies. Some of the Gleason's people had known Gatti and liked him a lot and were a little bewildered by his sudden death. Some reports said that his wife had strangled him to death. But it was hard to believe, given his legendary trilogy of fights against Mickey Ward, that a small woman could have killed him in a manner that required so much physical strength.

Alexis got in the ring forty-five minutes before she had to check in for her flight. "She'll never make it," I said to Sonya, who agreed that she was pushing her luck.

Then the fight started. Alexis immediately seemed stronger and more grounded than Patricia and was forcing the pace, making her move and catching her a little off balance at times. Patricia didn't sit down on her punches so much, and she used those runner's legs to escape the attack. But Alexis managed to corner her and tee off, landing combinations in the way that she hadn't been able to against Christina Cruz the night before.

Alexis won the fight and looked to be enjoying the moment, in no rush to get out of the ring. When she made it back to our corner, she started to cut her bandages off.

"You can fly with those on," said Alicia, and Alexis grabbed her stuff and was out the door in her fighting gear—blue shorts, shirt, and boots.

"They're gonna think I'm crazy at the airport!" she shouted on her way out.

Meanwhile, Jackie arrived wearing a hot pink tank top and black satin shorts. I was also wearing pink. Jackie's body looked sensational, like a thoroughbred in the mounting yard. I was happy that she looked so good. The only thing I noticed about her that might have hinted that she was closer to fifty than to forty was a slight stoop. Other than that you might say she was in her thirties. I was hoping that the running and the effort she'd made to drop some weight would tell on her. But I didn't expect it would. I opened my jacket and showed her I was also wearing pink, and she laughed.

"We should have consulted," I said.

"What?" said Sonya. "You didn't get the text?"

We went to the glove table together. "Good luck," I said. "You're one of the most likable people I've ever met." And she smiled and said, "That's what Anne said. She told me, 'You two ladies are gems.'" She made Anne sound like a nice woman who served tea and cookies. But it was Anne "I'm going to destroy you" Wolf she was talking about.

Never had there been so much good will between me and someone I was about to fight. When I expressed concern about this to Yvonne and Bonnie, they said, "It doesn't matter. This is business."

I'd had no feelings—neither positive nor negative—about the woman I'd fought the night before, and I preferred it that way. But what could I do? I was sure that this wasn't the first time at one of these tournaments that people had made friends and then had to fight each other.

Suddenly we were in the ring, and we had a referee who I'd noticed because he had a face like Fred Flintstone's. He came over to check me, which like all pre-bout inspections was neither comprehensive nor even very specific. I opened my mouth and showed him my mouth guard. He turned my palms up and inspected my gloves and then turned them over, and I noticed that they were ten-ounce gloves. After all the bullshit with Masters rules and glove sizes, they'd given us gloves that were too small even for our weight class, which in this case was being described as 152 lb. even though Jackie weighed 142.5 lb. and I was just over 141 lb.

"Wait a minute. Not ten-ounce gloves," I said. "No. We're meant to wear twelves!"

He looked confused. Then I wondered whether Jackie was wearing tens or twelves. Had I possibly just given away an advantage?

"Hmm," Alicia whispered to me. "Maybe you shouldn't have said anything."

Then he checked Jackie's gloves, and it looked like she was wearing tens too. So then Kevin Franklin, the head of the officials, came over to confirm they should be twelves. Then one of the glove guys came over to take them and said, "They should be twelves," as if it had been our fault they weren't. "We're the ones who told *him*," said Alicia. "And why didn't he bring the twelves over with him? Now he's got to go back and get them."

Finally, Fred Flintstone brought us to center ring, and we touched gloves and went back to our corners.

I boxed cautiously in the first round, perhaps overly so. But I wanted to see what Jackie had in terms of power and reach and what she did with it. Would she come "right at me" as Alicia had cautioned she might, or would she play it more like a boxer? I'd told Peter that I had an unofficial policy that for the first twenty seconds of any new encounter I would time my defense, feeling out punches and biding my time about what to do next. So I let her be the first to throw and stayed mobile for the first few seconds. She sure did have a long, long jab. It unfurled like a black snake. I wouldn't be able to stand and match it with her by throwing jabs or she would beat me to the punch—that much was clear. So I just kept moving around as she kept throwing.

I was wary about getting too close to the danger zone. I caught her with a right, and I remembered her saying how she gets mad when she gets hit—and she did. But she also stiffened up, and it slowed her a little. I landed maybe two clean right hands in that round and maybe she landed two clean punches as well—and one of them looked bad for me because she caught me as I moved in. But her punches weren't quite as hard as I'd expected them to be, nor were they as fast. We bumped gloves at the end of the round and went back to our corners.

The second I sat down I got slapped on the side of the head like I was a ten-year-old caught picking her nose. "This isn't a sparring session," said Alicia. "You have to throw more punches. She's racking up the points right now. Don't try and throw that one right hand." Then she jumped out of the ring and said, "Stand up." I thought I could get a few more seconds so I ignored her.

"Stand up!" she repeated. And I did.

I began the second round with more vigor and urgency. I dropped down a lot more under her jab and moved in on her. Within about ten seconds Jackie stumbled back and fell into the ropes.

"Holy shit," I thought. "What have I done?" But I moved in on her some more. I recalled fighting a big girl in Australia who was wearing a cumbersome breastplate that seemed to be bothering her. At one point she dropped her hands to adjust it, and not only did I *not* take advantage of it, I kind of felt sorry for her. I thought I'd won that fight by staying mobile and jabbing, but I didn't win it and was angry about the decision for a long time. Someone said to me afterward that it looked like I could have done more. With that memory embedded somewhere in my fight brain I tried to do more now and to not feel too much sympathy for the stumbling Jackie. Better her than me. I don't know if it was my punch or a slip or maybe a bit of both, but if the ropes weren't there she would undoubtedly have gone down. I know that much. She bounced off them and floated away. I managed to break through her defense at times to land clean shots, and she kept her punches long, but those sleek arms were unfurling a little too slowly and not very accurately now.

Alicia seemed more satisfied after the second round, and although she waved the spray bottle before me like it was a pistol, she squirted my face more in good-humored service than as a form of punishment.

In the last round Jackie was clearly tired and so was I. But I was able to outwork her. The stuff coming back at me was much less forceful and less frequent, and I could move in more easily. I knew that it was the ability to work when I felt fatigued that made all the difference. The running she had done to make weight must have taken its toll. Her clothes were loose, and I thought she looked gaunt again, like she had

Camille and Alicia.

in New York. She still looked like a sprinter at her peak, but maybe it all concealed a fatigue that she wasn't expecting to feel. I sensed the last round was my best. But as usual I wasn't certain about the whole fight. Alicia, however, seemed more confident.

When they called the blue corner at the end of the fight, I was ecstatic. I had to look over and confirm that I was from the blue corner, and there was Alicia's smiling face to confirm it. I had won! I hugged Jackie so hard I made her squeal. I couldn't stop thanking her. I told her she was a great boxer as she put the medal on me, and I held the ropes open for her to step down from the ring.

The doctor asked me how I felt.

"Tired," I said.

"No pain anywhere that you didn't have pain before, no headaches? Vision problems?"

There's really no point in asking these questions immediately after you've had a fight because you feel nothing. If you win, you feel elated, and if you lose, you feel thrilled to have survived. Better to ask the next day. But in actual fact I didn't have any pain or injuries anywhere from the fight. Nothing. Not that night nor in the days that followed.

Mostly, I felt euphoric about the win, especially because back in New York I had been cast as the underdog. But another part of me felt that I hadn't really earned it. I don't know why, as I had certainly done my time. All the hard training, all the running, the sprinting, the sparring, the careful eating—all of it must have counted for something. Maybe Terri was right, perhaps luck has nothing to do with it. As Muhammad Ali famously said, "The fight is won or lost far away from witnesses, behind the lines, in the gym, and out there on the road, long before I dance under those lights."

What *did* make me feel lucky was the fact that I was fighting Masters. Camille had to fight fresh, hungry, fit, and seasoned 132-lb. girls in their twenties who were as determined as she was. She'd clearly won her first fight, and in her second fight she was completely dominant against the "dude" girl who had a poor defense and a slightly front-on stance. Camille's punches shot straight through and her opponent ate them each time. It was a shut-out win for Camille and her best display of boxing skill yet. Those first two bouts had both been busy four-round fights, and now she had one more to go against a waitress from California.

In her third fight, Camille fought her heart out but didn't get the decision. She took it hard and blamed herself, but I couldn't see what more she could have done. It was clear she had done the best she could; the other girl just edged her out with her strength.

Sonya won the final in another hard-fought contest in which she managed to get a stoppage.

It had been an amazing three days, seeing all the girls together, both in and out of the ring. On the final night, after the belts and medals had been awarded and the pictures taken, I watched as everyone returned to the lobby in dresses and high heels and went out into the Saturday night air to celebrate. Just ordinary girls now to look at them, I thought. No one would ever have guessed what they had been up to earlier in the evening.

11 THE HEAT IS ON

AFTER THE tournament, I came back to earth as if I were only now arriving in Florida, as if the Hilton had been a strange parallel universe in which women's physical power was acknowledged and celebrated.

I had planned to train with Bonnie for a couple of weeks before heading to Ringside, so I moved out of the Hilton to the Angelfish Inn, a small hotel on Hollywood Beach in Fort Lauderdale. The natural climate, which had been kept at bay by the Hilton's air conditioning system, started to drain me within a few hours, the humidity and the baking sun sapping my strength like some chronic illness. There didn't appear to be any shade, the narrow strips cast by the ubiquitous palm trees making a mockery of the very idea of shade. The glare coming from the pavement seared my retinas. My constantly squinting eyes reminded me of Clint Eastwood's in *Pale Rider*. I was sprouting crow's-feet by the minute.

I lost so much fluid during my first session at Bonnie's gym that I had to wring out my clothes afterward. And it felt like someone had replaced my blood with glue. Even body-punching with three nonfighting and relatively unfit females proved hard work. The ring floor felt spongy and slow, and the air was like mud. The women were aggressive. Of course they were—Bonnie encouraged them to attack constantly. Since they weren't trained boxers, they fought with an unpredictable rhythm, and I had to find a way to fend them off without hurting them. Bonnie said she always told her fighters it was up to them not to get hit in these unbalanced encounters. The women were at the gym for fitness training—they weren't expecting the violence of boxing. Nor did they realize how strong they were or how challenging it was to neither hurt them nor be hurt by them.

The owners of the Angelfish Inn, Karin Valentine and her husband Stephen, were both regulars at Bonnie's boxing and kickboxing classes. It was odd to be punching the landlady within a day of moving in. Karin was a tall, straight-talking, good-humored, Virginia-born Jewish girl in her late forties with a hearty laugh, a mass of thick hair, and two teenage daughters. She'd run the hotel for the last ten years, becoming a true Floridian in the process, and she enjoyed getting to know her guests and hearing their stories. I liked Karin right away, and she became my unofficial tour guide during my stay.

The day I moved in I borrowed Karin's pink bike on which I trundled down the boardwalk along the beach, enjoying the pastel colors and the sea breeze. Hollywood Beach was predominantly a working-class holiday spot, geared toward budget accommodations and family vacations, unlike Miami, which was only an hour's drive away. Looking at the shirtless strollers, I suddenly felt how far I was from New York City. The obesity epidemic I'd heard about was impossible not to notice. Australia has just as many overweight people as America, but the typical obese Australian just isn't as big. I'd never see people *this* big. I started taking pictures, as if these Floridians weren't people but some unusual form of wildlife. And the pictures didn't really convey how big the people looked to me, as if the camera's lens couldn't quite gather in the shock I felt.

The Angelfish Inn had a homey, seaside feel to it, much more my speed than the Hilton. There were some long-term tenants but few guests, since it was the off-season. Guests usually ended up together talking, smoking cigarettes, and drinking beer in the courtyard, which featured a big tank of turtles, some massive cacti and palms, and a shaded eating area with an overhead fan.

My room was small but thankfully cool, which was all I really cared about. And it had a kitchen, so once again I could feed myself. I'd been getting a bit sick of restaurant salads comprised of iceberg lettuce drowning in cream cheese accompanied by bread that tasted sweet. I yearned for fiber that wasn't drenched in sugar.

Karin took me to Publix, the local supermarket, and let me loose in the produce section. At the register, the attendants couldn't help commenting on my basket of goods.

"This is all healthy stuff here," one of them said to the other.

"Look at this, there's nothing sweet here."

"Yes, there is," I interrupted. "Berries, apples, bananas. They're all sweet."

The women shook their heads as if they'd never seen anything like it.

The day I moved out of the Hilton, aside from being a little tired after a late night, I certainly didn't feel like I'd just had two fights in two days. I didn't have a single mark on me. I didn't even have a stiff neck. I'd come out of most of my sparring sessions much worse for wear. Physically, there was no reason not to fight again soon. In the meantime, I was eager to get back to some semblance of a gym routine. The days at the Hilton had been euphoric, but also strange and disjointed. There'd been a lot of napping, waiting in line, pancake breakfasts, then the sudden bursts of energy with the fights, then back to resting again.

If anything, the fights had given me a new starting point. I had broken the ice, returned to the ring, and not just survived but triumphed. And yet I felt that I'd still held something back, that my victories hadn't been quite emphatic enough. My boxing "voice" needed to be louder in the ring, my presence more dominant.

I'd seen much younger women simply go for it, sitting down on their punches, hitting as hard as they could, pushing the boundaries of their power, wearing hard punches as if they were mere irritations, and responding quickly. Women half my age were unapologetic about their power and resilience. The whole charade of an innate feminine fragility was gone. And yet femininity itself had survived. No one was discouraging them from giving it their all.

I hoped that Bonnie might help me become more emphatic, that she'd help me become a fighter instead of the restrained boxer that I was.

I felt more at ease with Bonnie now than I had the year before, when I'd found her quiet reserve a little hard to read. Now that she'd seen the extent of my love of boxing she seemed to open up to me more. And now that I'd seen her generosity and her determination in making certain that as many women as possible discover boxing, not just to keep the sport alive, but to help it grow, I guess I opened up to her more.

Boxing often feels like it is just too vulnerable—like a creature out of some moving tale, always on the brink of death, constantly derided, misunderstood, ridiculed, and misrepresented. And so those of us who believe we can bring the best out in boxing feel we're here to help keep it alive. In this Bonnie and I recognize each other as fellow travelers. She lives at the prominent end of that work, and I inhabit a more peripheral position half a world away. But our feelings are the same. Just like the late champion Alexis Arguello, we are protective of the sport. "See, I respect boxing because it has given me so much," Arguello once said. "And that's why I will never allow anyone to mistreat the sport of boxing if I can help it."

And now we were both looking forward to having two whole weeks together instead of the couple days we'd had the year before. "You know," Bonnie said, "this experience will help you pass on more to other fighters if you want to train them. I can say to my fighters that I've been in situations and that I understand . . . I've fought when my hands were wrapped too tight and I got blisters, I've been in there when it's felt like a dream, or when it's felt like it's been a part of me. I know what it's like to be nervous, when I've had sleepless nights. I've been there when I've been too strong even."

Almost immediately after I moved to the Angelfish Inn, Terri Moss began trying to convince me that I should fight at the Georgia Games the following weekend. She followed up with an e-mail telling me that Susan Dunn was ready to rumble. I turned to Bonnie for advice. "A champion would take the opportunity," she said. "You have the opportunity to fight, you should take it."

That night I called Terri and booked my flights. I was bound for the Georgia Games.

The sport was heavily populated with people busy making lists of reasons not to fight or, as I found in New York, saying they wanted to fight but changing their minds at the last minute. Amateurs were accustomed to tournaments in which they had to fight whoever they drew. But professional careers were all about plotting the course of lowest risk in order to capture the big payday fight. But Bonnie had never been such a fighter. She was pure warrior, fighting, above all, to test herself. When she wasn't in the ring, the spotlight had made her uncomfortable. She was a creature of the gym.

USAdojo.com, the martial arts website, once asked Bonnie if she had any regrets, and she told them, "Not a one. I wanted to be in this atmosphere, I wanted to eat it, I wanted to breathe it, and I got there."

For Bonnie, boxing was a way of life.

She spent some time with me one-on-one giving me the close attention and the skills work that she dedicates to her fighters, and I

felt honored to be in that position. The gym was on a side street off
Dania Boulevard that reminded me of something out of a Tom Waits
song: the small dark bar across the street called The Wayside Inn; the
empty apartments all around, victims of the foreclosure crisis that was
sweeping the country; the abandoned sofa on the pavement adding
to the hungover feeling of it all. Up a flight of stairs, Bonnie's gym was
clean, bright, and extremely tidy. Through the windows that surrounded the ring you could see the fickle Florida sky swell with
clouds, then suddenly clear up. Floridians joked that it could be
raining in the front yard and sunny in the back.

I sensed the work in Bonnie's gym might be more demanding
physically than what I had been doing at Gleason's, but even if it
weren't, the climate was sure to make it feel that way. While it did
turn out to be more grueling, there seemed to be a greater margin
for error and less unforgiving pedantry. Bonnie, despite her reserve,
was actually extremely encouraging and positive. She recognized
effort as much as results.

She showed me some drills that were variations on what I had
done before and some new ones I'd never tried. There is, for example,
a common drill that involves tying a rope between two points and
imagining that line as the trajectory of a punch so you can practice
moving forward and bobbing, weaving and dropping under the
punch, and then doing the same moving backward along the line.

What Bonnie did was tie the ropes diagonally across the ring
and ask you to shadowbox around them facing outward. When
you got to the corners that was when you unleashed your attack,
unloading and weaving under the rope while your imaginary
opponent was trapped in the corner. And then you moved on with
your lateral journey.

Another drill she showed me would hopefully give my punches
more impact. It involved stomping with the same foot as the hand
punching. In other words, if you punched with your right hand,

you'd stomp with your right foot. This encouraged you to give greater emphasis to your punches, "sitting down on them" as the saying goes.

"But it's just a drill," she cautioned.

After we finished, we sat on the edge of the ring, and I tried to drink enough water to avoid dehydration.

"What happened to Michelle Straka?" I asked her. "She never came back."

Bonnie shrugged and shook her head.

"She came here to spar, and even Ruby beat her up. My girls were so excited. 'Yay, we beat someone up.'"

Ruby was one of those quirky people that become fixtures in gyms. She was a wiry woman who I guessed was in her late forties or fifties and who seemed to be present at every class Bonnie held, from the morning boxing circuit to the kids' karate class. She had abundant, wavy brown hair with thick bangs that gave her a kind of sheepdog look, and she walked stiffly with a slight stoop. In between classes she lingered in the gym and made remarks that didn't really refer to anything specific, non sequiturs that floated in the thick air. Boxing gyms are havens for oddballs like Ruby. Lost souls can often find a sense of belonging and I was moved by Bonnie's kindness toward her.

When I'd done some body-punching with Ruby, she'd surprised me with her strength. I had an opportunity to find out more about her when she gave me a lift home one evening. I was shocked to hear she was only thirty-eight.

"What do you do for a job, Ruby?" I asked her.

"I don't know," she said.

What did that mean, I wondered? I waited a little to see if she could explain.

"Oh, well, you know, I work at the gym," she said. "At Bonnie's old gym on US 1."

"That's Bert's gym?"

"Yeah."

Bert Rodriguez had been Bonnie's trainer and also, once, romantic partner, business partner, and then, briefly, mortal enemy before finally settling into the status of old friend. He'd visited her gym when I was there the year before, climbing the stairs on creaking and bowed legs, both knees shot and his hands knotted like old tree roots. He appeared bound and patched together with straps and bandages. He had a flat nose and a nut-brown Cuban complexion and was wearing a baseball cap. Bert and Bonnie were friendly to each other. I knew they had once run a gym together but fallen out over something. I'd walked around the gym with them while they told me the stories behind all the posters and belts on the wall.

There was one picture that I had always admired of Bonnie in which she is sitting in the corner of the ring, resting her right elbow on her knee. She is looking down at the floor in a moment of calm between rounds, her mop of curls falling over her face and her body in tremendous shape, with a washboard stomach, shapely legs, and imposing arms and shoulders. Either she is drawing deeply on inner resources or bored, depending on your point of view.

"I like this one," I said.

"Yeah," Bert said. "She looks like she's thinking about what she needs to get at the store."

The next morning Bonnie was already at work doing exercises when I arrived, dressed as always in baggy black basketball shorts and a black sports bra. I started wrapping my hands when she moved to the cross trainer in the corner.

"Entertain me," she said.

So I asked her about her fight with Alicia and if she could make me a copy of the video recording she had of it. She'd shown me a few rounds of it the year before, and now that I knew both fighters better I was keen to see it in full.

"I was let down by my corner in that fight," Bonnie said. "I didn't have the morale in my corner."

"What do you mean?"

"Bert was my trainer, and I fell in love with him," she said. "We were together for ten years. Then he started offering to commit and everything until I found him with Kathy Rivers."

Kathy Rivers is a six-foot-tall blonde fighter who Bert is still married to today. The way Bonnie told it, she was happy when Kathy came along, and the two of them trained together for a while. Had Rivers trained to fight or to be Bert's wife? I wondered. According to Bonnie, although the two women got along, on the occasion of her fight with Alicia, the preparation leading up to it had been difficult. She and Rivers were both on the card, and it became apparent that Bert was not as interested in Bonnie by then.

The relationship between fighter and trainer is an intimate one that requires trust. A trainer gets to see the fighter stripped bare, and the fighter is dependent on the trainer for almost everything in the corner, from water and an honest appraisal of how the fight is going, to encouragement when things are bad and reassurance when they are good. But even before it gets to that point the focus on one another during training is so intense and physical that romance is often inevitable. There are many examples of women hooking up with male trainers. I've always wondered about how this relationship plays out between men, about the homoerotic undertones that might lurk in this very macho game. But maybe that's taking the idea too far. Since I have had more women in my corner now, I see the relationship in a different light. It's like few others in life. Romance may often be a by-product of all the time spent together and of the intimacy created, but not always.

When Bonnie finished her time on the cross trainer, her veins were pumped full of blood and her body looked even more amazing, especially since now she was closer to fifty than forty.

"Bonnie, you look better than women half your age," I said.

She smiled and pointed to the frown line between her eyebrows. "Except for this," she said. "I got that from all my fights."

"Ha," I said. "That's the result of fifty stare-downs."

As we began work that day, Bonnie told me that the amateur judges were more likely to score the punches when fighters stepped forward.

"I saw in your fight that Jackie was moving back, and you were coming forward and stepping in on your punches. You were scoring because you were stepping in. Just like a white girl."

"Yeah," I said. "A short white girl."

Bonnie, herself a blend of Italian and Puerto Rican, had her racial classifications. White girls were aggressive, black girls were loose and fluid, and Latinas cut angles just like Belinda Laracuente and, the best boxer she had trained, a woman called Ada "Ace" Velez, who was soon to make a comeback.

I'd seen some footage of Ace, and she was formidable.

"She's gifted and she knows it too," said Bonnie. "Just like Melissa and Belinda. They're hot and they know it."

And then she pointed to Yvonne who had just arrived at the gym.

"She is definitely not gifted. But if I were in a war, I know who I'd rather have by my side. She never gives up."

"For amateur boxing, you're good," said Bonnie. "You're great."

"Really?" I asked.

"Yeah," she said.

They were just the words I needed to hear before I set off for Atlanta.

12 ON A MISSION

BY THE end of the week I found myself at Terri "The Boss" Moss's home in Decatur, one of the oldest parts of Atlanta, Georgia. Her elevated postwar timber home with bare floorboards reminded me a little of my own home back in Melbourne. Terri had scooted out the door that morning to take a class at her gym, warning me that we were in the 'hood and that I probably shouldn't wander outside alone or I might get mugged or shot or worse. The violent-crime rate in Atlanta is higher than that of most other American cities, but I couldn't see any obvious danger around me. Terri had been a police officer, and I thought her warning was a product of the paranoia that goes with the job.

It didn't look like any 'hood out there to me. It looked like a pleasant, leafy, middle-class suburb, but what did I know? Inside her place I was bathed in dappled light that seemed so gentle after the harsh glare of Florida. I was a prisoner since she wouldn't let me leave, but it could have been worse. I was surrounded by greenery outside, her fridge was full of salad and fruit, and I had my espresso machine. I was happy. And thankfully, the weather in Georgia was going through an uncharacteristically mild patch that week so outside it was pleasant and breezy. Not that I got to sample it much. Terri had picked me up at the airport the night before, set me up on her fold-out sofa bed in her spare room, and ordered me to get plenty of rest.

Terri had been married and divorced three times and had a married daughter, Melissa, and a baby grandson. She was the most youthful grandmother I'd ever met—slim, lively, and attractive. Nonetheless, she was done with men, or so she said. Not that she was in the least bit interested in women, though. Most of her fitness clients and fighters were gay. Another distinguishing feature of Decatur, apparently, was its large lesbian population.

"I don't know about you, Mischa," she said, "but I could never fall in love with a woman."

When she described the rest of her family—her single mother, a semireformed party animal, and her brother and sisters—they sounded like characters out of the movie *Deliverance*. She said they engaged in a cultural phenomenon that I hadn't heard of called "hating." "You know," she explained, "like 'don't be hating on me.' You never heard that expression?"

"In Australia we call that the tall poppy syndrome. We like to cut down tall poppies. But I always thought it was just us."

When I asked her about her father she laughed. "I have no idea," she said. "Every time I ask my mom, I get a different answer."

Terri now lived alone with a tortoiseshell cat called Betty. Actually, the cat was originally named Bennie Briscoe, after the Philadelphia fighter whose training tricks Sylvester Stallone stole for the Rocky Balboa character. But Melissa had misheard the name as Betty Briscoe, and it stuck.

Like Briscoe, Terri's business partner and former trainer Xavier Biggs is also originally from Philly, a city that was known for breeding slick fighters who were also notoriously tough. Philadelphia gym wars were famous for their merciless sparring. Fighters cared more for their gym status than they did for their world ranking. Many of the gyms are now gone, but the wars, it seems, continue. I saw a Louis Theroux 2008 documentary called *Law and Disorder in Philadelphia*, so named because parts of the city are overrun with drug dealers and there are more than four hundred murders there a year.

Tyrell, Xavier's brother and Olympic gold medalist, had been one of the famous Philly fighters. Unfortunately, he'd completely gone off the rails and had become addicted to drugs and alcohol, repeatedly going and in and out of rehab. In the mid-1980s Tyrell was demolished by Mike Tyson and recovered from the loss only to resume his downward slide. Xavier suspended his own eight-fight career in the early 1980s to help Tyrell. During that time Xavier stayed in camp with his brother and kept honing his skills, sparring Meldrick Taylor, Pernell Whitaker, Johnny Bumphus, and the like. Without the highs, Xavier didn't have the same kind of lows and has been able to use what he'd learned to train fighters, which he's been doing now for more than twenty years.

There was no romantic connection between Terri and the almost taciturn Biggs, but she joked that they fought as often as a married couple. They ran the gym along gender lines. He trained the men and she trained the women—the "boxing chicks," as she called them—and the two groups never mingled. Biggs was frequently on the phone to her. She seemed to have an earpiece permanently in her ear with him on the other end. Often she was either rolling her eyes or taking furious notes. Sometimes when it rang she would hiss at it. But she'd answer it anyway.

When she left me that first morning she said, "If a big black guy walks through the door and helps himself to what's in the fridge, don't worry. It's just Biggs."

He had a key to her house and used the computer to burn CDs.

She apologized for her old car and her modest house and complained that Biggs could be a little demanding at times. But mostly she was cheerful, energetic, and great company, clearly happier with her life now than when she was an overworked law enforcement officer.

"I used to have a proper career before this you know," she said. "I was a narcotics investigator."

Before boxing, which had begun late for her when she was in her thirties, she had been a typical cop, smoking cigarettes and eating junk food. She even looked a bit like Angie Dickenson with her blonde bob and her attractive features.

The hard-bitten journalist in me enjoyed the hard-bitten ex-cop in her. We had a kind of meeting of dispositions that made me feel as if we had known each other a long time.

That night she filled me in a little more about Susan Dunn. "She's kinda annoying," said Terri. "I mean, she says she's gonna turn pro, and she hasn't even had one amateur fight yet."

Terri was a little sensitive about people who made such claims, perhaps because she was a world champion professional boxer who had battled hard for acceptance and respect from the tough elites who had moved in Biggs's circle. Impressing Philly fighters was no easy feat. I suspected Terri wanted me to teach Dunn the kind of boxing lesson that she should have already learned in the gym. It was one of respect, respect for the sport and the decent people in it. This was about protecting the sweet science from being inappropriately exploited—even if it was by a small-time comedian no one had ever heard of.

People who make unsubstantiated claims about themselves and their achievements or have unrealistic aspirations when they have no idea what is involved tend to be seen by boxing professionals as dangerous to the sport. They don't like seeing the sport mocked by such pretenders. Terri had convinced me that fighting Dunn was a chance to set her straight about how dangerous the sport could be and that I would be doing this for her own good. It had become, over the last few days, somewhat of a crusade, even a mission, for Terri.

In the meantime I checked out Dunn's website and saw that she did indeed claim to be a professional boxer. It also made plenty of other extravagant claims that had nothing to do with boxing. In one photograph, she sported a mullet and what Moss called "root rot"—dark roots growing out of bleached hair. "Very Tennessee," Terri observed.

"Finally," her website announced, "a female stand-up comedian who specializes in political comedy." Was it possible for a lesbian comedian from the South to be a redneck and also claim to be a savvy political observer?

A sampling of her jokes included:

"I thought about going into politics, but I never learned embezzlement or doubletalk in school."

"I'm very religious. I worship myself."

"You know what?" I said to Terri. "She's not actually funny."

"And what about those eyebrows!" she said. "And that damn root rot."

Meanwhile, Terri Moss and Xavier Biggs were attempting to organize a very ambitious reunion show of the 1984 U.S. Olympic boxing team, which had won nine gold medals, one silver, and one bronze. The team had become known as the greatest Olympic boxing team in history. It had included Biggs's brother Tyrell, Mark Breland, Evander Holyfield, Meldrick Taylor, Pernell Whitaker, Virgil Hill, Henry Tillman, Paul Gonzales, Jerry Page, Steve McRory, and Robert Shannon. Terri and Biggs were not only trying to get them all together for the show but, in the midst of a financial crisis, were trying to sell five-thousand-dollar ringside tables, secure sponsorship, get broadcasters on board—all with only a few weeks to go.

Some of the members of the team, like Tyrell, were apparently a bit worse for wear and needed the show, which was scheduled to take place at the Atlanta Marriott Century Center, as a morale boost as much as anything.

"Have you heard Meldrick Taylor speak?" Terri asked. "This is a dangerous sport."

Pretty quickly I got sucked into the whole reunion drama. Since I wasn't allowed out on my own, I became Terri's sidekick. It felt as if we were in a version of *Thelma and Louise*, racing around in her old red BMW, going to the farmers market, the gym, and a café to meet Biggs and discuss the show. I was at her side all the time.

"Don't let me scare you, Mischa," she said as she careened across three lanes of traffic in a sudden grab for the freeway exit. "I know what I'm doing. You learn things about driving in the police force that they don't teach regular people."

"So, how did you start boxing?" I asked.

"Let me educate you a little," she said, turning to me with her Jackie O sunglasses. "I guess you think that America is the center of the universe for boxing, right? Well, let me tell you it's unregulated and crooked, it's full of thugs and con men, Mischa. You know what a meat man is?"

"Uh . . ."

"A meat man is a guy who trains people to fight someone's up-and-coming fighter. You know what a matchmaker is?"

"Um . . ."

"Well, I'll tell ya. He's the guy who works for the promoter to match the fights. He's little better than a meat man. Actually, he's almost what you would call like a street person. He's basically a hustler, you know what I'm saying? They have what they call cat fights here in bars, you know what they are? Girls who aren't trained boxers fight each other at, like, strip clubs, and that's where the matchmaker will get the meat from. He'll go to a titty bar—I'm sorry, that's what we call them—and the matchmaker will go there, and say we've told him it's $500, he tells the meat man to train the girl and it's $300, and in the end they give the girl $150 for the fight, you know what I'm saying? And she's had maybe two weeks in the gym preparing for it.

"There's meat and there's dog meat and then there's the five-hundred fighter. They'll be like a 2-28 record or say a 3-32. They'll fight the distance, but they won't be able to win; that's for a fighter who's coming up and needs a test. A fighter who's taking a step up from fighting the meat."

Terri, of course, was talking about professional boxing. Up until this point no one had given me the low-down on the state of affairs in the American scene, not like this anyway. It felt like she was briefing me for some complex undercover sting, which was exactly the kind of work she used to do in the narcotics branch.

I was getting a picture of professional boxing as a dangerous mix of mobsters and thugs and gold-digging women, where the athletes were chewed up and spat out, leaving once-great boxers mumbling and dribbling about what was left of their lives on the streets. Even great champions could end up on the scrap heap and that included some of the Olympic champions who would be reunited in only a few weeks' time. The fact that human dignity could still find its way to the surface in such swill was a miracle. In Australia professional boxing was so marginal and the money so puny that the sharks had better things to do with their time, like deal drugs and run e-mail scams.

"So, basically," said Terri, getting back to the original question, "my first trainer was a meat man."

Like for so many women boxers, Terri's first foray into the sport had been motivated by a desire to get fit. She'd joined a friend who thought it might be fun. The meat man got her some fights, which of course she lost, three in a row, until eventually Xavier Biggs saw her sparring and thought she deserved a chance. And she'd won her next three fights, now with Biggs in her corner.

When I met Biggs the next morning over brunch, he said of Terri, "She's the best woman boxer I've ever trained. I knew from that first

Xavier Biggs.

time she was a fighter. It was just that someone had to teach her how to fight, know what I'm saying?" Biggs was tall and very black, with dark glasses and a towel around his shoulders. When he smiled he revealed a rather appealing gap between his two front teeth. He wore a bandana wrapped around his 1960s flat top, sported a pencil moustache, and had a toothpick jutting permanently from the corner of his mouth. Terri said that Biggs was a real loner, estranged from his wife and in only occasional contact with his son. If he wasn't in the gym or with her, she guessed he was probably alone.

After saving her from the meat man, Biggs remained in her corner through the whole fighting journey that included trips to Hungary, Madrid, and Baton Rouge.

I was intrigued by their relationship. They seemed to be a fascinating blend of partners and siblings, with maybe a father-daughter dynamic as well. I found myself constantly wanting to photograph them for the visual contrast. Terri was small and blonde and dynamic, while Biggs was tall, languid, and reserved. They really couldn't be more different from each other. They would stand together discussing the upcoming Olympic show, both of them looking crisp and taut for their ages, Biggs already over fifty and Terri forty-three.

Most of the time Biggs wore T-shirts with slogans on them—"I'm the one," "Only the strong survive," or "100 percent champion." Sometimes Biggs would replace his sunglasses with black framed reading glasses, and he'd look more like Spike Lee or the American essayist and cultural critic Gerald Early. He was a jazz connoisseur, and he'd come to Terri's house to burn CDs on her computer for the gym each day, usually jazz and funk mixes. Biggs was cool but tolerant of the more excitable Terri. She and I would joke around, and every now and then he'd flash his gap-toothed smile, rolling his tongue over the toothpick and shaking his head. At times like that, Terri and I felt like we were a couple of silly little kids and he was our dad.

"He's so cool he doesn't even know how cool he is," she said one day.

"That's the epitome of cool," I added.

He seemed to like the sound of that. He also liked that the jazz and hip-hop artists he collected were some of my favorites. For him boxing and music goes together, and it has always been the same for me too—anything with the right beat, usually music by black artists.

Biggs thought that the jazz musician Jimmy Smith was actually boxing in musical form, using the rhythms of flurries and jabs—pop, pop, po-po-pop. His Hammond organ called the shots. "If you punched like he played, you'd be the best boxer in the world," he said.

This was an idea that had also appealed to the jazz great Miles Davis, who wrote an album based on Jack Johnson, the first African-American world heavyweight champion, and who attempted many times to kick his heroin habit by training alongside fighter Sugar Ray Robinson. To him the syncopated rhythms of jazz and boxing were connected.

Biggs made me a couple of CDs while I was there, one with some of the artists we had discussed and another with classics like Ella Fitzgerald and Frank Sinatra. Whenever I set foot in the Decatur Boxing Gym the music on the sound system just did it for me. I wanted to move around, shadowbox, use the ring. I've always thought that boxing is a form of expressive dancing for men, who need the excuse of a violent sport before they can simply express themselves. And the music drove home that point. Part of me wanted to enjoy that dance and learn what the best fighters knew about it, more than I wanted to fight.

WEIGH-IN AND registration for the Georgia Games, which were a legacy of the 1996 Atlanta Olympic Games, were held on a Saturday at the Doraville Arena. A huge crowd gathered, about 80 percent black and Hispanic. And once again, I couldn't help noticing the high proportion of overweight people among the officials, the trainers, and the spectators. Anyone who wasn't actually boxing was a blob. It made the boxers look like an altogether different species.

Atlanta, I was reminded, was the home of Coca-Cola, probably a leading contributor to the obesity epidemic. It was one of the hearts of the civil rights movement, the birthplace of Martin Luther King Jr., *and* the childhood home of James Brown.

Krichele and Crystal, both 118 lb., met us at the arena. Patricia Alcivar had driven from North Carolina hoping to get a match, and there was another woman slightly heavier than her at 125 lb. who had registered.

Susan Dunn had already arrived and was complaining about how she'd struggled to make weight, which was a surprise to hear because Terri told me she claimed to be below 138 lb. and I was anxious to stay at that weight. She also complained that the drive all the way from Tennessee had tired her out. She appeared to be holding Terri responsible for both these problems. Her voice was incredibly high pitched and monotonous, and she was loud, like a squealing tire. Her hair was just as bleached and her roots just as dark as they were on her website pictures. She also seemed to be just as funny as her jokes had suggested she would be.

Terri had been amusing me all day with comments like, "This could be a comedy of errors, but you're gonna deliver the punch line, Mischa, I know it."

"You know," I said, "in Australia the slang for toilet is dunny." Terri liked that and from then on we referred to Susan as Dunny the Unfunny.

Her trainer wasn't due to turn up until that evening, and it still wasn't clear if we'd fight on Saturday or Sunday.

"I was 145 pounds yesterday," she whined. "You told me I had to be 138 pounds."

"No, I didn't Susan," said Terri. "I told you that the Masters have a ten-pound differential and not to worry about the weight."

Once again Kevina Franklin was in charge of weighing the women. So instead of standing in a long line with the men, the small group was ushered into another room, which was air conditioned to arctic conditions, where we all stripped to our underwear. Susan and I both weighed

Me, Evander Holyfield, and Patricia Alcivar.

138 lb. Once we had been checked out by the doctor, we were told we would be fighting the next day. Krichele and Crystal were matched against each other, and Terri decided not to let them fight. Patricia was willing to give away weight to the other girl, but her would-be opponent had gone home with an upset stomach. Patricia and her husband were going to meet us later for dinner and then drive back to North Carolina.

Terri was worried about Patricia turning pro. "She's what we call a train-iac, you know, one of those mental people who just don't know how to stop. I'm not sure how much she'll listen."

Indeed Patricia's Facebook updates made her seem pretty obsessive, and in person she was excessively cheerful.

We spotted Evander Holyfield regaling the crowd, and Patricia was keen to have her picture taken with him. I didn't care one way or the other, but I thought I could ask him on her behalf.

"You coming over?" I asked Terri, who shook her head.

Holyfield looked like I'd just told him someone had smashed into his car when I said Patricia would like a picture with him. And his expression in the picture said it all. I went back to where Terri was standing and said, "He didn't like us much."

Nearby were a couple of cops, one of whom recognized Terri from her previous career. They asked her if she was making better money now than she did on the force. She laughed when she told me. "That's America," she said to me. "All we care about is the money."

After the weigh-in we met Biggs for lunch at a bakery.

"You know," I said to Terri when Biggs got up to go to the bathroom, "I think *I'm* a black man."

"Me, too," she said.

"What, you think I'm a black man or you're a black man?"

"We're both black men," she said. Then Biggs came back.

"Have you heard that song he plays in the gym that starts off, 'How cool can one black man be?'" Terri asked me. And we laughed, and Biggs ignored us, chewing on his toothpick.

How cool can one black man be?

The next day when we arrived at the arena I noticed Dunny sitting in the crowd with her trainer. She was dressed in white satin shorts and looked a bit weary like she'd been watching the fights all day and had sat through all sixty bouts on the card the previous day. Meanwhile I had been at Terri's house relaxing. We didn't even get to the arena until the afternoon.

The day before Terri had allowed me out for what she called a Bennie Briscoe run. It was really a short slow jog around a lake, not more than a mile or two, and she followed me the whole way telling me to slow down. I was already one of the slowest runners on the planet, so this felt like strange advice to be getting from her.

"You all right, Mischa?" she would ask me from time to time. "You feeling well rested?"

Then she showed me an e-mail from Dunny that read:

Hey Terri, Ringside e-mailed and called me and said they got an application from a woman in NY who is 45 years old and weighs 138. Did your fighter sign up for the tournament in August? Anyway, you have got to love my week. Started off on Monday sparring with Courtney (great style, she's pretty to watch). By the second round she was done. I barely went after her and every time I did she was scared to death. Regina told coach she would be in Thursday because when we sparred before she was holding back. Then Tuesday Hayley (powerful hitter, volleyball player and strong leg muscles) was scheduled to spar with me and she came in and all of a sudden got sick. Larry a kickboxer jumped in and basically he was just really aggressive with me to see how I would handle it. Please, if you are too aggresive I will get away and then attack you. Duh. Wednesday, I got a pep talk from a

boxer who tried to scare the hell out of you, kind of like you do, and he keep saying a real fight is nothing like sparring or drills. You have to be okay with the crowds and the pressure. Then I looked at him and said, "you do know I'm a comedian don't you?" Yesterday, Regina told me it was a bad idea to go all out before a fight so we will spar when I get back. Courtney and Hayley got belly piercing, so they couldn't spar. I'm not kidding. Today, who knows? I do love it. It's hysterical . . . I will be there for weigh in at 8am. My life is beyond hysterical . . .
Susan

"God," I said. "She thinks she's pretty good 'cause she's got Courtney and Haley running scared. But who the hell are Courtney and Haley?"

"She's annoying, isn't she?" said Terri.

Now in the arena, after Terri bandaged my hands and I started to warm up and shadowbox, I realized we were back in the real world. The land of the Women's Golden Gloves in Florida was probably an aberration. It was back to being in a man's world. A couple of boys told me they were excited to see a women's bout because they hardly ever saw them.

Biggs was standing with his prized protégé, the teenage sensation Carlos "Kitten" Monroe, who, just like his mentor, didn't say much. The two of them stood side by side, surveying the crowd. The coolest dudes in the arena. Meanwhile Terri was bouncing around me saying, "It's a pity you can't stay for longer so I could teach you some tricky shit." I started bouncing around too.

"Never mind, maybe after the fight," I said. "I'll be here for a few days."

We did some punch combinations on the pads, but it felt too rushed, as if we hadn't had time to tune in to each other.

Fighting Susan Dunn in Atlanta. DEAN HESSE

At one point we looked over at Dunny, and her trainer seemed to be giving us the evil eye.

"What's he doing?" asked Krichele. "He trying to psyche you out?"

Before I knew it, Terri went over to talk to him, and he was smiling. So I went over too and shook his hand. I think he just had poor eyesight and was squinting at us rather than trying to stare us down.

"Well," said Terri as we walked back to where we were. "He's not as dumb as she is."

Then we resumed our warm-up. "She could be like a wild cat," said Terri. "Or she could just stand there scared stiff. You can't tell."

"You can't," I said. But I knew how to ride out a storm.

"If she comes out wild though, what will probably happen is she'll shoot her load real quick, that's what Biggs calls it. Either that or she'll be terrified and won't do anything."

"Or she might be a good boxer," I suggested.

"Yeah, she might be. We just don't know. Mischa, tell me, do you feel OK? Do you feel like you've had enough rest?"

An older black man who reminded me a bit of Sydney Poitier was watching me warm up and said he'd make sure to stay and watch my fight.

Finally, it was time, and we were in one of two rings. Sure enough, as soon as the bell went off, Dunny came out, not so much like a wildcat but more like a flailing robot. I spent the first minute running around the ring as she stomped after me, throwing sloppy punches, none of which landed cleanly, and then, as predicted, her load was shot, and my jabs started landing.

I went back to the corner feeling confident about the next round.

"That's good work," said Terri. "Now try a right-hand lead this round and follow it up with a left hook. She comes out with her hands up, but then after a few seconds, she drops them, so take a little step to your right and throw the right hand. You all right?

Alicia Ashley

This is another cakewalk for you. You want me to get you coffee and a bagel?"

That was the first time I had ever laughed in the middle of a fight.

In the next round I was landing at will and virtually nothing was coming back at me. I didn't quite believe it and wasn't sure how to time my punches. Every time I landed one flush, Dunny's head would snap back and her eyes would roll around as they tried to refocus and her hands would flap around at her sides. It looked like maybe she was either showboating or bluffing. But actually I think she was just trying to stay upright.

I went back to the corner and announced, "I want to stop her. I think I can stop her."

"I think you can too," said Terri.

And in the third round I thought of Bonnie's stomping drill and started grunting with each punch like all the girls did at the tournament. I tried to put everything I had into each one of those punches. About midway through the round, Linda, the referee, decided that Dunny needed a break from the onslaught and gave her a belated eight count. Personally, I would have stopped the bout at that point, since most of the blows were unanswered in any meaningful way. But Linda was tough. After the count, the fight ended.

Immediately afterward we both went to see the ringside doctor. "Wow," the doctor said to me. "Did you even get hit?"

"I don't think so," I said.

"Me neither," said the doctor. "You beat the crap out of her, though."

I wanted to give Peter the news and went outside to call him when I couldn't get a signal inside the arena. Standing outside was the Sydney Poitier look-alike.

He flashed his movie-star smile. "I'm glad I stuck around," he said. "I like the way you box. You could have finished her off, but you chose not to. You did it with your boxing skill instead. I like that."

When I went back in I saw Dunny coming out, and she looked a mess: her nose was cut, and her face was red with marks from my gloves. Whatever else she claimed to be, there was no doubt she was one tough cookie.

Soon after, a man who had been in her corner approached me and said, "That was a real good fight. Thanks for taking it easy on our girl. You could have hurt her, but we appreciate that you didn't."

Huh? Why was everybody saying that? Couldn't they see that I'd been trying my absolute level best to knock her out?

When I saw Terri back inside she said, "Biggs was laughing all through your fight. That's a good sign. It means he liked it. Hey, chick, you brutalized her in that last round. She was blocking punches with her damn face. And you were barking like a little puppy. Yap, yap, yap."

Then Biggs appeared.

"Good fight," he said. "You look like a pro."

After the fight, Dunny was back on the email. Her emails came with such frequency now we had dubbed them, "The Dunny Diaries." This one had been addressed to another friend of hers and she'd cc'd Terri, who forwarded it on to me. In a long rambling paragraph it explained that she'd so weakened herself getting to the fight and making weight that she was fighting me at half her usual strength. She also said she was looking forward to a rematch with me in two weeks.

"Was she always like this?" I asked Terri. "Or did I do this to her?"

On the following Monday I spent some time at the gym sparring Krichele and Crystal, both of them more of a challenge than Dunny. Terri started showing me some of her "tricky shit," but we would have needed more time than we had for me to settle into the routine and really learn much of it. A few days after I returned to Florida I got a phone message from Terri. Former two-time world champion Vernon Forrest had been shot and killed in an attempted carjacking not far from her place. He was only thirty-eight. "Wow," I thought. "She really was in the 'hood."

13 BACK TO THE SWAMP

ON MY first morning back at Bonnie's Florida gym I felt slightly more comfortable, despite the oppressive humidity. The temperature had fallen a degree or two, and there was a breeze coming through the back door. It's amazing how small changes under extreme conditions can have such a dramatic effect. Or perhaps it was just that I was well rested and still on a high from winning.

I was gaining a greater appreciation for small adjustments all around, though.

Bonnie was pleased to hear that I thought the preparation at her gym had helped me in the fight, particularly when it came to stepping up my attack. All that stomping may have helped me sit down on my punches more. But I also told her how concerned I was that people had perceived that I was deliberately holding back, when I knew I was putting all I had into it.

"I wasn't holding back. I really tried to stop her," I said. "But I just couldn't."

Bonnie smiled. "Oh yeah," she said. "It's hard to stop the women. I tried to finish off every one of the girls I fought. But they don't give in. Men you can stop, but women are tougher."

"Also, we had a female ref," I said.

"Ah-ha," she said with another knowing smile.

Male referees tended to be a bit squeamish about women getting hit too much and intervened sooner when it came to counts and stoppages than they would if they were reffing a men's bout.

The referee in Atlanta, Linda, was a petite woman in her fifties and a Masters boxer herself. Although she moved around the ring on her toes as if she were modeling the latest spring outfit, she was as tough as an old prison warden. I thought she'd been a little too tough, actually, planting yet another nail in the coffin of the myth that femininity was burdened by excessive nurturing instincts.

The whole gender question got a new twist that day when I called Dave Lubs, who was coordinating the Ringside Tournament. He told me cheerfully that a few more women Masters than he'd expected had registered.

I had contacted him before leaving Australia, and his response then had been pessimistic. "I wish I could say come and join the fun," he'd written me in an e-mail. "After all, this is the greatest amateur boxing tournament in the world. However, the chances of getting a bout are not very good. Last year we had three women Masters enter. Two did get a bout. They were both in their fifties, same weight, with no fights. Just a lucky situation. In 2008 we had two women Masters enter, both ladies were 125 pounds and the same age and both had no bouts. Again, just a lucky situation."

But as the registration forms started coming in, the situation began to look more positive. This was the first time I'd gone from "can't do" to "can do," instead of the other way around. Dave sounded on the phone like he might be a rotund man in his forties. He mostly used a speaker-phone, and I imagined him doing half a dozen other things at the same time in his Kansas City office, maybe putting a golf ball into a cup, maybe pouring himself a scotch on the rocks.

"Lemme see," he said when I called him that day. "We've got four women at 132. What are you?"

"I'm at 138," I said. "But I could maybe come down."

"Now, hold on a second. There's one here that will probably come up to 138."

Then the line went silent, as he took himself off speakerphone. When he spoke again he sounded as if he were speaking close to the mouthpiece, as if he didn't want anyone to hear him, as if he might be covering his mouth with his hand.

"Let me tell you something, though, Mischa. It's kinda interesting," he said. Then there was another pause.

"This one used to be a man."

"What?" I exclaimed.

"He's had the operation. So, he/she is registered to box as a woman."

"USA Boxing has allowed that?"

"Yeah. No one is prepared to say no. Not USA Boxing or the LBCs"—the Local Boxing Clubs.

"What, are they scared of getting sued?"

"Yeah, I think that's it. It's kinda interesting, don't you think?"

"Dave," I said, "that's very interesting. But is it fair? What about that woman tennis player who was a man?"

"Billy Jean King?" he said.

"No, no," I said. "She *was* a woman. There was another one."

"Oh, yeah, I remember that."

"But this is boxing," I said. "You know, strength is a factor."

"I dunno," he said. "Maybe with the hormones he takes . . . I gotta stop saying he. It's she."

"But is it?" I asked.

I heard the sound of shuffling paper. "Well," he said, "he's fifty-five years old, and her name is Pauline. It used to be Paul."

"I don't know. I mean, did he box as a young man? Maybe he has a lot of experience? Plus the strength. We spar with men in the gym, but this is a fight."

"I got another call," said Dave. "I gotta go. Just keep this to yourself for now, Mischa, OK?"

"OK," I said.

The very next person I saw was Karin of the Angelfish Inn, who was giving me a ride to the gym in her Mustang convertible. "Hey," she said.

"Hey," I said. "They're lining me up to fight some kind of transsexual person."

"Huh?"

"A woman who apparently used to be a guy."

"They can do that?"

I shrugged.

"Wow," she said. "That's interesting."

Once I got to the gym, I also told Bonnie. Later that night, when I got back to the Inn, I called Alicia and told her. Then I told Terri Moss. I nearly even told a complete stranger in the Laundromat, but thought it would take too much explaining.

Naturally, everyone found it interesting.

Bonnie shook her head. "I don't know," she said.

Alicia, as usual, was circumspect, only mild surprise in her voice. Maybe living in New York had made her impossible to shock.

Terri Moss, however, was shocked. Shocked but also intrigued.

"If this person wants to box, why the hell didn't he do it when he was a man? Don't take that fight, Mischa," she said.

Back in Florida, Bonnie was trying to be as nonjudgmental as it was possible to be about my gender-bending opponent. "People shouldn't be condemned for being different," she said. "They should be accepted for who they are. But this is boxing."

She said I should hone my skills and prepare for fighting a much stronger person, even if we didn't know exactly what gender that person would be. That shouldn't be a problem, I thought, since everyone in her gym hits so damn hard, every punch fully loaded. I'd managed to avoid the previous Saturday sprint and sparring session by fighting in Atlanta. But the coming Saturday loomed as a challenge greater than my three rounds with Dunny, whose descent into bitterness and rancor had also taken another interesting turn.

She was now directing all her rage at Terri, as if she were responsible for her loss somehow, and saying that she wanted to fight me again at Ringside.

"I won't lose to her in Kansas City. You can bank on it," she wrote, referring to me.

> One of three things is going to happen, she will be knocked out, I will put her in a coma, or the referee will stop the contest. That's just the way it's going to be. Before this weeknd [*sic*] I would have simply outboxed her. I'm a stronger, faster, and smarter boxer than her. For ever [*sic*] punch she landed on Sunday I'm going to place 5 on her in Kansas City. Count on it . . .
>
> I'm going to knock your girl out in the first round, even with 16 ounce gloves. Bank on it. I lost that fight, she and you didn't win it. Tell yourself whastever [*sic*] you need to, to sleep at night. Kansas City will be a very different day for her. I hope and pray if you are there you work her corner, you need to taste a real lose [*sic*].

Terri, who said she didn't think she would make it to Ringside, was changing her mind. Between Dunny and Pauline, it was getting too hard to resist. When it came to Pauline though, she was skeptical as ever about the authenticity of her claims. "I wanna see me some vagina before you get in the ring with him."

In preparation for my coming battle of the sexes, Yvonne Reis spent three rounds shoving me around with a punching shield that became so slippery from my perspiration that I felt like I was being stalked by some giant jellyfish—a smiling jellyfish, that is, because Yvonne clearly enjoyed the job.

After the first day there were no more cool breezes, and I went back to feeling like I was losing condition because of how the humidity was affecting me. But from what I had read, training in humidity was a serious problem only if you were losing more fluid than you could replace or if the perspiration wasn't making contact with moving air and couldn't act to cool your core temperature. Acclimatizing generally took two to three weeks, and I hadn't been in Florida quite that long, so it wasn't surprising that I felt a little flat. But was this inability to train at my peak causing a loss of fitness too? I couldn't tell and neither could anyone I talked to about it. Everyone conceded that the weather didn't help, but no one could tell me whether my fitness was deteriorating as a result.

One of the medics at the Florida tournament, Vanessa Ramos, also trained at Bonnie's gym. She worked as a firefighter paramedic and had served in Iraq. Although she had been seriously injured in a bomb blast and spent months in hospital, she was consistently cheerful and extremely helpful. Vanessa suggested fluids with electrolytes might help keep me properly hydrated. It was possible that I wasn't keeping pace with the amount I was losing through sweat. She told me to try Pedialyte, which wasn't as strong and sugary as some of the sports drinks.

The next afternoon, Karin's daughter gave me a lift to the gym on her way to volleyball practice. I was amazed at how people seemed so happy to drive me around. I was more than willing to catch the bus, but the truth was that the buses were unreliable. I'd once waited nearly an hour for one to take me from the gym back to Hollywood Beach, standing in the searing sun with no shade around. That bus never came. An older black man with bandages on his arm had been waiting along with me.

"It should be here by now," he kept saying.

Finally, out of patience, in need of a shower and some food, I flagged a cab.

I was in the passenger seat of the Valentine family's pick-up truck when Ringside's Dave Lubs called again.

"Now Mischa, you're gonna find this real interesting," he said. "I just spoke to Pauline and he/she said—darn it, I should just say she, I'm going to blow that, I know it, and I'll probably do it in front of her. Anyway, she said that she wants whoever is going to be fighting him/her to give her a call, and she can explain everything. He says that he—I mean she—never lived as a man and was declared female at birth. Anyway, she lives in Daytona, so if you want, I'll give you her number and you can give her a call."

"OK," I said to Dave. "I'll give her a call. By the way, how did he sound on the phone? Like a man or a woman?"

"You know," said Dave, "she sounded like a feminine man. Mind you, I've heard women who sound a lot rougher than her."

Jackie was also planning a trip to Ringside. We'd been in e-mail contact, and she always signed off "warm hugs."

I told Jackie about Pauline. "Don't do it, Mischa," she said. "Fight me."

Ever since I'd assured Dave that I'd keep my mouth shut about Pauline, I hadn't stopped talking about her. I'd told about ten people on two continents.

That night I called Pauline.

"Hi Pauline, this is Mischa, the Masters boxer from Australia."

"Oh, hi," she said. "Dave said you'd be calling. What did he say about me?"

"He said you were once a man," I replied.

"I was. Yes, sort of. I had to have an operation to become a woman," she said.

She sounded just like Dave had described her—like a feminine man. She reminded me of a character from the 1989 film *Last Exit to Brooklyn.* Everything came out all at once, as if she'd never told anyone the story before.

"I was born with equipment I couldn't use, you know what I'm saying? I was molested when I was young . . . I never dated . . . I was ninety pounds in high school and started weight training and all that. I had a miserable time. I got picked on a lot, and I used to run from fights all the time. I had the operation a year ago. But I don't have implants or anything. I'm all natural, you know what I'm saying? People that see me think I'm female. I have a boyfriend now too."

This all came gushing out of Pauline, fact stumbling over emotion, timelines jumbled together, life story jostling with biological fact.

The journalist in me was intrigued, while the fighter in me was concerned. The information she was sharing was not giving me a clear idea of what kind of competition she'd be in the ring. She really wanted to talk to me like she was one of the girls, establishing her feminine bona fides: boyfriend, petite frame, natural breasts, likes to flirt with men and they with her.

I interrupted her to ask why she wanted to box.

"Well, my mother liked boxing, and I take after my mother. When I knew I wouldn't have the strength any more, when I decided to be totally female, I decided to take martial arts classes."

"How long have you been boxing?"

"A little over a year on and off. How about you?"

"I've been boxing for a few years," I said. "Maybe ten."

"Oh, I see," she said. "What do you look like?"

"What do I look like? I'm about five-four, stocky build. Short hair. Female. Married," I added, "but no kids."

I didn't really have that many feminine bona fides myself, come to think of it.

"I gotta tell you," said Pauline, "when I decided to compete in boxing I wanted to compete against a man, but the USA Boxing doctor who examined me for the physical determined that I was female, I think because they didn't want me to get hurt. But a person like me is genetically both."

"But why do you want to compete in a tournament at all? Why not just train, enjoy it, spar a little?" I said. "And what do you mean, genetically both?"

"I'm fifty-five years old but really haven't started to live," she said. "I had female insides and male equipment that didn't work for me, you know what I'm saying? I've always admired women boxers, and that's what I want to be. I'm not so crazy about the men who box. I don't admire them so much. Men are assholes," she laughed. "I mean, I have a boyfriend, but he's an asshole too."

"OK, Pauline, I still don't know enough about your biology," I said.

"I don't really even know my own biology," she said.

"What do you mean?"

"When I was born, they called me . . . Oh, I can't even say the word, it upsets me too much."

"I think it would be good if you could just be straight with me," I said. "Just use the right words so I can get some idea what you're talking about."

"OK, well. Oh, this is hard. They said I was hermaphroditic."

"OK," I said.

At last, some kind of definition. But I still didn't know what the implications were in terms of her strength.

"Pauline, I don't really care anything much about breasts or implants or how feminine you look or any of that. It's none of my concern, and it shouldn't have to be. The only thing that concerns me is how you will be inside the boxing ring and whether you will have any kind of advantage there because of your strength."

That actually seemed to settle her down a little.

"The way I see it," she said, "you're five pounds heavier, ten years younger, and you have more experience than me. I mean, I might lose."

"Don't talk like that, Pauline," I said.

"But I don't really care because it takes guts just to get through those ropes. As far as I'm concerned, you're a winner just getting in there."

In Pauline's garbled biography there was also talk of therapy, ripping doors off refrigerators in a hormone-fueled rage, combined with stories of victimization and sexual abuse.

"I don't blame people for not accepting me," she said. "Counselors say—and I've had a lot of therapy over the years, believe me—they say they don't understand how I've come this far without committing suicide. Boxing is hard to learn, particularly if people don't want to teach you."

It sounded like Pauline hadn't trained long, hadn't sparred much, and wasn't being taken seriously in her gym in Daytona—not exactly a place known for its progressive values.

"We don't have many girls boxing, mostly they do Muay Thai. I prefer conventional boxing, but the guys are all bigger and if they hit hard, their punches really hurt."

I was starting to feel that I might be the one with the unfair advantage.

But then she said, "I have to tell you everything. People like me have more strength than most people in my weight class. I'm like a machine that doesn't want to quit. That's why I can do this at fifty-five. I do take female hormones, though, because they make my female parts more sensitive. I developed breasts on my own. They're not real big. If I didn't work out, they would be bigger."

"OK, OK," I said. "I get the picture."

"I set this as a goal for myself and just got hooked on boxing."

She told me she'd get her boyfriend to send me a photograph, and I could see for myself. The next day she sent the pictures with an accompanying message that said it had been nice talking with me and that she hoped we could have a match. The accompanying photos depicted a small person with very strong, shapely legs in white running shoes with red laces, white shorts with a ribbon belt, a cherry red sports bra, red boxing gloves, and a floppy red cap posing in a boxing stance. Her hair was long and frizzy, had a lot of what Terri Moss would call "root rot," and there was some makeup on her face. The pose was odd. The person looked odd. Not like a drag queen exactly, but certainly not like a woman of fifty-five. The shot reminded me of a Diane Arbus photograph. I had mixed feelings; the situation was pushing me back into the status of "novelty." I had nothing against Pauline. She sounded genuinely excited to be able to live the life she'd always wanted, and her love of boxing also sounded real and heartfelt.

But why did people in America always want to run before they could walk? In a country where everything was already larger than life, there was a tendency to overplay one's hand. The cars were big, the people were big, the meals were huge, the houses massive—and yet there was such a sense of desperation that people would frequently go beyond their limitations in order to be noticed. It made my little adventure seem rather tame and sensible. At least I actually knew how to box. Why did Pauline need to fight and draw attention to her ambiguous gender? Couldn't she just enjoy her training?

"It sounds like a mismatch in your favor," said Peter when I recounted the conversation and sent him the pictures.

I also forwarded the pictures to Terri Moss. "That's a damn man," she wrote back. "There is no doubt about it. USA Boxing should be ashamed of themselves sanctioning men to fight women. I'm sure your skill will work for you, but chick, do *not* mix it up with this guy. This is crazy. His flailing punches will be very rough. Biggs would never let me fight someone like this. I'm with you, though, if you want to do it. Practice the chicken-stick-'n-move *a lot*."

Mixed matches in boxing are not unheard of. Bonnie said she'd fought a man she trained with a few times but always felt that he was stronger, and when his skill failed him he could always use that superior strength. There were countless stories going back to Barbara Buttrick's time, when there were so few women around that there was often no choice but to fight men. But there was always some doubt about how genuine the encounters were. The frequent victories going to the women in these clashes were cause for suspicion that the men weren't fighting to win.

The great Lucia Rijker, who never lost a kickboxing or boxing fight to another woman, was knocked out cold by a man in his prime, Somchai Jaidee, who already had nine knockouts on his record. This bout, from what I have seen of it, was genuine and quite competitive until Rijker got caught while attacking Jaidee. If Rijker couldn't do it, then I doubt anyone else could.

Mixed matches have usually been pretty inconclusive with women either matched against lighter, inexperienced men or against men who were clearly not using their weight and strength to their advantage. Certainly many such matches have drawn a crowd. The German bantamweight Regina Halmich, already a popular main-event fighter in Germany, broke TV presenter Stefan Raab's nose in the fifth round in front of 7.5 million viewers in 2001. In the rematch in 2007, Raab looked to be landing some punches on the tiny Halmich without even really trying, while she whaled away at his body. He reacted to each punch she landed like a seasoned WWF performer, selling the move, just in case anyone missed it. It looked like a fix to me, and it proved nothing.

I've rarely felt as if I could beat any man I was sparring with—unless they had no experience and were a lot smaller or really hopeless. From time to time I may have landed a good clean punch or managed to hurt them a little, sure, because I know how to throw correctly. And there have even been some I've managed to outbox. But I'm not sure the outcome would be the same if we were fighting instead of sparring. Strength isn't the only factor in boxing, but it's significant enough to render mixed matches either unfair or unrealistic.

And it's really a no-win situation, especially for the men, who end up either looking like bullies or cowards. Freddy Roach said if he had to choose, he'd rather play the bully.

Now, when I looked at it, I had three potential opponents in Kansas City: one was a woman who felt like my best friend, another had vowed to put me in a coma, and yet another of uncertain gender who wanted me, more than anything, to know how convincingly feminine and pretty she was.

It was getting more and more, as Dave would say, interesting.

Back at the Canino Boxing and Karate studio, the dreaded Saturday of track work and sparring was fast approaching. And it was not a day for the fainthearted. This time Tara Wood collected me, and we went together to the track. Tara had only been training with Bonnie for three months and put in a good showing at the Golden Gloves in the 165-lb. division. She'd been one of the white Amazon girls I'd categorized at the draw and was pleased to hear that I'd thought she looked tough. She had long red hair and was built like a basketball player, which is exactly what she had been. Originally from a Mormon family in Utah, she had small-town friendliness and big-city smarts.

She was about the fifteenth person I'd told about the man/woman thing. "Get out of here," she said. "They want you to fight a man?"

Tara had moved to Dania Beach from Sarasota where the trainer at the gym she'd been going to had said, "You don't want to box. Why do you want to mess up your looks?"

That prompted her to search for another gym. She'd already broken her nose twice playing basketball, and she wasn't very concerned about it. She did a Google search and found Bonnie. Three months later, she was in the ring fighting a forty-fight veteran in the quarter-finals. And she won. But she was beaten in the semis in a dubious decision by the shorter Elissa from Kansas City.

"Hey Bonnie!" she shouted as we got out of the car. "You should give your abs names. Bonnie and the kids."

After the four laps we did three 400-meter runs, and Bonnie and Tara led the way, both of them with good, track-athlete running styles. I kept pace for about 200 meters and then fell back. A few others had joined us. Yvonne was doing her own version of sprinting, and Ruby was trotting around in her own world. The few men remained quiet and focused, doing all they could to keep pace with Bonnie and Tara.

Then after that we did three 200-meter runs, and that was it. One more lap to cool down, as much as one can cool down in such a climate.

We went to our respective homes for about an hour—not long enough for a proper rest—and were scheduled to regroup at the gym for sparring.

Bonnie was old school. And that is a hard school. Sparring in Florida was nothing like it was in New York City. In fact, I was relieved that this wasn't a weekly thing for me. I was already bone weary from the sprinting before I even wrapped my hands. And I was feeling a bit wary of Yvonne.

"When we spar here you leave your ego at the door," she barked. "That's guy shit." But somehow I wasn't so sure about that.

Yvonne was 152 lb. but had mostly fought at 165 lb., mainly as an amateur and early in her pro career. She'd won silver at the first amateur women's world championships in Turkey in 2001 and finished her amateur days with a respectable 14-3 record the next year. Age caught up with her, and there wasn't a female Masters division then, so she had no option but to turn pro. After cutting her teeth on some unremarkable fighters, like Shelley Burton and debutante Alexandra Moloy, she went up against some real luminaries like Germany's Kazakhstan-born 21-0 super middleweight Natascha Ragosina and the veteran Dakota Stone, as well as the daughter of Detroit Lions great Charlie Sanders, Mary Jo Sanders. Yvonne had also faced perhaps one of the most decorated of all female boxers, Trinidad and Tobago's Giselle Salandy, who held WBC and WBA titles, as well as WIBA, WIBF, and IWBF belts as a light middleweight, and was undefeated in 107 rounds of boxing over seventeen fights, but was tragically killed in a car accident in 2009 at the age of twenty-one with the world of women's boxing in the palm of her hand. Yvonne couldn't beat the classier fighters and was stopped by a couple of them, ending up with a 7-13 record with 1 draw. But she had generally conducted herself like a trooper. Yvonne Reis always battled hard despite her limitations. She was finally rewarded with the WBC middleweight title in Africa against the Kenyan Conjestina Achieng and became a local celebrity during the time she was there, with crowds following her and calling out her name. Fifteen minutes of fame among the Masai.

While we were shadowboxing one day Yvonne told me she had once been knifed in the shoulder while traveling in Greece.

"The guy told me to get on my knees and give him a blow job." When she refused he stabbed her in the shoulder. She then pulled the knife out of her own shoulder and slashed his Achilles tendon before running away.

"There was no way I was going to suck his hairy dick," she said and began stomping on her punches.

Unluckily for her but maybe luckily for me, Yvonne had been knocked out cold by a knee in a recent mixed martial arts bout and so was not sparring too hard. But everyone else was. Jovita, another ex-military girl, who was out of shape but determined to make it to the Gloves the following year, put everything she had into our two rounds. I would have preferred it for both of us if we had been more relaxed. I hit her harder than I really wanted to, but I didn't have much choice.

And then, finally, I did my two rounds with Bonnie. Her punches felt like hammers, and they came in bunches. One punch—I think it was an uppercut—landed on the side of my nose, and I feared that its shape had been altered by that punch, though she assured me that it was fine. Bonnie also threw her body behind all her punches. I think she is possibly the strongest woman I have ever sparred. She just didn't feel like 125 lb.

"I'm looking forward to fighting now," I said. "It's gotta be easier than this."

With a bruised nose and a sore jaw, I went back to my Angelfish hideaway, had a shower, got something to eat, and promptly fell asleep until Tara came back to pick me up to take me to Bonnie's to get my haircut. At home, in her lush garden, Bonnie seemed to have such a sweet nature, such a calm and steady disposition. She never seemed to get angry or upset, or even hold grudges when perhaps she should. She let people go when they got poached by other trainers and forgave others for betrayals that many wouldn't tolerate.

But when she hit you, she hit hard. She hit like a man, but was perhaps even more dangerous than a man because she wasn't holding back and had a greater regard for what women could tolerate than men usually did.

Yvonne proclaimed that in Bonnie's gym, the men don't baby the women because they've all tasted Bonnie's strength in the ring. "And she whoops their asses," said Yvonne.

On my last day I asked Bonnie what she might have done with her life if she hadn't been a fighter and she drew a blank. I looked at her face and tried to imagine her behind the counter at a hairdresser's salon or with a bunch of children, married, maybe chain smoking.

"What if you'd been born thirty years earlier and fighting wasn't an option?"

She shrugged. "Well, it would have been something physical because I'm a very physical person," she said, unable to offer me even a hint of an alternative life.

On Sunday Tara and I went to Miami just to check it out. She thought my fixation with photographing the fat bathers on South Beach was hilarious.

Tara was great company that day, and on my last night in Dania Beach she hosted a farewell dinner for me, inviting my new friends—Bonnie, Jovita, Aileen, and Vanessa—to bid me farewell. It was fun to relax with them now, after training with them and hitting them. I would miss them all, although I had to confess that I wouldn't miss the weather. I was flying out early the next morning to Los Angeles.

14 PATTY BOOM BOOM

I HAD only a vague idea of what worried Terri about Patricia Alcivar until I saw her skip gaily into Hollywood's Wild Card gym wearing hardly anything at all: skin tight gym shorts and a tank top. I immediately felt the urge to throw something over her.

I'd been at the dinner at which Patricia and her husband, Brian, spoke to Terri and Biggs about turning pro. She clearly had an independent streak and was used to arranging her own sparring just to get some work. That was what alarmed Terri the most.

"It's not like amateur boxing," said Terri.

I sat quietly, biting my lip, thinking of all the gyms I had been to alone, both here and in Australia, and of all the people I had sparred without a trainer to watch out for me. I understood Patricia's desire for independence, but I could also understand Terri's reasoning.

"You're different," Terri told me. "You're in the Masters."

That was true. I was older, less exploitable. No one was going to profit from my success or failure. I was just in my own happy little world, really.

I was always a little grateful for the mask middle age gave me and how it rendered me invisible to leering men. And I wondered if all these attractive young women were aware of how the men drooled over them. For some reason, this was more obvious to me here, at the Wild Card gym, than at other gyms I'd visited. Had I also been oblivious to it in my twenties or had I liked it? Was there something that genetically predisposed young women to either being blind to it or flattered? Now I saw it for what it was—kind of revolting.

Patricia kept our Monday morning sparring date, and she brought with her Martin Snow, a big, six-foot-five truck of a man with a fog-horn Brooklyn accent who had been her trainer in New York. Ever since she came to his box-aerobics class and winded him when she punched him in the solar plexus, the two had been an inseparable team, working together through countless tournaments. Patricia is the only fighter Snow has trained, and she has stuck by him despite the urging of others to find another trainer. She can trust Martin. He has never hit on her and has been somewhat of a father figure to her. But Martin was in no position to have her turn pro, as he was too busy running his gyms in New York and Los Angeles. His Trinity Boxing Club was around the corner on Santa Monica Boulevard, so he was able to meet her at Wild Card while we did our rounds. The minute I saw him I breathed a sigh of relief. As long as he was nearby she would be safe in this bear pit.

I ended up in LA because I'd gone west on a wild-goose chase to see Melissa Hernandez fight, but it never happened. I'd been there once before and I enjoyed returning now to the Vagabond Inn next door to the gym at the raggedy end of Vine Street. The area had character and some of the urban grit I'd missed in Florida. And the breezy, sunny climate was such a relief. At last I could run with some pleasure through the streets of West Hollywood.

The Vagabond was managed by a friendly Fijian Indian called Sanjay. Across the road from the gym there was a Social Security office, a Goodwill store, and a place called Big Dollar that sold unbelievably cheap junk from soap to a pack of four socks for ninety-nine cents. Up the hill toward Sunset Boulevard were a few pawn shops, another shabby shopping mall, a Pollo Loco, and an ArcLight cinema, leading eventually to a Borders, a Bed Bath and Beyond, and a Japanese restaurant. By the time you crossed Sunset, the skankiness was replaced by the fresh gloss of recent gentrification. But I preferred it down the hill, where all the transvestites, lunatics, and hobos were. One man spent the morning standing on his bedroll shouting like a demon on one side of the street and then crossed to the other side in the afternoon to do the same thing. The first time I walked past him I almost jumped out of my skin. But I realized pretty quickly that I was simply not in his world. The area reminded me of a neighborhood I had once lived in. At the time, it had been Melbourne's most notorious red-light district, but like the area beyond Sunset, it, too, became gentrified.

I was getting ready for Ringside and had managed to coordinate with Patricia Alcivar to spar. She had been at a Tony Robbins Seminar in San Jose. By happy coincidence Dee Hamaguchi was also in the gym, enjoying a little West Coast summer vacation, living in Hollywood and training at Wild Card. Dee was a Yale science graduate who now taught high school physics and math in New York. Originally from Canada, she had been a long-time resident of Harlem and was one of Gleason's pioneering women. She had been pivotal in forcing the *Daily News* to accept women in the Golden Gloves tournament in New York in the mid-1990s. She was giving me water between rounds, telling me to use my jab more, while Martin's deep voice rumbled continuous instructions to Patricia.

Later that day Patricia and I went to Starbucks, where I learned more about her. I'd picked up snippets about her boxing career, but I was curious to hear more. Either she was still a bit charged up from her Tony Robbins weekend or this was just her—bright and

Dee, Mia, me, and Patricia at Wild Card.

shiny like a new penny, teeth glowing white, her smooth skin luminous with good health.

As we sat talking, I learned that this dimple-faced woman with a permanent smile had had a less-than-sunny past. "I grew up dirt poor," she began. But that was just the start.

"My parents came from Colombia, and they moved here when they were in their early twenties. My mom, I really feel for her 'cause she's had a rough life. She was dealt a bad hand, she really was. She married my father, who turned out to be a monster. He was a physically abusive alcoholic.

"My father—I don't know why and I think I'll never know why—but my father chose to be physically and sexually abusive to me. We were all girls, the four of us. We were all really close, me and my sisters, and I got the worst of it. I really got the shit beat out of me. Really. I mean, it was horrible."

"From what age?" I asked.

"The youngest I can remember, I would say somewhere around four or five years old. I still have scars on my back from the beatings I took. It was always over something so stupid."

Patricia was telling me this as if she were recounting a family picnic, not the horror of what it was. And I was totally spellbound by the incongruity of it. Patricia's Pollyanna disposition was unsettling when she was speaking about her abusive past. If there was ever any doubt in my mind that human beings are inherently contradictory creatures, here was the proof. It was one thing to think that femininity and boxing were contradictions, which is true on so many superficial levels. But this one human being's defiance of the darkness that had been her introduction to the world was breathtaking. It made the simple yin-yang novelty of being a female boxer seem rather trivial by comparison. I thought about the relative consistency of someone like Anne Wolf, who had lived with killers and eaten out of trash cans. She didn't have Patricia's cheer and glow.

Instead, Anne's personality was in keeping with her life's narrative. Disturbing though Wolf's early life experience had been, it was far more disturbing to hear these nightmarish details coming from such a sunny person.

"The sexual abuse probably started at a very young age," she said. "I know it was somewhere around two."

"You're kidding!" I gasped.

What kind of a man sexually abuses a baby? That Patricia had not only survived but flourished became more and more remarkable to me the more I learned about her.

When Patricia was nine, her father had tried to molest her younger sister. "I called the police on him and that was it. They removed him from my house. I haven't seen my father since I was ten years old. He's still in New York. He lives in Brooklyn, and he still has the same job—he works in maintenance at IBM. I don't hate him. I don't really have any feelings for him. I'm way past that. Something Martin has always told me is that the best revenge is success. You know, just move on and do the best that you can in life."

Patricia had taken that idea and run like the devil with it. And she'd run and run and run.

Her antidote was sports, at which she excelled. First she participated in gymnastics; then full-contact karate, winning the 1994 world lightweight championship; and then boxing, winning two New York Golden Gloves finals. Sports had been her salvation and, as she says, her "Prozac." And she'd needed something, because the suffering didn't end when her father left.

"My mom became very bitter and miserable. She was under so much pressure supporting four girls by herself. So it was rough growing up. She used to really torture me. Her way of torturing was, on a beautiful Saturday or Sunday, instead of going to the beach, she'd say, 'OK, go clean windows, go do laundry, go do chores, go wash clothes, go scrub the bathroom,' and stuff like that. I was living like a prisoner. I didn't have any friends. I grew up isolated. It was mental abuse. At the time, my mom worked the evening shift as a maintenance person from 4:00 p.m. to midnight, and we didn't have a car so she would get home at 2:00 a.m., and if she found one cup dirty, she would wake me up and tell me to finish my chores.

"At the age of about fifteen I was miserable, and I thought I'd rather live alone and in peace than do this. I felt singled out by my father and then by my mom.

"One day I'd just really had it. I thought, 'You know what, I'm done.' I got my things and I got out. I found a room in Queens with an old lady."

The catalyst for her departure was the Los Angeles Marathon, which she had been watching on television with her mother one Sunday afternoon. She was spellbound as Olga Markova crossed the finish line to cheers and adulation.

"Everybody was, like, going crazy, and I thought this is what I want to do one day. And my mom was always, always unsupportive. She was like, 'That's not for you. You'll never be able to do something like that.' And I remember my eyes filling up with tears, and the next morning I got up by myself at five o'clock and I ran, I ran maybe like five blocks, and I thought, 'OK, I'm just going to keep doing this, I'm going to run a block or half a block farther each day.' I had, like, sandals. I didn't even have sneakers. Sneakers were just too expensive."

Patricia got a job, coincidentally in a sneaker shop, and was able to pay the rent and finish high school. And buy some sneakers. At the age of sixteen she competed in her first New York Marathon.

When she finished school she got a job as a receptionist at a battered women's shelter, of all places.

Patricia's identity had been defined by struggle and her ability to get to the finish line, no matter what. With her innocent, underdog appearance, boxing had been ideal for her, really, a reinforcement of her already-proven resilience, a public display of the ability to triumph over adversity, an ability that she had already proven by surmounting the obstacles of her childhood.

"When I first got into boxing I was about eighteen years old," she said. "And I looked like I was fourteen. When I first went into Gleason's gym everybody was like, 'What's this little girl doing here?' And in my first fight my opponent comes out, and she's this girl who had just gotten out of prison. And then I came out, and everyone was like, 'Oh no.' And this one girl said, 'Don't get into the ring, you're going to get hurt.' And that's why I keep getting into the ring, because it was like, 'You guys think I can't do it? You have no idea what I've been through. I can do this.' The more people told me I couldn't, the more I wanted to do it. Same with professional boxing."

But how long, I wondered, would she be able to keep getting up at four thirty in the morning to run ten miles and have enough energy left for a boxing session at night? Wasn't she running the risk of burning out?

Then she told me that in her twenties she'd started experiencing heart palpitations and had begun to gain weight and to feel fatigued and sick.

"I went to twenty-five different doctors," she said. "Something was clearly wrong, but they didn't know what it was. I was giving it all I had, but it wasn't good enough. The amount of oxygen in my blood was off, and the only cure for that was medication, but the medication was going to prevent me from being a competitive athlete. They were about to do a very invasive test."

Then two things happened to change her, she says. First, she went to church and, second, she started seeing a nutritionist who told her to drop her vegan diet and start eating more protein. Gradually her health began to improve. But she never discovered what it was that had ailed her exactly.

"I said to myself, 'God puts certain things in a person's path. Nothing is by accident. Everybody has a purpose.' I honestly believe I went through what I went through so that I would have a good story to tell. There are so many girls, young girls, including my sisters, who lead a rough life and don't know how to find a healthy outlet, and they turn to drugs, alcohol, sex. My sisters live half the life I live, and they are all single young moms. I used to offer to pay them to come running with me in the mornings, and they wouldn't get up. I was basically on my own."

It was strange for me, an atheist, to hear about religious faith helping someone find answers where there were none. Who was I, with my happy childhood, to dismiss religious faith when so many individuals gained strength from it? So what if it was a fiction? Maybe some horrors in life are too incomprehensible to be rational, and people need to have a sense of a grander narrative and purpose before they can endow their lives with meaning. But what kind of God would direct such horrors to happen? And for what reason? Give me secular humanism any day. Sometimes things happen for no good reason.

"My therapist once said to me, 'You know what you need? You need to go to an incest survivor group,'" Patricia said. "So I went to this group, and I was shocked. All the women there were either drugged, recovering alcoholics, had some sort of addictive behavior, were depressed, or suicidal. And I was like, 'This is not me. What the hell are you doing sending me to one of these groups?' These women were hopeless, just hopeless.

"I'm doing what I was destined to do. My background is a source of strength for me. I have the authority to inspire other women. If someone can look at me and say, 'If she can do it, then I can do it,' then my life's purpose has been realized. It's a rough road, and I'm willing to take it," she said.

The next day, when I sparred Patricia again, it felt a little different to me. Her resilience was much more obvious, and I could see something in her eyes that was harder, darker. I couldn't help thinking how, compared to all she had been through, getting hit by me with a boxing glove was nothing. But no one, looking at that face of hers, unmarked by any visible sign of pain, with not even a frown line on her forehead, could have any idea of exactly how tough she really is. Not me, certainly, and maybe not even Terri.

15 AND NOW THE WORLD

"DANG," SAID Terri. "It sounds like a real cluster fuck out there, chick."

I'd been describing to her the scenes that had greeted me at the KCI Expo Center in Kansas City earlier that evening. It was still August 2009. From LA, I had flown to Kansas City for the Ringside Tournament there. People of all shapes and sizes were milling around everywhere, crowds gathering around the bracket sheets pasted to the wall at the building's entrance. Many people were either in their fight gear or carrying gym bags. Others were in team T-shirts or official USA Boxing uniforms. It was as though the whole world was about nothing but boxing. Men, women, children—everyone had morphed into boxing enthusiasts. There was no financial crisis or climate change or war in Afghanistan or health care debate or real estate collapse or subprime mortgage catastrophe. All that mattered in life had been reduced to gloves, head guards, skipping ropes, satin shorts, and mouth guards, and all roads led into the ring. Nothing else existed. Human worth was now measured by punch counts and slipping skills. Was it possible that even I, the embodiment of a boxing fanatic, had finally reached saturation point?

Inside the center was a Ringside shop that sold everything a boxer could possibly need and lots more stuff they didn't. Should anyone run low on boxing boots or shirts or trunks or gloves or punch mitts or key chains with boxing gloves, or gauze, or Ringside caps and T shirts, here was a ready supply. There was also a small café that sold the usual garbage masquerading as food and farther inside the massive bunker that everyone had come for, a vast, artificially lit concrete space with six full-size boxing rings where fourteen hundred athletes would battle it out. The battle had already begun for some. The tournament had been going for two days, but Friday and Saturday were the semifinals and the finals. The Masters, of whom there were fewer competitors, were not required to arrive until Thursday night to register. It was freezing cold inside and hot outside.

"Tell me," said Terri as I walked around the lobby trying to get a better signal on my cell phone. "Have you seen Dunny anywhere?"

I had. I first saw her when I'd arrived at the center, having caught a lift with a car full of guys from Washington, DC. One of them had kindly given up his place in the car for me, since I was hurrying to make the registration deadline. Despite being without a car, I kept finding plenty of people willing to help me get where I needed to go.

"Oh my God, there she is," I'd said out loud as the car approached the center. "I can't believe she's come after I beat the crap out of her in Georgia."

The teenagers sitting next to me thought that was hilarious.

Then, once I was inside the center, Dunny appeared out of nowhere and slapped me on the arm, a bit too hard to be friendly, I thought. After the coma e-mail, I wondered if that was meant to be some kind of message.

"Hey," she said in her tuneless falsetto. "How ya doing?"

And then she vanished.

A little later, I was standing with Jackie Atkins, my perennial companion on registration lines and at tournaments, when Dunny reappeared in the middle distance.

"That's her," I said. "The one from Atlanta."

"Where?" said Jackie.

But Dunny was out of sight again.

"Sorry," I said, looking around. "I've lost her again."

"And what about the other one?" said Jackie, leaning in close and batting her long lashes. "You know"—she paused for effect—"the *guy*?" She raised her eyebrows. "Have you seen him?"

I searched along the line and there seemed to be a lot of Masters men and quite a few women. But nothing in between. "Not yet," I said.

Then I saw a woman who looked flat chested and a little masculine but more understated than the flamboyant Pauline had been in her photos. But it could have been her.

Standing there in the line I started to feel exhausted and hungry. It had taken me all day to get from LA to Kansas City, and I was possibly going to fight twice over the weekend. When was I going to rest? I'd only managed a quick glance at the bed in the Econo Lodge, but the stench of stale cigarette smoke, the likes of which I hadn't experienced since some time in the mid-1970s, had made me slightly nauseous. I guess the whole world once smelled that way to me, particularly my house and car. But after fifteen years as a non-smoker, I now found the smell worse than someone who had never smoked at all. I was astounded that there were such things as smoking rooms still available in American hotels, and that it was permitted in casinos, because it was banned virtually everywhere in

Australia. The smell gave the place a sad, deadbeat, end-of-the-line feel. But I couldn't dwell on that. Otherwise, it seemed clean enough, and I had to get to the Expo Center.

And as soon as I entered the building, like a recurring motif, there was Jackie, Irish Liz, and Ekne Montalvo, Jackie's friend who'd been in her corner when we'd fought in Florida. This time he was weighing in to fight in the 165-lb. division. This was something, I gathered, he hadn't done in a very long time. It was hard to tell. Ekne was an exceptionally friendly, good-humored man, short and powerful across the shoulders and in good shape. But I couldn't understand a single word he said. He got his message across with sounds more than words, smiling and gesticulating all the while.

It was so cold inside the expo center that Jackie was dressed for a ski trip, wearing a jacket with the collar turned up and a peaked cap. It was summer in America outside, yet the expo center was cooled so aggressively that you had to pack as if you might encounter a snow storm. We moved along the line, which led to a table where people at computer screens sat taking in stats.

Pretty soon Jackie and I got to talking with the woman in front of us who had a body builder's physique, tattoos, and shoulder-length, dirty-blonde hair. I couldn't help but notice that she also had a conspicuous pair of quite obviously synthetic boobs. She was with a man in a peaked cap.

She introduced herself as Kathy Hungness and was in my weight class. "I weigh 141, but I can be 138 by the morning," she told us. Kathy was from Illinois and looked to be a fairly well-preserved forty-year-old. She said she'd never fought before, but that she was one of the coaches at their club. She looked to be in good shape, very lean but also strong. Her veins twisted around her forearms like pipe cleaners. The three of us immediately started speculating on various likely match-up scenarios and who else might be in the mix.

I kept spotting Dunny, who would appear and vanish like the white rabbit in *Alice's Adventures in Wonderland.*

"There she is," I'd say to Jackie whose head would spin left and right. "Nope, sorry, she's gone again."

Then I zoned in on a mannish woman I'd spotted approaching us. I scanned her neck for an Adam's apple and any other telltale signs.

"Excuse me," I said. "Are you Pauline?"

"No," she smiled.

"Sorry," I said. If only she knew I had pegged her for a hermaphrodite.

Then I heard a slightly familiar-sounding voice say, "Oh no, I'm only 125 pounds. I've tried eating donuts to get heavier, but I keep losing weight."

The speaker was standing before the official's desk, a small and wiry person, wearing a cap with the Ringside insignia, a T-shirt that said "All American Girl," and a pair of red-rimmed, slightly outdated spectacles that magnified her eyes. Her brittle hair scribbled around her cap like a clown's wig.

"That's her," I said.

"The one from Atlanta?" asked Jackie.

"No," I said. "The other one. That's the *guy*. You know."

I gestured toward the registration desk.

We both stood staring dumbly.

Finally, I was in front of the officials handing over my book. I introduced myself to a man everyone was addressing as Dave. The robust, portly fifty-something person I'd imagined Lubs to be turned out to be a considerably older, slight, snowy-haired figure in a blue shirt and glasses.

He gave me a warm hug like a distant relative I had come to visit.

"Have ya seen Pauline?" he asked, and I nodded.

"People who don't know, can't pick up on it, ya know," he said.

I found that hard to believe, but once you knew, there was no going back. You couldn't un-know, I suppose.

What followed was like something out of a 1960s surrealist film. We were all directed into a small room for a Masters meeting comprised of John Brown, the founder of Ringside, sitting before us in shorts that showed off his tanned, athletic legs, while we all waited. And waited. Brown was the star of his own series of boxing instruction videos that he sold through his Ringside website along with everything else from apparel and safety gear to heavy bags and even boxing rings. He was possibly in his sixties, maybe older, but fit and trim. He looked a bit like an old school army sergeant. He also spoke with a slight lisp, due to what looked to be a harelip. He was flanked by a couple of women, one of whom had fought Tara Wood back in Florida and the other, a slim woman in her thirties with a short, pixie haircut.

At one point Brown read out some names and asked those people to say how many bouts they'd had.

This was a tricky question to answer. Many didn't know if this meant Masters bouts or total bouts in a boxing career that may have been interrupted by a twenty-year layoff. Others may have simply continued into the Masters from the open section without a break. A few people sought clarification, but I got the impression that most people preferred this matter to remain as vague as possible so if confronted, they could say, "Oh, I thought you meant *Masters* bouts."

Some, when asked, called out "none" or "zero" or maybe "five." And then someone said "fifty-two." That made the others sound like bald-faced liars. I hoped he didn't call out my name. And thankfully he didn't. I wasn't sure what my answer would have been.

After that nothing happened for a long time. And it continued that way for more than an hour. Everyone sat in the room, but no one knew why.

"What's going on?" I asked Jackie, thinking if anyone knew, it would be her. But she shrugged.

"I think there's a meeting," she said.

During this time, Pauline, who, with those red-rimmed glasses, looked to me like a petite version of Dustin Hoffman in *Tootsie*, sat herself right next to me.

She picked up from where we'd left off in our phone conversation and went over some of the same ground, referring to the "operation" in Thailand and the "equipment" that didn't work.

Every now and then she would look around and say, "Wow, this is so cool." But I was listening less to what she was saying and focusing more on how she appeared. Her hands, I noticed, were massive, almost out of proportion to the rest of her. Great square blocks with raw skin on the knuckles. Her body language was complex. On the one hand, she had a lot of what looked like contrived feminine gestures—crossed legs, hands demurely in her lap, and she smiled a lot as she spoke, holding my gaze unnervingly with those magnified eyes. Yet she was also quite muscular and solid in a very masculine way. But we were at a boxing tournament, after all, where femininity wasn't at issue, and actually it didn't matter if she looked a little masculine, as some women clearly did. But she was battling against anything that might betray her secret. The truth was that, technically at least, with or without male equipment, she had chosen to be female. It made for a rather uncomfortable tension, and I found it fascinating at first.

"Have you always felt that you were a woman?" I asked, and she nodded tentatively as if she weren't quite sure. But her social skills were clumsy, as if she weren't used to making general small talk. So we hit a kind of conversational dead end.

"I'm also autistic," she added after a long and uncomfortable pause.

"Really?" I asked. She shrugged and smiled and stared at me with her goggle eyes.

I got up to go to the bathroom, and when I returned I saw that

Pauline and Dunny were deep in conversation as if they'd known each other for years.

What a crazy place this is, I thought. Where else in the world might you see a middle-aged lesbian comedian and an autistic, post-operative transsexual in her midfifties getting ready to enter a boxing ring? And here they were, sitting together and chatting like old pals. I was looking forward to going home but was a little worried that Australia might seem dull after all this.

Then, finally, Brown spoke. He said that it would be many, many hours before the brackets were done. It could go as late as two or three in the morning, and so he suggested it would be best for people go back to their hotels, get some rest, and come back at 6:00 a.m. to check in before the weigh-in at 7:00 a.m. I couldn't understand why he didn't just say that in the first place instead of making us wait all that time.

It was 8:00 p.m. when I was recounting all this to Terri on the phone. I was waiting for Jackie and her troupe so that I could go with her to see if I could get the extra room at the Marriott that Jackie had reserved and leave the Econo Lodge.

I was telling Terri about seeing Dunny and Pauline together. I wondered aloud if they might have known each other before the tournament.

"Maybe it was because of Gays at Ringside," said Terri.

"What?" I said. "I can't believe there is such a thing as Gays at Ringside."

"No," she said. "Dave. Dave Lubs. Dave at Ringside. He would have told them about each other."

I really was tired. I told her I was working on getting a better room at the Marriott. "It's a bit of a rat hole," I said of the Econo Lodge.

"You mean like a flea bag?" she asked.

"And it stinks of smoke."

"And you know," she said, "that's not just smoke. That's a whole lot of deadly, toxic chemicals too. That always sets off my asthma."

"Did you ever smoke?" I asked.

"Are you kidding? Two packs a day."

"Me too," I said, laughing. "And now listen to us."

I got off the phone and joined Jackie in front of the KCI Expo Center and we walked up the street to the Holiday Inn. Jackie charmed the pants off the Holiday Inn shuttle driver, and he happily took us to the Marriott. She addressed him by name, asked about his wife and kids. How did she get to know him so fast? She'd obviously done this kind of thing before and knew the secret of wrapping five-star hotel staff around her little finger. On our trip to the Marriott, Jackie suggested that I should actually stay at the Holiday Inn so that I could check the brackets early the next morning and tell everybody whether or not they were fighting. That way, only one of us would have to show up.

So, just as soon as we arrived at the Marriott, where everyone behind the front desk seemed to melt into a smile when Jackie greeted them, the front desk gladly called the Holiday Inn, and what a miracle, they had two rooms available. What would I do without Jackie Atkins? I wondered. I passed on dinner, grabbed a sandwich, and the driver took me to the Econo Lodge where I checked out. Then he came back and took me to the Holiday Inn. I got excited because I would save on travel time and cost to the KCI and I also wouldn't have the headache of trying to sweet-talk some shuttle driver into giving me a ride. Cabs were charging ten dollars each way, and it was a two-minute trip. But when I arrived at the Inn, Mike (I had learned from Jackie to read name tags) at the front desk said there had been a mistake and that there were actually really only . . . Well, the situation was that there were zero rooms available.

I must have had a homicidal look on my face at that point, because Mike quickly said, "Don't worry. I'll fix it."

I waited and waited while the nervous Mike made calls and looked furtively over at me with my bags at my feet. I then tried to call Jackie to see if I could get back that Marriott room I'd forsaken. I had her on the phone when Mike told me that the Marriott had a room and that the driver would take me there.

It was 11:00 p.m. by the time I landed in the Marriott's soft bed, utterly done.

Cluster fuck. You can say that again.

Five hours later my cell phone woke me up, alerting me to a message. Terri had missed her flight.

I crawled out of bed to weigh myself, and I was 141 lb. I think I needed to make 138, but who knew, the rules were so rubbery and Ringside seemed to have its own set of rules. There was that ten-pound differential, but would they invoke that here or not? If I wanted to be safe, I had only half an hour to go for a run and try to sweat it off.

But first I rang Terri to find out what had happened. Her flight had been scheduled for six in the morning. She had gotten up at four, she told me, but when she tried to start her car she discovered her car battery was flat because she'd left her lights on all night. She needed a jump-start. But no one was answering their phone. Eventually, Lynne, a sixty-year-old boxing chick friend of hers, answered. "You know her sister has been sick so she keeps her phone on."

"Yes, yes," I said, "and—?"

"Well, Lynne drove me to the airport, and I'm sure I would have made it to the gate on time. But you know what happened?"

"What?"

"You know the airport train? Well, it broke down."

The flight hadn't left, but they'd closed the boarding gates and she didn't make it. She'd had to pay for a flight change.

"So," I said, looking at my watch and trying to get my feet into my running shoes, "what time are you getting here?"

She rummaged in her bag and said, "I lost the itinerary, can you see the flight times on your computer?"

"I haven't got wifi in the room."

"You haven't? Oh, here it is," she said finally. "Three o'clock. But how do you feel, Mischa? Do you feel rested?"

I laughed.

"I'm OK," I said. "I'm a bit over weight, so I'm going to go for a little jog."

"But you can lose weight lying down."

What did she think I'd been doing all night?

"I haven't got time to lie down!"

"But you need to r—"

"I gotta go," I said.

I had twenty minutes to drop some weight before meeting Jackie in the lobby to get to the weigh-in.

When I got outside the muggy heat was tempered by a light and pleasant breeze. For fuck's sake. Of all the times for a breeze! It was the last thing I needed—something to cool me down and stop me from sweating. Any other time in the past five weeks, and it would have been a godsend. But not now. Ringside was feeling more and more like an obstacle race tacked on to the end of a half marathon with a cross-country challenge in the middle for good measure. Just when I felt close to hitting the wall, everything started getting even harder. And here I was in Kansas City, and all the place was to me was a collection of hotels and the KCI Expo Center. I jogged around what was a manmade lake on a tree-lined path for about twenty minutes wondering what the place was actually like. I had the number of novelist and philosopher Clancy Martin but didn't think I'd have time to even talk to him on the phone. I got back to my room, jumped on the scales, and nothing. There was no change. I hadn't lost a single ounce.

When Jackie and I arrived at the KCI Expo Center, the place was swarming with bodies clambering over each other as people tried to read the bracket sheets. It was like a scene from a Depression-era movie in which unemployed men were trying to get work at some struggling timber yard. There was an air of desperation. We joined the throng.

It looked like Jackie and I had been matched against each other, and Dunny was fighting the body builder with the boobs. Because Jackie weighed 145, that meant that it didn't matter that I was over after all. I was hungry and tired and couldn't wait to get back to that super soft Marriott bed.

But the weigh-in line was endless. It snaked around the center lobby and folded in on itself by the women's rest room. To make matters worse, it was moving at a glacial pace. And it was all women, too—it wasn't tacked onto the end of the guys' line. There were scores of women and girls, young and old, lined up to box. I couldn't imagine what was slowing it down, but at least Kevina Franklin was keeping everyone entertained with her intermittent announcements.

I started chatting with a black girl from Detroit called Kiki who told me she was twenty years old, which meant she was just eight years old when I started boxing. She said people were always telling her she was too aggressive for the sports she played, so her mom sent her off to learn how to box.

"I wish my mom had sent me off to learn how to box," I said.

The biker chick with the boobs, Kathy, was sweaty from running, and she looked a little weary. I thought it strange that she was wearing black eyeliner at this time of the morning and for such a nonevent as an amateur weigh-in. When she got on the scales she took off her shorts, revealing a thong and a pair of muscular buttocks.

"Sorry everyone for my ass," she said.

"But it's very nice," I said, and a few people laughed.

She looked so much like a body builder that I guessed she might also fight like one. I'd seen plenty of them in my old gym and talk about gassing out. They had about ten seconds in them before their aerobic system virtually shut down. Although she looked fitter than that and had been for a run, I guessed she might be slow, thinking she had a lot of power in all those nicely shaped muscles. People in her gym had probably told her that she would be stronger than most women, and that this tournament would be easy for her.

After the weigh-in we went into the freezing cold arena to get in line for the physical. Now we were all mixed together, and I was lined up behind a bunch of twelve-year-old boys, which made me feel a bit strange. What the hell was I doing there with all these children? When was I going to grow up?

Boxing doctors everywhere basically just checked that you were alive. They squeezed your hands and poked your nose and your cheeks and asked you if you had any pain, dizziness, or headaches, as if anyone would tell them if they did. Some take your blood pressure and resting heart rate. But sometimes they take their examination a little further. Here, after the small and very wrinkly female physician listened to my chest, she asked me to stand with my feet heel to toe and close my eyes. She then instructed me to open my eyes and move my finger from my nose to her finger, which she held out in front of her, and then back to my nose, then back to her finger, and so on. Then she started moving her finger. At that point I thought I was done for. But it seemed to amuse the doctor, who gave me the all-clear anyway.

"You're good to go," she said. "Fit to box."

When we were all clothed after the medical check, Kathy stopped to admire Jackie's "striations," the muscle fibers that are visible only when body fat percentages are low. What does she think this is? It's not a muscle posing contest.

Ekne appeared, looking a little tense. "You make weight?" I asked, and he nodded.

Terri Moss wearing Ringside headgear.

"Who are you fighting?"

"The shiny guy," he said, laughing.

"The shiny guy?"

"*Chinese* guy," said Jackie.

"Oh."

Before we returned to the Marriott, we decided to go shopping. I still needed to get the mandatory, Ringside Masters headgear. Inside the shop, a male Masters boxer was complaining about it, too. Not just that the contraption itself was too thick and heavy and restricted vision, but that it was compulsory and Ringside was the only supplier.

"It's a bit sneaky of them, don't you think?" I said.

"Yeah, it is," he said. "Very."

But what could we do? I forked over my seventy dollars for a red helmet that I would wear maybe twice in my life and never again. Jackie and I then headed back to the Marriott and had a buffet breakfast. I had to remind myself that we were fighting each other that night. I couldn't hang out with her all day, as if we were best buddies. I needed to get at least a little distance. So I went back up to my room and got into bed to rest until Terri arrived.

A few hours later there was a knock at the door. I put on my head guard and opened it.

"The only good thing about this," I said, "is that it makes your head so big it has a slimming effect on your body."

"Let me see," Terri said, like she'd been there all along.

I took it off, and she tried it on. It looked even more ridiculous on her because she already had such a miniscule body and she was wearing her Jackie O sunglasses. She looked like she was wearing a bug costume for a fancy dress party.

"Have you checked the brackets?" she asked.

"Yeah," I said. "It looks like we'll be fighting around eight, so we should probably head over there in a couple of hours."

"Is there a shuttle or something?"

"We might have to get a cab," I said. "It's alright, I'll pay."

By now I was resigned to just handing out money left and right—to the cab drivers trying to screw you because of the tournament, to Ringside for their helmet, to the five-star hotels with their outrageous rates and room service charges for cheap, stodgy food, and to anyone and everyone who so much as lifted a finger for you. Money was just hemorrhaging from me, but I was too tired to worry about it. I was also worn down by the ceaseless good cheer being delivered by all and sundry in anticipation of a generous tip. All the "Hi, I'm Cindy and I'll be your wait person for today" speeches and the "look at me bending over backward for you" service. I was missing the surly and sarcastic Melbourne waiters and the laconic nature of the Australian hospitality industry. I longed for the absence of all these niceties.

"Do you think Peter will come with you next time?" asked Terri in the car on the way to the KCI.

"I dunno," I sighed. "I don't think he could take all these "have a nice days." It would make him want to hit someone. And he hasn't even experienced "have a *great* day."

Inside the KCI the six rings were all in use. High-pitched electronic bells were going off constantly. Boxers were shadowboxing or warming up on mitts, the smack, smack, smack sound of leather hitting leather like the sound of corn popping. The burble of voices, occasional shrieking and screaming, the high-pitched squeals of groups of children, and the baritone of shouting men all echoed around the massive concrete cavern. The ring announcer's voice would break through it all in disjointed bursts: "In the red corner . . . from Miami, Florida . . . weighing in at . . . 152 pounds. . . . Masters bout . . . all the way from . . ."

People of all ages, genders, shapes, sizes, and nationalities were either getting gloved up or de-gloved; wiping off the sweat after a bout or nervously shadowboxing before one; or sitting, dressed in shorts and shirts, jiggling their legs, white iPod wires trailing from their ears. On the periphery, I'd occasionally see someone walk by with a steaming plate of muck purchased from the café, a woman nursing a baby, people sitting in groups on foldout chairs as if they were at a picnic, others piling onto the bleachers, some standing stock-still, fixated on the action.

I had no prefight nerves at all. There was no one for me to impress or disappoint. Maybe I was just too exhausted. But that was fine because the whole fight would only be three minutes long, a kind of microfight.

I spent a lot of time shadowboxing. It was a bit contagious. Everywhere you looked someone was doing it. Then I'd think it was too soon to warm up, so I'd stop and sit down and talk to Terri. At one stage Pauline appeared, still wearing a cap (could she be balding?) and attached herself to us like a devoted fan. I'd missed her fight that afternoon, but she said she'd lost.

"I'm still glad I did it, though," she said.

I wondered if her opponent knew that technically she'd beaten a guy. I was finding Pauline strange in ways that had nothing to do with her ambiguous gender. She seemed a bit of a lost soul, all alone in this massive cluster fuck with her camera in her hand and no one to photograph. She showed me some shots of her fight, but they were a blur. I was curious about how it was going to look, but I'd decided that after the late night, early morning, all the travel, and playing musical chairs with the hotel rooms, I'd needed rest more than I'd needed to see Pauline's fight.

I asked her if she could film my bout and showed her how to use my camera. "Do you think you can do it?" I asked. She nodded but didn't fill me with confidence.

In the meantime, we had been joined by a local man who had come to check out the tournament. He was a tall, good-looking ath-

Me and Pauline.

letic guy in his late forties who had a nice smile and laughed easily. He told us he used to box when he was younger, so I tried to persuade him that he should compete in the next Ringside tournament. Pauline seemed to like him and this amused Terri to no end. She winked at me as they went off together to get something to eat.

He came back alone, and I wondered if perhaps I should have him film the bout instead of Pauline. He appeared slightly more on the ball than she did. I handed him my camera and gave him instructions, and he seemed to take them in.

We were bout number twenty-five in ring five, and the time was getting close, so Terri and I went to the glove table to get my big, white, sixteen-ounce gloves.

Luckily, I had already had my hands wrapped because when we got back to our spot, Jackie was gloved up and heading toward the ring with a big black guy and Ekne.

I looked over, concerned. "What's going on?" I asked.

"We've been moved up. Now we're bout twenty-three," said the big black guy.

Where did he come from? I wondered. Actually, he looked like he'd come from central casting. In a rush Terri put my gloves on, we did some very perfunctory warm-up moves, and then we clambered into the ring.

"I'm OK. I'm fine," I said, bouncing up and down.

I looked at the ring next to us and saw that Dunny and the body builder were about to get under way. "Look!" I pointed them out to Terri. The bout started, and I saw the body builder flailing and Dunny flailing a little less effectively and the referee stepping in to give her a count. That was all I caught before I had to come to center ring to begin my own bout.

I went on the attack from the first bell, but I couldn't tell if she was catching me with clean shots or not. Between the padded head guard and the heavy gloves, I had no sense of what was going on.

They rendered me numb. The one-minute round flew past, and I went back to the corner to a rather pessimistic Terri.

"I don't know about that round," she said. "You need to calm down a little, Mischa, and just box more, scoop that jab. I think you took too many shots in that one."

"Really?" I said. "I couldn't tell."

Round two felt better although Jackie seemed to be trying to box more herself this time and was pretty mobile, forcing me to try to cut the ring and trap her in a corner, which I felt I was managing to do quite well. I also noticed Jackie had adopted the Hurricane's whoop-whoop war cry, which sounded completely wrong coming from her. It just didn't seem to fit her personality. It was funny, and I thought, "I must remember to tell Melissa next time I see her."

I went back to the corner.

"That was better," said Terri. "But I don't know. I still think she might be ahead."

"I can't feel anything in this fucking gear," I said. "I can't even tell if I'm landing."

"It was better. Just keep doing the same thing, keep your head movement going."

At the end of the fight, Terri still seemed unimpressed. "I don't know," she said. "I've seen you do better."

When I thought about it, I realized that Terri had been there at each one of my US fights and in the corner now for half of them. She was getting to know what I could do pretty well. She kept telling me that I had talent, but I felt the need to correct her each time.

"No, it's not talent," I said. "I've never had any talent. It's just experience and that I've been persistent. I'm just dogged, that's all."

"No," she said, "it's talent. You're a no-bullshit boxer. You've got a good jab and you've got rhythm. You know how to box and move. I wish I could spend some more time with you, chick, I could teach you some real tricky shit."

In center ring, waiting for the announcement, I was reconciled to the fact that Jackie had won. But it was my name that was called out and my hand that was raised. Wow, I thought, that's never happened to me in more than a decade of boxing. I'd never been on the right end of a robbery before. Not ever. Not that it was blind robbery, exactly. Maybe because I was on the front foot, being the aggressor, and they saw me making the fight more. But I couldn't wait to see the tape just the same. Fights can often look completely different to how they feel.

"Sorry, Jackie, I thought you had that," I said as we stepped out of the ring.

"Me, too," she said.

"Well, we can always have a third fight," I said.

"Uh-uh, no way," she said. "No more."

That seemed a bit churlish. Maybe she'd change her mind about that after a little time had passed.

But then I started to wonder if it wasn't such a bad decision after all.

Straight after the fight her corner started carrying on like it was the WBC championship of the world that had just been snatched from them. It seemed a bit too much. The big black guy was nice to me—"You're a class act"—but he was furious about the incompetent judging. He and Jackie tracked down John Brown and, last I saw, had buttonholed him and were giving him the lowdown. A few people in the crowd who'd seen their reaction told me they thought the decision had been fair.

"I think you deserved that," a few of them said.

The handsome guy handed me my camera, and Pauline stared at me with those owl eyes, beaming.

"Good job," she said.

I'd been on the wrong end of such decisions so often that I felt this was my due. Fate owed me this one, I reasoned, for the times when I had been stiffed. I had been boxing for so long now and had worked so hard, coming from nothing, with no athletic background, in my late twenties. Surely I deserved one dodgy decision to go my way. Jackie would live to fight another day. She was a successful forty-eight-year-old woman with a great job, lots of friends, and enough money to splash on a Marriott suite and first-class plane tickets. She had a daughter, a gym of her own, a great set of guns, custom-made leather boxing boots, a loving husband, and oodles of charisma. What more did she want? Did she deserve to be on her way to being a champion in only her second fight? She couldn't have everything. But still she was pissed.

Mostly she was complaining about the cost.

At breakfast the next morning, which was positively frosty compared to the day before, I tried to make her feel better. "If it's any comfort to you, this sort of thing has happened to me too, plenty of times. It's just the way it is. It's what people mean when they say, 'That's boxing.'"

But it didn't really help. The whole situation seemed to be testing her capacity for unwavering niceness, so I thought I'd better go back to my room.

I couldn't really say much about the fight because the tall handsome man I had handed my camera to turned out to be a complete imbecile. He'd thought when I'd asked him to film the fight that I wanted him to take photos even though the camera had been set to movie mode. So what I got was about five seconds of fight and then fifty-five seconds of the cement floor, which included his rather large feet in a pair of black flip-flops, his hairy muscular legs, and parts of his apricot-colored T-shirt along with the backs of a few heads in the crowd.

When I realized what he'd done, I couldn't believe it. Terri was on the phone to Biggs at the time, still trying to tie up the Olympic reunion, and I was swearing and cursing this man's stupidity as I replayed the clips.

"How could he be such a fucking idiot?!" I shouted.

Terri was laughing as she spoke to Biggs, saying, "Sorry, Biggs, I'm not laughing at you." Then she got off the phone, still laughing. "That was so funny," she said. "You're cussin' and I'm laughing and Biggs doesn't know what I'm laughing at and he's cussin' too."

We later found out that Dunny had been stopped by Kathy in the second round. How did she stop her and I didn't? I could only conclude that the referee was a little more cautious at Ringside than in Atlanta and didn't want Dunny to go down so they intervened before it came to that. I'd have to check the brackets for the time of the bout at the weigh-in the next morning, but it was me versus Kathy in the final.

Again the bout was scheduled late on the card, number twenty-something, which meant I would be in the ring sometime around eight. That posed a problem because Terri's flight was leaving at six. The weigh-in line was slow-moving. This time I was next to two girls from the New Zealand team, Alexis Todd and Eske Dost. They made me homesick. Even though New Zealand is another country, they had the same low-key, reserved, modest qualities that typify antipodean sportspeople. Eske was a sports dietician by profession in the 138-lb. open class, and Alexis seemed the quieter of the two. Their team included three females and a few males, and they had raised money themselves through donations to pay for the trip. We started comparing notes on American-style boxing, the obesity epidemic, and the audacity of calling it a world championship tournament when really it wasn't. International teams were invited, and there were a few of them there, but mostly this "world" was America.

After the weigh-in, I found Kathy and her trainer and asked them if they'd mind if we moved the bout to an earlier time. They agreed.

"I'll go find out how to do that and come back. Will you be right here?" I asked and they nodded.

I went over to the Holiday Inn to the administration room, but it was empty, so I went back to find Kathy where I'd left her, but she was gone.

I called Terri and told her. She said, "Come back here and get some rest, and I'll get the bout rescheduled. Don't worry, Mischa, it'll work out."

So Terri and I tag-teamed. She went to the center and I went back to bed. When she came back she told me she got the bout changed but hadn't been able to get hold of Kathy. I rang the ever-helpful Dave Lubs.

"By the way," he said, "did you see Pauline fight?"

"No," I said. "I had to miss it. I heard she lost. What was she like?"

"Terrible," said Dave. "Just terrible."

"I have to say that to me she looks like a guy."

"Well," he said, "she didn't fight like one, I can assure you. She didn't even fight like a half decent woman."

I was getting more and more anxious about finding Kathy in time.

"Don't worry," said Terri. "If she doesn't show up, you'll win by walkover."

"But that's not fair," I said. "To change the bout time and win because she doesn't know about it? I don't want to win that way."

We started calling hotels at random, but I could see it would get us nowhere. There were dozens of them. I looked at Terri. Maybe we were both a bit burned out—Terri from trying to organize the Olympic reunion and dealing with Biggs, and me from five solid weeks of training, traveling, and fighting.

"This is hopeless," I said.

"Mischa, I can tell you just want to go home now. You look tired," said Terri.

"I am," I said. "And I do. I miss Peter. But we have to find Kathy."

I changed into my fight gear, and we got another high-priced cab over to the KCI and broke up to go hunt for Kathy. The words "needle in a haystack" came immediately to mind. It felt like an episode of *M*A*S*H* after Radar called, "Incoming!" The bells going off sounded like bombs falling, and the noise of the people created a sense of anarchy.

I went outside, and I saw John Brown himself, back from a run with a towel around his shoulders, and approached him, explaining the situation.

"Who did you fight yesterday?" he asked.

"Jackie Atkins."

"Did you win?"

"Yes."

"Oh, yes," he said. "That was controversial."

"Yes, she didn't like the decision."

"Did you hit her?"

What an odd question. "Yes," I said, "I hit her."

That seemed enough for him, and he called someone on his cell phone, explaining to them that my "handlers" had to catch a plane and that I'd needed to have the bout changed. "Now she's concerned that the other side might not know." He seemed to be getting a number for Kathy. He gave the number to me. I went to get changed and called her, but her phone went to voicemail. I left a message telling her the bout time had changed and hoped for the best.

Inside the arena, I tried to call Terri again, but I couldn't understand anything she was saying through the noise and the bad signal I was getting. The time was getting closer.

And then, as I returned to the spot near the ring, there she was, with her trainer, already fitted out in her blue corner gear.

Once again we were caught by surprise, and the fight seemed to be ready to start when I had only just put my gloves on. Kathy looked a lot bigger in the ring than she had on the ground, for some reason. On the back of her shirt were the words "The Zone." I had only seen a few seconds of her in the flailing match with Dunny, so I didn't really know what to expect.

After my rush job with Jackie I started the round cautiously, just moving around the ring, while Kathy tried to keep up with me, moving left, then right, then left. She was pretty flat-footed and didn't have any idea how to cut the ring. She stomped after me as I moved and eventually ran out of patience and threw a haymaker right hand that I blocked and countered. The next time she made an attempt, I beat her to the punch with my trusty jab. And the next time she did it, I ducked under it and countered, and she spun around a full 360 degrees.

Anyone who thinks fighting someone with no idea how to box is easy is mistaken. It was halfway through the round before she threw her first jab, slow as molasses, and then a second one, just as slow. I just took a little step back, and it fell short. After sparring the likes of Patricia Alcivar, Bonnie Canino, Ronica Jeffrey, Sunshine, Alicia, Camille, and Terri's amateurs, this was awkward. It was hard to time my punches.

"She sucks," said Terri, when I plopped back down on the corner stool. "Just let them go, don't worry about her."

The next round I did more of everything, more moving and punching and weaving and hooking. But still, it was hard to time my punches against the slow moves of this biker chick. It reminded me of a little kid who is about hit you—he brings his hand back and then never lets it go. Now? Now? Here it comes. And when she threw one hand, the other hand dropped down, and she almost threw herself off balance. I didn't think she was managing to hit me, but I couldn't be completely sure with all the padding. It did appear, though, that all those well-proportioned muscles didn't amount to anything useful in the ring.

"I can't believe she's a coach," said Terri. "She doesn't even know how to throw a damn jab. Imagine what they must be like at her club."

Midway through the third round I decided to stay inside and bang a little. When I did so, her arms started flapping around all over the place like she was trying to take flight. I think she might have even tried to throw two hands at the same time. The only reason the flurry ended was because her arm got tangled up with mine. Then when the final bell sounded, it seemed too soon, and I wasn't even sure if the fight had ended.

Terri was laughing when I went back to the corner.

"Are you sure I've won?" I said.

She nodded.

And, indeed, the Ringside world championship belt was mine—the same belt that retails on the Ringside website for $149.99. For $100 more you can get the deluxe version.

I was also awarded a pair of extra large trunks and a shirt with the Ringside logo. Kathy was given the consolation prize of her own trunks and shirt, but she seemed uninterested and surly. Being a sore loser had become a kind of theme for the weekend. She looked angry, even when I tried to tell her she had done well considering her first and only previous fight didn't even go the full, arduous three minutes. But she didn't care. She looked like she wanted to get out of there as quickly as she could.

Terri, meanwhile, was trying to get Liz, who had filmed the fight, to take a picture of the two of us in center ring with the belt. But I could see a little kid already in Kathy's corner, ready to fight, so we ran around the ring like a couple of headless chickens, while I argued that we should get out, and she told me I was a world champion and had every right to hold things up if I wanted to.

"Calm down," said the referee. "You won, OK? You survived."

I carried my bundle of stuff out to where the New Zealanders were.

"Good fight," said Eske.

"That was one of the weirdest fights I've ever had," I said. "Those gloves!"

"I know," she said. "They look like marshmallows. It's hard against beginners, too."

"Yeah," I said, "you can't time anything."

Eske rolled her eyes. "And she was throwing both hands at the same time."

Terri and I sat with the New Zealand girls after my fight until Terri had to go to the airport. I was going to miss her, but I knew we would meet again. If ever there was a way to bond with someone, it's in a boxing ring, so I was certain we'd stay in contact. I wished her good luck with the Olympic reunion and decided I would stay at the KCI until Eske fought and then get out of there. Really, I couldn't wait to go home.

I sent Peter a text message: "I'm 5 and 0 in America, baby! World Ringside champ."

It was interesting to watch Eske against one of the stars of USA Boxing, Queen Underwood, whose name I'd first heard mentioned back at the Florida Golden Gloves by Melissa Roberts, who had also made it through to the Ringside finals.

It was a close and high-caliber fight, and I felt a little embarrassed about the level of my own competition. I'd gone from one minority to a whole new minority, from gender to age. Eske looked great, throwing sharp straight punches that popped out like arrows, while Queen stayed mobile, using the ring.

I could see sixty-year-old Masters men stumbling around in the ring behind them and wondered if, perhaps, there should be an upper age limit, if only for the sake of human dignity.

Queen won the fight and continued her reign.

When I got back to Australia, I kept wondering about the fight with Jackie. I asked her if she could send me a copy of the tape, but she never responded. I tried to work out what had gone on from the few seconds of footage that I had, all of which looked like I was on the attack.

It wasn't until some months later, when I was thinking about John Brown's question—"Did you hit her?"—that it occurred to me that if I didn't feel the punches, then neither did Jackie. Was it possible that she believed she'd won the fight because she thought I hadn't hit her?

16 THE HUMAN ANIMAL

LUCKILY FOR me, when I finally met the most dangerous woman on the planet, her fighting days were over. I'd been hoping to simply run into Lucia Rijker at the Wild Card gym, but ultimately I had to engineer a meeting. Via e-mail we had agreed to a week of one-on-one training sessions at the LA gym in October 2009.

I arrived early for our first meeting and began skipping rope to warm up. I didn't know what I was in for, but I was expecting something tough. I thought of those fierce arched brows I'd seen on YouTube and in documentaries, the deep concentration in her eyes, and the ruthless destruction that she had dished out in a lifetime of fighting. Over the years I had watched everything I could get my hands on. I'd watched *Shadow Boxers* countless times and, more recently, clips of some of her fights that had been uploaded. Even as the talent pool grew, Lucia continued to stand out. I was apprehensive, bracing myself for a hard week.

But the person who greeted me had an open and trusting expression, wide-set brown eyes, and distinctive, full lips that smiled warmly.

I had just finished wrapping my hands when I saw, first, tight curls escaping from beneath a cap, then those unmistakable high, broad cheekbones, features she had inherited from her Surinamese father and Dutch mother. As I moved toward her, I was struck immediately by her easy geniality. I had been expecting someone intimidating, aloof, and a little stern. I think that at one time or another she had been all those things and more—but not anymore. The hand that had delivered thirty-six knockouts extended toward me in friendship.

"Good to meet you after all these years," I said, which must have sounded odd. I meant all these years of my admiring and knowing about her, of trying to mimic that cool and efficient style. After fifteen years of long-distance admiration, here she was right in front of me, looking just like a normal human being.

Only thirty minutes or so had passed since Manny Pacquiao and his entourage had left Wild Card, and it was open again to us mortals—the usual disparate cluster that included some of the world's finest athletes, along with what looked like hobos and a sprinkling of Hollywood celebrities thrown in like glitter on a grungy carpet.

Although my visits to Wild Card always seemed to coincide with preparations for Pacquiao's next big fight—this time it was against Miguel Cotto—I didn't particularly care about seeing him. But I was the exception. There were so many fans and onlookers that Freddy Roach had to close the gym while Manny trained. The night before I'd been astounded to see fans crowding around the windows of the Thai restaurant next door to the gym—a scruffy little place—just to watch him eat.

When I mentioned this to Sanjay at the Vagabond Inn, he told me Pacquiao used to sit in the cramped motel foyer eating breakfast all alone. That was before he became famous. "Right there," Sanjay said, pointing to the nook where a self-serve continental breakfast was provided with plastic bowls and spoons. Now his face was on Hollywood billboards half a mile away.

I was a little miffed that Lucia was being overshadowed by Pacquiao, but almost immediately people approached her wanting pictures, others told her that their daughter watched clips of her before sparring.

"Sorry," she said to me, shrugging.

I was glad it wasn't just me. I wondered how many other women also lived with a sense of Lucia Rijker driving them, reminding them how good they could be. Those tight, explosive punches delivered with the kind of leverage that can turn the shortest, most unassuming action into something lethal. And who had not thought, "I want to look like that, I want to *be* like that?" I read that one female fighter had Rijker's name and the words "A sword is useless in the hands of a coward" tattooed on her back. I wasn't alone in thinking there was something a bit special about Lucia Rijker.

And here we were now, sitting side by side on the low edge of Wild Card's big central ring. "So," she said, "we didn't have a chance to chat. Tell me what you want to get out of this."

I explained that I didn't have the edge I wanted. I yearned to be more dangerous, I told her, both in sparring and fighting. I wanted to be able to finish a fight.

"I look like I'm holding back," I said. "I do *something*, I don't even know what it is. But it seems to water everything down. Maybe because I've done a lot of sparring over the years. Maybe I'm too practiced at that sparring mentality. It's too friendly. People say to me, 'Oh, you could have stopped her if you'd wanted,' and I'm actually trying to. But I don't look like it."

"Have you had any time off?"

"Occasionally."

"You're a gym rat?" she asked, grinning.

"Yes," I said. "I suppose I am."

"Maybe you need time doing something else to get that hunger back."

What was she saying? I'd spent time doing other things. I was on a roll now. Back in the game. "But I *enjoy* fighting," I said. "And I won all the fights."

I realized that I might be giving the impression that I'd been losing. "Oh," she said. "But have you ever taken a week off?"

"Not really. Sometimes. Usually not unless I'm sick."

She smiled knowingly. She of all people knew how powerful the pull to the gym could be. Since she was six, when she started at judo, she had been forsaking all else for training. At nine, she'd begun karate, eventually attaining a black belt in Kyokushin. At thirteen, she became the Netherlands junior fencing champion. When she moved to Los Angeles in her early twenties, it wasn't long before someone zoned in on that remarkable talent of hers and lured her into the embryonic world of women's boxing. She'd already had a stellar kickboxing career over ten years winning four world titles. I'd read stories about how intensely she trained. Two hours of wordless focus. So, you know, she could talk.

She explained she would take me through some exercises that would show her how well my mind and body were coordinated. Oh no, I thought. That sounds ominously like a test. I was immediately worried about making the grade. Jetlag hovered as a ready excuse should I need it, which no doubt I would.

"It's all about this, up here," she said, pointing to her head.

"That's what bothers me," I said.

As soon as she started moving, it looked to me like Lucia was in control of every fiber and sinew, not just the major muscle groups, but the fine, hairline threads as well, every pulse and synapse. When she took off her jacket and was down to a tank top, she looked well sculpted and fit, but not overly muscled. Not as packed with coiled strength as she'd been in her prime, when she had turned Dora Webber's face into a bloody pulp. But in good condition nonetheless. When I looked at us side by side in the mirror, I thought we looked similar in the upper body, although her legs were longer and her hips much narrower than mine. But probably the differences between us were not about what was happening on the surface. She was freakishly talented. Her left hook had been calculated to be harder than a man's of the same weight, according to a test done by the *Sports Science Show* on the Discovery Channel.

But she was no longer in that almost superhuman state of a peak-performance elite athlete. For her, her peak had turned out to be as vulnerable as it was resilient. This had been revealed suddenly and dramatically when, eleven days before her million-dollar showdown with Christy Martin, her Achilles tendon had snapped during sparring and immobilized her for six months. Now, four years had passed and though, outwardly, she still had the appearance of a fit athlete, she was a different Lucia Rijker. Now she inhabited the real world instead of that self-sacrificing cloister that had been her life as a fighter, the one in which she had pushed all normal desires to the edge. Six weeks after the Achilles tendon injury her mother died. By the time she emerged, she was changed. The momentum for the Christy Martin fight was lost, her career had ground to a halt.

The phenomenal explosive strength that Lucia had wasn't simply physical, though. It was not just the composition of muscle fiber. It was more like a connection between soul and fiber, between being and acting. I felt that all my years of boxing had lead me to this point, side by side with the greatest female fighter ever, the woman who had turned around enough hardcore, macho boxing heads and shown them it can be done, that we women can do it as well as any man can. Just watch us. So it was a particular honor to be taken seriously by Lucia Rijker, to be taken seriously as a fighter. The timing was right for us to meet. That wouldn't have been true two years earlier, or even one year or six months earlier.

Before my American fights I wouldn't have known what I wanted from her, and the meeting might have been wasted. I would have

Lucia Rijker and me.

assumed my deficiencies were due to a lack of talent or athleticism. But I had come this far and even triumphed in my own small way over being a late starter and a slow learner, over being easy to hit and sluggish on my feet, over my own uncertainty and ambivalence and my aging body. I still believed I could improve. There was still time, I told myself. I hadn't reached the end yet. Meeting Lucia felt almost like finding the beginning.

First she asked me to do some rotating actions, isolating first my upper torso and then the lower, doing figure-eights sideways and then front to back. These were very unusual movements to be doing in a boxing gym, very subtle amid the thump and thwack, the rattle of heavy bags on chains, the speed bag rhythm, the expulsion of air like many small freight trains. In the corner someone was punching a medicine ball on the floor as if it had killed his mother. Some men were sparring in the second ring, others were doing pad drills. The air seemed thick with noise and sweat. Yet together we inhabited a little pool of serenity in the middle of it all, the eye of the storm, maybe.

Lucia had become a Buddhist in 1994, around the same time she had moved to Los Angeles and become a boxer.

"I needed something to tame the beast," she said.

Her beast was a powerful one. No woman has ever beaten her. She has always seemed so different from all the others, not just the ones of the early era but those that had followed, too. Maybe it was Buddhism that gave her her intense focus and diamond clarity. I wondered if her ability to hold the extremes of her personality in balance gave her the perfect physical balance she had in the ring. I always felt that my own balance was fine, but I was feeling a bit rocky now.

Lucia asked me to rotate my hips from side to side as if I were throwing hooks, while leaving my arms loose and swinging. Because punching power comes, not from bulked-up biceps, but from the whiplike action of the torso, it begins with the feet.

"Think legs," she said. "Don't use your arms."

I wasn't feeling very much in control of my body, still full of fluid from flying and a little foggy headed from too much sleep. And I was just a tiny bit self-conscious.

She got me to do some slashing actions as if with an imaginary sword. I was facing the most dangerous woman in the world, and she was smiling encouragingly, asking me to mark an imaginary X on her body.

Then she went to her bag and pulled out something called a "Bodyblade," a yellow, winged, flat sword about the length of a baseball bat with a black rubber handle in the center and black rubber ends. She asked me to hold the center handle with both arms straight and then shake it so that the blades flapped like wings. If I tried to use my arms or didn't adequately engage my core, I lost the rhythm. First I held it above my head, then out in front, and then, hardest of all, with one hand, standing on one leg while wobbling the blade and moving it diagonally across my body. I seemed to overbalance repeatedly and felt as if I was always on the brink of toppling, and indeed had to put my raised foot down many times as I struggled with all the elements required of me: balance, slow movement, and rhythmic movement.

"You know what this tells me?" she asked.

"That I have no balance?"

"No," she said. "It tells me that all the parts of your body aren't working together. Your arms are working separately from your legs, so when you're thinking of one thing you lose track of the other. We need to bring it all together so that you can use your instincts better and don't think too much about what's going on. When you fight you need to draw on your animal instincts."

Something about her hybrid accent—a blend of BBC English, the hard consonants of her native Dutch, and the lazy Californian cadence—gave the word "animal" a certain weight and sensuality.

"It's an animal world," she said. "It's all about scanning and sizing up and making choices from instinct, not from intellect. We live in a world of animality, not just in the gym. It's all about survival of the fittest, especially in a capitalist country like America, where the strong dominate the weak either physically or financially. That's the animal world."

At that point I suddenly saw her as a kind of Jane Goodall character, working in the field like Dian Fossey in *Gorillas in the Mist*. I realized that she hadn't just been like one of Gerald Early's obsessives the whole time she had been in the gym. She'd also studied the human species in one of its most extreme and naked states. She had thought carefully about the world she was in and what it meant. This might have been the most unique training session I'd ever had. Lucia appeared to take a very tangential approach to diagnosing my weaknesses as a boxer, but the truth was it was unnervingly accurate. I'd never had someone lead me into a boxing session in this way. The usual procedure is pads on, gloves on. *Jab, jab, jab. Left-right. Left-right-hook. Faster, harder, more, more, more.* Lucia's approach was both more methodical and more intricate. She was looking as carefully for symptoms and responses as a surgeon would who already had his hands and instruments inside your body. And going far beyond the goals of any surgeon, she was observing the biomechanics, but also the intent.

She asked me to shadowbox for a round. At last, something familiar, even if it was the most self-conscious round of shadow-boxing I'd ever done in my life.

"Good," she smiled, when the bell rang. Then she asked me to do another round with more feinting, more head movement, faster and more erratic, and to turn my knuckles over and tighten my fists when I threw punches.

She could see I wasn't imagining an opponent and what they were doing. I needed to visualize them and aim my punches at them. The fictional other in a shadowboxing routine can so easily be forgotten, especially by those who have become a little blasé about it. I'd seen groups of people chatting incessantly in Gleason's rings, their arms flying out in combinations while their eyes scanned the gym for distractions.

I was just as guilty. But this time, instead of looking for distractions, I was wondering, "What is she thinking?" And, "I hope I look OK, passable, not beyond help . . ."

Next we worked on the pads. Ah, the pads. Would Lucia turn out to be my ultimate pad man? Would I have to fly fourteen hours and pay thousands of dollars to get my fix? The pads were white with little red leather hearts sewn onto them, and the letter "L" on one and "R" on the other. Was that left and right or Lucia Rijker?

She embarked on refining my left hook, getting the snap, the leverage, the pull-back, the elbow up, the knuckles coming down, the hand coming back to my chin. For a while I was "slowly stirring a giant imaginary cauldron of cement-thick soup" in an attempt to get the action right. I liked the way she used images and metaphors. It appealed to the writer in me.

Toward the end of the session we did more balance work using a Bosu ball, which is like a Swiss ball cut in half. You can stand on the flat part or use it to do push-ups. My balance, again, came up short, and I thought that maybe there was something seriously wrong with me. The fact that I had been boxing so long might have concealed some much more fundamental deficiencies. Mind you, my body should have been sleeping, given the time difference and that I was still on Australian time. Maybe that was it. I was meant to be horizontal, not vertical.

The final stage of the session involved running my hands over my own body from head to toe and then up again, mimicking what she did as she stood in front of me. It was more like something you would do at the end of a yoga class. When we'd finished, she extended both her hands to me again and held mine. Her dramatic features melting into a smile.

"Wow," I said. "That was the most amazing training session I've ever had."

As we gathered up our gear, I asked her if she could recall an Australian boxer named Amanda Buchanan from the mid-1990s. Amanda was a smaller version of Lucia, her parents also of mixed races—her mother from New Guinea and her father Scottish. She'd been one of Australia's most talented boxers and told me once that she had trained with Lucia in LA.

But Lucia said, "In the mid-1990s I was like this," and she frowned and looked at the ground. "It was like a jungle in here. I didn't talk to a lot of people because I thought I wasn't going to like them. I used to be very moody, and it's so hard in LA with everyone, 'Hi, howya doing?'" she demonstrated the forced smile. "It was good to come to the gym, touch knuckles, and grunt."

"That seems to be the standard Wild Card greeting."

"Yeah," she said. "Thank God it's not a kiss."

We were back at Wild Card the next day, sharing the second ring with other people, and she had her hands up, palms facing me in what she'd described as a defense barrier, like a cat with its paws up. Her eyes were unblinkingly focused on me and mine on her. The exercise was to follow her around, no punches, just legwork, and for the first time I was seeing her body language as an opponent might have seen it, although the expression was eager, friendly, and alert rather than menacing. "Jesus," I thought. "I can't believe this, I'm moving around the ring with Lucia Rijker." But the strangest thing was that I felt like I'd known her for years. Mimicking her moves, her quick feinting, and sudden changes in direction felt like the most natural thing in the world for me to be doing.

"I'm sorry if I'm a bit awkward," I said. "But I'm a little in awe of you."

"Really?" she said, sounding genuinely surprised.

"Oh, yeah," I said. "Everywhere I go you're the one that has inspired people."

She laughed. "When people put me on a pedestal I always worry that I can only fall off. I'm human, I have my faults."

"Of course," I said. "But we don't need to know what they are."

The postfighting Lucia had decided, after much soul searching, that she would be a coach. A natural teacher, she had always worked as a trainer. But now she had decided to commit to working with fighters. "When I was here [at Wild Card] I was always working the mitts and then sparring, and I was getting my ass kicked. I thought, you don't need to lose brain cells to learn, there has to be something in between. I mean, how can you tell if someone has heart if you don't give them some defense?"

Later that day I sent her links to two of my fights, the one against Jackie in Florida and the one against Dunny in Atlanta. Before I sent them I watched them again and then watched a clip of her against Sunshine Fettkether. My heart sank a little. Lucia and I were on different planets. On her planet the punches were fast, the movements just right, the combinations deadly accurate. On my planet everything looked much slower and more diluted, a little more accidental.

But when we met the next day I was keen to hear what she thought just the same. "Did you watch the fights?" I asked.

"Yeah," she said. "Not bad. Good. But in one the other woman was a lot slower than you, and you just kept doing your thing, instead of responding to what was going on. That's the third level of listening. Do you know about that?"

I shook my head.

"The first is all about me. 'How do I look, what am I doing? How is my hair, do I look OK?' That level is useless. The second level is you. 'There you are, you're listening, you're frowning, you're concentrating.' And the third level is us, what's going on between us. And that's a sense that you can develop. Actors have it and comedians have it. They throw it out, and they see what kind of reaction they get. They can't just stand there as if they are alone. They have to sense what is going on in the audience."

During the session I threw punches at a rolled-up newspaper that was reinforced with tape. She warned me that she'd slap me if my left hand didn't come back fast enough. That bloody left of mine! And of course the slap came, and it was stinging. She was the second female world champion boxer to slap me. First Alicia and now Lucia. I was feeling blessed.

"I had a trainer who did that to me once, and he left the mark of the newsprint on the side of my face," she said. "It's very humiliating, I know. That's how you treat a dog. But it taught me to keep my hand up."

The next afternoon Manny Pacquiao was holding up the gym. I was due to meet Lucia at 4:00 p.m., when it was supposed to reopen. A crowd of impatient boxers had gathered at the bottom of the stairs, and a group of Filipino fans were waiting reverently with their posters and T-shirts and cameras ready for their hero.

I saw Lucia and walked over to her. "Is there somewhere else we can go?" I asked.

"Yeah," she said, and I followed her to her car, a white Mercedes that was parked in the street behind the gym.

"It's good for Freddy that he has a name fighter and that Manny is doing so well," she said as she started the car. "But this is the downside—that the gym hours are restricted and then these fighters get demanding and everyone else has to wait."

"It's incredible," I said, "that people watch him eat dinner every night."

"People go crazy over fame in this country," she said. "It's not the same in Holland. If you're a great athlete or actor, we respect that, sure. But it matters more that you are a good person. And the bigger they get, the more these leeches are around them, too."

Wild Card was crowded with boxers who had to negotiate, not just the scarce available space, but also the sharks that hovered

Martin Snow.

around the edges. And it was hard to tell from looking at them what their intentions were. Were they fight fans, just curious onlookers? Or were they matchmakers looking for meat? Maybe they were hustlers, drug dealers, criminals, or perhaps fight promoters with cash to splash. I'd started thinking of fighters as artists who had to work under the constant scrutiny of these shadowy figures. No other kind of artist would tolerate this intrusion, but for boxers that's just how it is. They're used to working under difficult circumstances—noise, heat, distractions—and with hoodlums and other questionable characters mixed in among honest managers, promoters, hangers-on, and fans. The night before there had been a power blackout, and everyone just ignored it and carried on.

Lucia and I had already finished anyway. And as she packed her bag, she said, "If this happened in a normal office, people would go home now. But here they keep going."

"I tend to think that in boxing everyone's a little crazy," I said. "Aside from me and you, of course," I added quickly.

She laughed heartily. "Yeah," she said. "Also, the crazier *they* are, the more you can hide your own madness."

Eventually, when it was almost too dark to see, Freddy ushered everyone out and closed the gym.

Now, as Lucia maneuvered her car out of a tight parking spot, I asked her if she'd had all the leeches and hangers-on when she was fighting.

"No," she said. "I always wanted to be alone. I liked the solitude of it. I wanted to live almost like a monk."

Her car had a pristine pale leather interior, perfectly clean except for a green tea health bar wrapper on the floor. As we headed off down Santa Monica Boulevard it felt as if we did this every other day. It felt like we were becoming friends.

I remembered that Martin Snow's Trinity gym was not far away. He was Patricia Alcivar's trainer in New York, and his gym was near the Whole Foods store where I got my salads. I'd stumbled across it the day I arrived and spent a little while chatting with him. I asked Lucia if she wanted to try his gym, and she agreed. It was funny that I, who really knew no more of Los Angeles than these few miles between Vine Street and Fairfax, was taking her to a gym she'd never been to before.

I called Martin and asked if I could come and train there with Lucia.

"Sure," he said with his gravelly Flatbush accent. "When did you want to come?"

"Now?"

"Not a problem. See you soon."

When we got there Lucia looked around. She seemed to like the gym. It was airy and comfortable compared to Wild Card, and there was a small group doing a class with Martin. The ring was very high up, like a stage, and there were signs and sayings handwritten on the walls.

"I like that," said Lucia, pointing to one of them.

It said, "Everyone wants to go to heaven but no one wants to die."

After our warm-up she put on a small pair of yellow leather Everlast gloves, and we got in the ring. First of all, she asked me to throw jabs into her glove whenever she held it up. *Pam!* "Too slow." *Pap!* "Too slow. Very good."

Then she asked me to defend her jab to my chest. "You want to wear a mouth guard?" she asked. "It's just light and to the chest."

"No." I trusted her to do as she said she would.

It was strange being hit in the chest, and her jabs were so damn quick. I was trying to see some signal, even the tiniest sign of a telegraph, but there was none. Her fists went from zero to a hundred in an instant. *Ping! Pop!* No warning.

I changed direction and moved to my right.

"Uh-uh. Don't do that," she said.

"What?"

"You're opening up to me, square on. Don't ever do that."

I thought I had my hands up, defending, but she said it was important to keep a side stance all the time.

Then it was my turn to hit her. "Wow," I thought. "I'm hitting Lucia Rijker."

When the round bell sounded, she was beaming. "Good," she said. "Very good. It feels good to punch back, huh?"

Actually, I think she was enjoying herself as much as I was.

Then we did a round countering each other. First she would lead, and then I would. I wasn't entirely sure, but it felt to me like we had reached that third level of listening. There was a sharp sting in her punches, a jolt in my chest now and then, because the gloves were small and I could feel her knuckles against my sternum. Her control was superb. This was a fraction of what she could do, a thimbleful. I could feel that her natural inclination was to dominate. Even in a playful mode, her body wanted to inhabit my space. She couldn't relinquish it to me, even in fun.

When the round ended, Lucia seemed energized. "I haven't boxed in a long time. Not since 2005."

"Really? Not even training?"

"Just coaching, and this is just playing."

"Yeah, but this is the fun bit."

She told me it jarred her body to hit the bag, and she hated running. She only did now what she felt like doing, whenever she felt like it. After so many years of driving herself and pushing herself daily, she decided to be more intuitive about training.

The next round we threw left hooks to the body only. This time I could feel a bit more of that famous leverage. Her punches were short. "*Hup-hup-hup*," she said as she threw them. And they were sharp. They didn't travel far, there was no winding up, but I could feel my right shoulder getting hot from being peppered by that yellow glove over and over.

"It's good to see you fired up," she said to me after the round.

Yet again, I wondered how far I would get under her guidance over a longer period, not just watching her on YouTube, but having it on display all the time, feeling the speed and the power. And having her watch me with her razor eyes. She had the hardness of Bonnie, the looseness of Alicia, and Terri Moss's boxing brain all rolled into one.

Terri was keen to hear how the sessions were going. I gave her daily reports on the phone. I told her about throwing a tennis ball against a wall to improve my reflexes, using a skipping rope wrapped around a pole to increase punching speed, swinging my arms, and as best as I could, I described the Bodyblade.

"I want to be just like her when I grow up, too," Terri said.

The next day Lucia picked me up, and we went straight to Trinity. This session she helped me to get more range of motion in my shoulders, especially when I threw the right, to stop those looping punches and to give me more reach. But we didn't hit each other again. She watched as I threw basic left-rights, holding small hand weights and then, without them, moving forward and back, getting me to twist more into the right, particularly on the back move.

I was getting a stronger sense of what I needed. But really I think she was mostly helping me help myself. I almost felt as if I always knew what I should be doing, but needed someone to guide me, which I guess is how good teaching should feel.

After the session, Lucia stayed in the ring. She seemed to enjoy its elevated position. I clambered down, thinking she must be ready to leave for her next appointment. But she was in a storytelling mood, and so Martin and I stood on the ground below, looking up at her like a couple of preschool kids, and listened to Lucia tell us stories. She was standing in the ring as if it were a stage, regaling us, getting lost in the narrative, playing all the characters. She did frighteningly accurate renditions of slurring, brain-damaged fighters and of men admiring themselves in the mirror.

"You were like Darth Vader," Martin said with admiration. "You know what I'm saying? You were like indestructible, in a whole other league. At what point did you become Lucia Rijker?"

"I've always been Lucia Rijker," she said with a quizzical frown.

"What is a Darth Vader?"

"It's a character from *Star Wars*," I said.

"You were like invincible, you know what I'm saying?" Martin continued. "Like you could walk down the street and bullets would just bounce off you."

"Well, I've always been what my brother calls fierce."

Thinking about the footage of her fights I'd seen, she was not only fierce, she was heartless, too—brutal in a cold and clinical way. Her eyes, like lasers, would focus on one thing and one thing only: getting her opponent out of her way, whoever they were, just getting them out.

Before becoming a Buddhist she had been an angry fighter, she said. "Angry in the sense that I didn't care if I killed my opponent or not." But since becoming a Buddhist she has valued the lives of her opponents more.

"Where is the killer now?" I asked.

"The killer is dormant," she said. "It sticks its head up every so often. But anger, when it's not directed to create, is destructive. So the first part of my career, it was about destroying. The anger was more fear and dysfunction. In the second part of my career, when I became a Buddhist, the anger was transformed. I used boxing to be a better person and to transform my life."

She told us how eventually she had to give some ground. "I was like the firstborn. After me, girls started coming to the gym all dressed up."

She mimicked girls, strutting around with their breasts out, and followed with a mime act of the men looking at them with their tongues hanging out. It was astoundingly accurate, but also hilarious. She had obviously done a lot of careful people-watching.

"Freddy started training another girl and stopped paying so

much attention to me," she said. "I didn't like it. But he just reacted in this macho way, like, 'Hey, I got two bitches. You're just jealous.' I said, 'Maybe I am, but we should really be doing something between fights, maintaining some contact.' In the end I went out to lunch with the girl and told her how I felt. She really understood what I was saying because she had been an only child and her father had remarried. His new wife had children and suddenly she had all these siblings. I wanted to spar her."

"Did you?"

"No," she said. "Freddy wouldn't let me."

I didn't think it was for her sake. Lucia described sparring sessions as "life and death."

"I had diarrhea on the days I had to spar. The men would hit me hard. Because I was a woman and I could punch, when I hit them they wanted to make me pay. I would go home with blood everywhere, on my shirt, my shorts, my shoes, even inside my shoes."

Lucia didn't seem to have the kind of problems I complained about, the chivalry and the tippy-tapping. Maybe I didn't hit the men hard enough.

"Maybe I'm holding back because I don't want them to hurt me," I said.

"Could be," she said.

She had been so fearless by comparison that she had even gotten into a fight outside the ring with one of the male boxers at the gym where she trained.

"He was allowed to play his music while he trained," she explained. "But I had a fight coming up. It was the main event in Vegas, and I wanted to play my music. I was sick of being polite. Sick of thinking, I'll just move over here and not take up too much space like a good girl. I thought, no, this is my time and I want to play my music. And so I kept changing it and he got really mad. 'Fuck you, bitch,' and that sort of thing, and he came over."

As soon as she threw a punch, the boxer's friends grabbed her and held her while he hit her back.

"Did you have a short fuse?" I asked.

"No," she said. "I don't think so. But I had a strong sense of justice. He verbally attacked me and intimidated me, which made me think, 'I'll swing first.' And I swung, but I hit his shoulder and then I got grabbed. It's a tender topic because we talked it out and I apologized. I had to fight for what I thought was right. But I had to leave the gym and train somewhere else for a while and hire a bodyguard and a driver.

"Until then, I never realized that an entourage actually has a purpose. I thought it was just needy performers who wanted feedback, a lot of emotional support, people to carry their stuff, and whatnot. But I realized it's actually protection. If I go to the gym now, people want to talk to me, they want just a little piece of me. Before I would look down, I'd say hello, and never make eye contact with anyone because I didn't want to talk to anyone."

That clearly had changed because of her time away from boxing. Lucia was happy to talk now. And what an entertaining talker she was. This was something I hadn't expected, that Lucia "The Striker" Rijker would be funny and playful and generous.

"You know, Freddy said you were mean when I asked him about you," I said.

"That's true. I can be," she said. "And so can he."

By our final session back at Wild Card, I felt like I had regained my balance. Not only that, but the exercises with the Bodyblade, which had felt almost impossible at the beginning, were now coming to me more easily. I was managing to stand on the Bosu ball with my eyes closed without a problem. I'd been for a run and felt my torso working in a new and more connected way.

"I have no natural talent," I told Lucia. "But I'm very persistent."

"That you are," she said.

"Also, you know, I was old when I started. I was twenty-nine."

"Really, that's late," she said. "How old are you now?"

"I'm forty-five," I said.

"No shit!" she shrieked. "That's unbelievable. You're kidding me. Wow." She put her hands together in a prayer position and faced me and did a little bow. Then she gave me a high five. I could feel myself blushing.

"How old did you think I was?" I asked.

"I don't know," she said. "In your thirties."

This was by far the most unexpected thing that happened between us. My hero was heaping praise on me. I suddenly got a sense of how precarious a place a pedestal might be.

On my last evening in town we had a meal together. She picked me up in regular clothes, not the usual gym gear, and we went to a place up the hill on Vine.

That night, over lentil soup, she revealed that her dream was to open a center for women boxers where they can work together and exchange knowledge.

"I believe that when you train a fighter just to be a champion, you're not doing them a service from a holistic perspective. You're helping them drive a race car into a wall. After your career, there's the wall. So if there's no holistic approach, it doesn't make sense to me. Why teach a person how to kill with a knife, but not show them how to heal with it or how to make beautiful things with it? Buddhism taught me how to change poison into medicine. I think I'll be even better as a trainer than I was as a fighter."

"Wow," I said. "That's a big claim because you were a great fighter."

The greatest, I thought. Maybe the greatest of all time. The female version, anyway.

17 BAD BLOOD

"BOXING," PROMOTER Lou DiBella once said, "is a horrendous, miserable, vile business full of miserable, thieving motherfuckers."

That may well be true. All I knew was that trying to coordinate anything, especially long-haul air travel, based on the plans of a professional boxer, wasn't easy. I'd gone back to Melbourne in August 2009, returned to Los Angeles in October to train, and was now flying back to the States in December. Melissa "The Hurricane" Hernandez had appeared and then vanished from three different cards over the course of a few months. All I was trying to do was see her fight, and yet it was turning out to be a nearly impossible task. I'd already spent a rather strange weekend in Palm Springs because of these phantom fights. Now I was in Albuquerque, New Mexico, where Melissa was once again due to step into the ring.

But this time it seemed that a fight was actually coming together. I was sitting across the table from The Hurricane, who was only days away from fighting Holly Holm in what was shaping up to be

251

the female fight of the year—if not the decade—pitching a bad-ass Bronx ghetto-girl against a sweet blonde preacher's daughter.

As Sonny Liston once said, boxing is like a cowboy movie: "There's got to be good guys, and there's got to be bad guys. And that's what people pay for—to see the bad guys get beat."

This show had been dubbed "Bad Blood" and was getting plenty of exposure in New Mexico. Melissa's friends were flying in from New York, Atlanta, Oklahoma, and Australia. Sue Fox, the founder of WBAN, had come from Portland, Oregon, at her own expense.

Melissa was there with Belinda, with whom she appeared to have reconciled, and Jill Emery, the southpaw world champion from Gleason's who had been her sparring partner. We were all chewing over Holm's strengths and weaknesses. Belinda had fought her in Temecula, California, in 2007 and lost in a unanimous decision. Holm had also had victories over other luminaries, like French-woman Myriam Lamare, who'd had Lucia Rijker help prepare her for the bout, and of course she'd famously taken Christy Martin to school quite early in her career, which had made the cynics, who thought she was a protected pretty face, sit up and take notice. But The Hurricane was a tough match-up for Holm because Melissa was physically short and stylistically unique. Jill testified that it wasn't easy for a tall fighter to deal with that low center of gravity and the myriad angles that Melissa could create, as well as her strong body punches, her speed, her unorthodox maneuvers, and all her distracting ticks.

"She fought me in the amateurs," Jill said of Melissa. "And I think it was her first fight, and I'd had about thirty. I won, but she made me look pretty bad."

Jill has an almost genteel quality about her. A drama school grad-uate originally from Pittsburgh, she'd moved to New York to pursue acting and instead became one of the most decorated female amateur boxers to come out of Gleason's, winning accolades that included USA Boxing's 2004 female athlete of the year before turning pro and eventually winning the IFBA's welterweight belt. She is almost willowy, with fair, lightly freckled skin and a short bob with blonde streaks. You can easily visualize her playing the kind of roles that Geena Davis is known for or maybe Cate Blanchett. She often has an intelligent, thoughtful expression on her face and is amused by puns, easily falling into the kind of banter that made me miss New York.

In the gym, I'd seen Jill work with Melissa, rushing at her like a bull and Melissa, the matador, timing her defensive moves and low-angled body shots. They had spent the previous two weeks together training intensively at camp in Denver and adjusting to the altitude.

The phrase "pound for pound" came up a lot. This fight was to determine who was the best. Boxrec.com, a website that ranks fighters and archives their records, had put Melissa in the top spot and Holm at number two.

"At the end of the day," Melissa said, "it's not about being good, it's about being entertaining. It's an entertainment business. It's *violent* entertainment, but it's still entertainment."

As former British boxer Frank Bruno said, "Boxing is just show business with blood."

For this fight, Melissa didn't need to lose any weight. In fact, she had to come in as heavy as she could. This meant that one of her favorite pastimes—eating—was an integral part of her preparation.

Holm had fought at weights ranging from 138 lb. to 152 lb. and probably walked around close to 160 lb. She had the IFBA light middleweight and welterweight titles, the IBA light middleweight title, the WBC welterweight title, and for what it was worth, the WIBA welterweight title. She was a strong-looking junior welterweight for a woman, even for a man. Tall and broad-shouldered, she still had a little sweating to do before the weigh-in to make the con-

Holly Holm.

tracted weight of 140 lb. I couldn't help thinking that Melissa, at 132 lb., was a lot smaller than Holm. Too much smaller, actually, smaller than Pacquiao, the former flyweight, had looked against De La Hoya, Hatton, and Cotto. It looked instead like a match between Nonito Donaire and Kelly Pavlik—not so much a question of height but one of sheer physics. This is the reason boxers are matched according to such strict weight categories. Otherwise, you would have big people mowing down little people, and there would be no contest. After all, unless you are very special, you will get mowed down if you're small. Melissa, it seemed, was claiming that same special status that Pacquiao and Mayweather peddled. But the pendulum was swinging between bold over-confidence and pragmatic realism.

"To be honest, I don't really expect to win. I just want to expose Holly and make her look bad. I want people to see her flaws."

"So, you've got nothing to lose then, have you?" I said.

"Right," said Melissa. "I've got nothing to lose."

If it came down to styles alone, I would choose Melissa's over Holm's any day of the week. I would rather lose as Melissa than win as Holm.

Coincidentally, Maureen Shea was scheduled to fight at New York's Manhattan Center the day before Melissa's fight in New Mexico. They really should have been fighting each other in the Bronx, where they're both from, but as Bernie McCoy often complains, boxing is a rudderless ship. Everything is just chaos and nonsense until a good fight happens by sheer accident.

The fight against Holm had displaced a match that would have pitted Melissa against Ana Julaton, which had promised to be an interesting contest for the WIBA junior lightweight title. The scheduling of the Julaton match had come as a surprise to many. They thought it was too much too soon in the career of pretty Julaton, a Filipino boxer with a big airline hostess smile and a thick cascade of black hair who was being marketed as a female version of Manny Pacquiao. Julaton may have been polite and pleasant, but she also had a good amateur record and had demonstrated a level of courage that belied her humble personality. Not only that, she trained out of Freddie Roach's Wild Card gym—home to her compatriot Pacquiao.

Julaton was tough and liked to go to war in her fights. But Melissa was widely regarded as the stronger fighter and the most likely to win on the inside. Everyone thought Julaton was brave to agree take Melissa on. And she had nothing but respect for The Hurricane—she even had the same nickname. So while Julaton was politely praising Melissa's abilities, Melissa decided to change her nickname from The Hurricane to I Am Women's Boxing (or "Womyn," as she preferred to spell it), which was something she said all the time to annoy those who thought otherwise. And instead of praising Julaton in return, Melissa called Julaton a "punk ass."

When the fight was canceled, some speculated that Melissa's bravura had cost her an opportunity. Instead, Julaton fought the more seasoned, more polite "Road Warrior," a 41-9 fighter named Kelsie Jeffries, and beat her, which only helped boost her standing.

Trash-talking is common in professional boxing. Ever since promoters realized that people would pay to come and watch some smart mouth get his comeuppance, it has been used as a marketing tool. The men do it incessantly; Floyd Mayweather Jr., for example, the best pound-for-pound contemporary fighter, is known for his relentless trash-talking.

Social networking sites have only expanded the platform for such necessary showbiz spruiking that goes back, as Bernie McCoy reminded me, to the days of Maxie "Slapsy" Rosenbloom in the 1930s, but that really came into its own with the birth of television.

"The characters are the people who bring in the fringe fans who wouldn't usually go see boxing," McCoy said.

But it isn't so common in women's boxing. Everyone seemed to want their female fighters to be well behaved, sitting on their hands and zipping their lips if they don't have anything nice and respectful to say.

They weren't supposed to write on their Facebook page, "Hey team julaton. Walking at 130 hard body baby. With a beer in my hand. lol. I am Womyn's boxing. Wait till you get a load of me." And, "The training is dope the sparring world class. I'm ending this in 6."

They were supposed to be more lady-like. Maureen Shea's updates included a steady stream of sugary clichés: "Maureen Shea is feeling thankful, peaceful and appreciative after a great training session! 'What seems to us as bitter trials are often blessings in disguise.'" Another asserts that "too often we underestimate the power of a touch, a smile, a kind word, a listening ear, an honest compliment, or the smallest act of caring, all of which have the potential to turn a life around."

Melissa Hernandez wasn't acting like a lady. She was acting like a boxer. A guy boxer. There was no one else like her among the women, no one willing to push the boundaries so far, at least in public. She was a high-wire act all her own.

"Someone call team Julaton and tell them to sell ad space on the bottom of her shoes cause that's all they're going to see fight night."

The day before the Albuquerque weigh-in, at the official press conference, Melissa made what sounded like an off-the-cuff remark about being in "Hollyhood." "I'm happy to beat Holly in Hollyhood," she said with her slightly husky Bronx accent. You could feel spirits in the room lift. One Australian politician used to call this "feeding the chickens." With Holm—blonde, polite, earnest— feeding them the same line over and over again ("I don't want to get beaten by someone who talks like that"), they were starved for verbal inventiveness. The chickens in New Mexico were having a feast at last.

Melissa's earlier line had been that in the ring Holm ran like a rabbit, and it was hunting season in New Mexico. She made light of their substantial height difference, claiming to be five foot one when she's really five foot three, and jumping on a chair for the stare-down pose. She said that come December 4, "The tall will fall." Her talk wasn't exactly all that trashy, actually. Anyone who finds being called a rabbit offensive has probably been a bit overprotected.

The day after the official press conference, Holm tried, in her *Stepford Wives* way, to expand on her earlier remarks. "I mean, it's motivation in some ways," she said. "But I don't want to lose to any fighter, so it's just another fight. In the sport you get all different kinds of personalities and things. But I do prefer to try and stay very professional. A lot of women boxers talk about how we don't get paid enough. I think [we would] if we would just be a lot more respectful and carry ourselves more professionally."

Melissa was battling to get Holly to bite. "If only she brought in a pair of chattering teeth and called it Melissa or something," Melissa said as she rode in the back of the car on our way to the hotel after her last training session before the weigh-in. Maybe Holm should have consulted Melissa for some ideas.

That morning at Albuquerque's Jack Candelaria Community Center gym, Belinda sparred a local girl who trained there called Victoria, a tall, thirty-four-year-old welterweight. Belinda was suffering from a bad cold and was wheezing, squatting down between rounds, and coughing and spitting. Her cold was exacerbated by the effects of the altitude. Despite that, she made Victoria look like a beginner. I wondered how I'd fare against Victoria. She was a southpaw so I let it ride. But it made no difference to Belinda, who still slipped and countered, same as always.

The night before, Victoria had driven us back to the hotel, and I noticed how she touched the rosary hanging from her rearview mirror and crossed herself a couple of times, more like the actions of an obsessive compulsive, I thought, than a gesture of religious devotion. She told us she had two kids, a husband, and had thirteen fights with only two wins and two draws. She was a battler. It looked like she was honored to drive The Hurricane around.

Melissa had been charming the locals pretty well, at least those who didn't feel the blonde preacher's daughter was their cup of tea. She'd won over the shuttle drivers, the people in the gym, the Latino and Native American workers at the Isleta Casino and Resort Hotel in Albuquerque, where the fight was taking place, and best of all, members of the media. Everywhere we went, people identified with the feisty little Hispanic woman.

"Everyone loves the little Mighty Mouse," said Belinda.

Inside the Isleta, all the prefight palaver was feeling a bit lame and artificial, though, like an imitation of something grown-ups would do. Melissa was the only boxer of the twelve on stage for the weigh-in with a sense of theater. Only Jessica Sanchez, a leggy 125-lb. girl, did a variation on the muscle pose, a kind of Amazonian archery posture, when she was on the scales. Other than that, it was as exciting as, well, what it was: people stripping and stepping on scales and some dry voice announcing their weight.

The women did look incredible, though, their midsections carved into a craggy landscape of ribs, hip bones, and abdominal muscle—a rare sight in America even on a healthy female. It was strange to see the women wearing bikinis while outside it was twenty degrees and snowing.

Holm was half a pound over the 140-lb. required weight and looked like she couldn't work up a spit to save herself. Melissa was a well-fed and energetic 134.4 lb. You had to wonder how much all the sweating and starving was going to affect Holm, who was looking a bit surly. Melissa was giving her no choice but to be stiffly affronted. Holm strutted back into the room after sweating off a pound, dressed in a white hotel robe, her hair up, looking like a school prefect.

The impending contest was perhaps having more impact outside the Isleta than inside, where the atmosphere was flat. Even promoter Lenny Fresquez's efforts failed when he tried to ignite some sparks by quoting Chevelle Hallback, who'd recently said she'd held back when she fought Melissa because she was a friend and actually could have knocked her out instead of fighting to a draw.

Melissa grinned her way through these insults while Holm held her lips tight and stared straight ahead.

Someone asked how she'd manage the height difference. She laughed.

"Well, if you see my height, you can see that I'll be battling height mismatches my whole life. I believe I can definitely outpunch Holly. I mean, I didn't get the name Hurricane for no reason. I can be Manny Pacquiao, as I said before, or Mayweather. Whichever one needs to show up, I'll be that."

I wondered whether Holm would ever fight someone who was naturally twenty pounds heavier than she was, in *their* hometown. Height was the least of it. It was actually more about body mass. Holm in her tight, low-cut jeans and black jacket looked a lot bigger than Melissa, with her loose jeans, T-shirt, bandana, and her big rock-star sunglasses. I couldn't help feeling protective of Melissa and a little fearful for her. She had bitten off an awfully big mouthful.

On the day of the fight New Yorkers started to arrive: Julie Anne Kelly, Ronica Jeffrey, and some others from Gleason's. Terri Moss was there with Patricia Alcivar and a few friends from the Decatur Boxing Gym. Terri had agreed to take over for Martin Snow and Patricia was having her second pro fight the next weekend. Patricia had so far survived the cruel world of prizefighting under the careful watch of Terri's ever-suspicious eyes.

The morning of the fight, Brian "The Bionic Bull" Cohen, Melissa's new manager, took a group of us back to the gym at the

Jack Candelaria Center. Belinda, me, Julie Anne, Terri, Patricia, and a couple more of us all managed to squeeze into the car.

Patricia and I sparred three rounds, although she had learned earlier in the day that her fight had been canceled. Two days earlier Maureen Shea's fight had also been scratched when her opponent had failed the medical.

The most overused phrase in boxing that week was, "Everything happens for a reason."

Sue Fox told me that 2009 hadn't actually been a very good year despite the obvious growth in the sport over the past decade. There had been fewer female fights than in recent years. She felt the reason was that fighters or, more specifically, their managers were being too picky, and the good boxers weren't fighting each other. But the spate of last-minute cancellations seemed to be something else. All these brides being left at the altar—why was that? Was being stood up just a woman's lot in life?

Fox, who ran Fresquez's website as well as WBAN, was looking forward to the showdown, though. She'd never met Hernandez or Belinda or many of the fighters and former fighters in town for the event, which was a surprise to me. Apparently she'd had been viewing them all these years through the same kind of reverse tele-scope that I had. The night before the fight I went to dinner with her, the publicist Amy Green, and Trina "The Iron Butterfly" Ortegon, an ex-middleweight also from the local area, who had trained with one of the really early pioneers of what you could call the contemporary era, a woman named Irene Garcia who ran a boxing gym called A Woman's Place in Albuquerque.

On the way to dinner, Fox, who had a kind face and long auburn hair, told me she originally started the site because, despite her own fighting achievements in the late 1970s and those of others she knew, there was no record anywhere of their exploits, and she wanted to change that. She said women's boxing was now so big she could hardly keep up. Growth during the past ten years in particular had been exponential. Hundreds of thousands of pages were now archived on the site. Fox, another ex-police officer, seemed delighted to be in a world that she had only imagined for many years.

The four of us stood in the hotel lobby speculating about the future of the sport. The 2012 Olympics were ahead of us, and rising stars, who were still in their early twenties, like the Irish fighter Katie Taylor, would likely be participating.

"Oh, she fights like a guy," said Fox. "She's just incredibly talented."

Although it was late, we had trouble breaking away from each other after dinner. "It's amazing," said Sue. "Wherever you go in the boxing world, you have friends. It's because people don't understand us, they don't understand the sport. They think it's crazy. But we know what it takes."

Twenty-four hours later, I found myself running the gauntlet, surrounded by the poor and huddled masses who were sitting like zombies before the slot machines inside the casino, smoking their empty heads off. I literally had to run through the toxic, gray air holding my breath to avoid gagging on my way to the showroom where the fight was being staged. Terri, Lynn, Patricia, and Lisa were still fussing, as if we were going to the Oscars, but I wanted to be sure I got my press credentials and something to eat. The buffet line appeared endless and service in the restaurants looked slow. So I got my press tag and went back to my room and found an apple, yogurt, and some crackers and avocado. I knocked on Terri's door and found them all still primping as if for a ball. Patricia Alcivar looked like she was ready for a *Vogue* photo shoot, her long dark ringlets straightened and styled to fall elegantly across her shoulders and her runner's legs enhanced by high heels.

"Terri," I said as I watched her check her more conservative outfit in the mirror. "It's a bit of a cluster fuck down there."

"It is?" she said, still assessing her outfit. "Oh well, we should go then. But I don't really care about the first fight. It's just a guy fight, isn't it?"

Terri looked even smaller than she had in Kansas City. Was it possible that she'd lost weight? The Olympic reunion show had collapsed at the eleventh hour, and soon after she'd come down with pneumonia. I hoped that our Ringside adventure hadn't added to her stress.

"You look a lot better than you did last time I saw you," she had said when she'd first arrived. "You look rested." Hearing that made me laugh.

When we got to the casino, the line into the showroom had grown and seemed to go on forever, winding around the card tables and poker machines with their incessant, tuneless burbling. The shuttle driver had told me that Albuquerque was a last-minute town, and here it was, the last minute, and the throng had arrived.

Thankfully, the line moved quickly, and so in we went, through the security check. We came across Belinda, who handed all of us a Puerto Rican flag. I got a quick picture of me, Ronica, Kimberly, and Belinda waving the flags and then made my way ringside and watched "the guy fight" from the neutral corner. They were both local boys. One was like a raging bull in the first round and got knocked out clean in the second, flat on his back. The doctor and his corner men hovered over him, trying to shake him awake.

I went over to Terri who was sitting with her group half a dozen rows back.

"He shot his load," I said.

"Yep," she said. "He sure did."

She and Lynn decided to go off in search of a drink. I went back toward the ring and saw Belinda and Julie Anne and decided to join them. I hate being stuck at ringside. It's the worst position from which to see a fight, jammed up against the action. You can't see the broad geography and a lot of punches are hidden. There's also no atmosphere.

Belinda, me, Ronica, and Kimberly Tomes.

I watched the Jessica Sanchez vs. Amanda Crespin fight with Belinda and Julie Anne near the entrance to the changing room. The tall Sanchez jumped straight in and fought like a short person, throwing hooks and bombing right hands down at Crespin. It was clear that all she needed to do was jab and move to keep off Crespin, who had a little muffin top over her shorts and probably should have been fighting two divisions lighter. But instead it was a phone-booth encounter, Crespin probably the better boxer, but it went to a draw anyway. I knew Sanchez wouldn't be able to jab after I saw her spar her trainer at the gym. Another waste of long arms, I thought. Thank goodness so few tall people really know how to use their natural assets.

The next girl fight was Jodie Esquibel, who trained with Holm and had Mike Winklejon in her corner, against Suzannah Warner, who was from Gleason's and had Hector and Dillon Carew working hers.

I was standing near the curtains watching the fight when Bionic Bull's sidekick came out and said to me, "There might not be a fight. Belinda didn't get to watch Holm's hands being wrapped, and now they're not cutting the wraps off. She says she's not going to fight."

I took that information to Sue Fox who was at ringside, filming the bout with two cameras, waving them like shotguns in the air.

"There might be no fight," I said.

"Huh?" she said, clearly focused on filming.

The bell sounded for the one-minute break, and Sue put down her cameras. "What did you say? What's going on?" she asked.

"The main event. It could be off. They didn't see Holly's hands being wrapped, and now they won't cut them off and redo them."

On the face of it, hand-wrapping may sound like a petty issue. But recently there had been some controversy in men's boxing on the subject. Earlier in the year the former WBA welterweight champion Antonio Margarito and his trainer Javier Capetillo had had their boxing licenses revoked by the California State Athletic Commission because Capetillo had put a "plaster-like substance" under Margarito's wraps before he fought Shane Mosely in January. Although he lost the fight against Mosely, he'd knocked out Miguel Cotto the year before, raising the suspicion that the gloves had also been loaded for that bout. Some said Cotto wasn't the same afterward.

Anyone who has ever been hit with an eight- or ten-ounce fighting glove knows how hard it feels when knuckles connect with facial bones. It's not like sparring in the gym, where all the padding in the gloves slows everything down and dissipates the impact. It's like a pillow fight by comparison. To add extra hardness to those fists in the form of any "plaster-like" substance could be lethal. Already in the previous weeks the female welterweight Rita Figueroa had been rushed to hospital after complaining of a headache following her fight against Kita Watkins in Chicago and had had to undergo emergency brain surgery. We might be girls, but we're capable of hurting each other, possibly with fatal consequences. I was sure Melissa and Holm would resolve the issue.

I decided to watch a few rounds of Suzannah's fight from my squatting position next to Hector in the corner since I was already there. I'd met Suzannah at Gleason's and was fascinated by her lean, tiny physique. Basically she had a boy's body and a thick, long wad of dreadlocks tied behind her that probably added an extra two or three pounds to her weight. These were flyweights. Minuscule girls, both in purple-pink skirts. Suzannah—who was British, but of African descent—was an ex-soccer player and looked like she was dressed for a few sets of tennis at Flushing Meadows. It was a high-work-rate, action-packed fight, if a little sloppy at times. Hector shouted relentlessly: "Two hans, Soosie, two hans Don wait. Straight away. No hard ponches, Soosie. Joost fast. Two hans. Yes, dats eet. Keep goin."

Back at the hotel, Hector had had nothing but praise for Melissa. "She play a very good head game," he said. "You should a seen her in Panama. It take her three songs to get into the ring, she dancing and dancing so much and people love eet. Me, too. I love dat leetle girl, I tell you."

Suzannah was throwing everything at Esquibel, doubling her rights while Esquibel was on the move. But Suzannah was coming in with her hands up rather than coming in with the jab, which made it a close-range encounter. During the fight I looked up and saw Holm watching from the doorway to the stage. She was standing as still as a statue, her face greased and her Dutch milk-maid plaits in place.

They must have resolved the wrap issue. Surely, after all the pre-fight publicity and in front of a full house of paying customers, they wouldn't cancel the main event. It would look bad for them if it was all because they wouldn't cut the wraps and redo them.

At the end of Suzannah's fight, which she won on a split decision, retaining the NABF strawweight title, I went back to my spot next to Julie Anne. Then Belinda came by carrying a bucket and a huge wrapped-up Puerto Rican flag and said, "Melissa's gone back to the room, and I'm going up there now. They won't rewrap. She's not fighting."

Terri came to where I was standing near the changing room and I noticed Doris, Fresquez's assistant, talking frantically on the phone.

"Everything going smoothly?" I asked when she finally ended her call.

She smiled and said, "No."

"I've come a long way to see a fight," I said.

"Oh, you'll see a fight," she said. "Holly will be fighting tonight."

"You've got someone else?" I asked, and she nodded.

Terri and I looked at each other.

My heart started racing. Should I go up to the room and tell Melissa there was a substitute? Or should I stay out of it? Melissa walking out over the hand wraps would look bad for Holm, but

Holm fighting a substitute would look bad for Melissa. I wanted to do something, but what?

"What are you going to do?" asked Terri. "I don't really want to watch the substitute fight her. I mean, her boxing sucks. She fights just like that Jodie Esquibel. She just runs in and runs out. That fight between her and Warner was so ugly. I hated that fight. It makes me mad because they're in my weight class, and I know I'd just jab their eyeballs off. Neither one of them knew how to fight."

"I don't know," I said. "I'm going to watch it. I mean, I've come all this way."

"Well, I'm going to get a drink, anyway," she said. "There's a twenty-minute intermission."

I tried to work out what to do. I rang Melissa and got her voice-mail. Then I remembered I had Bionic Bull Brian's number, and so I called him and said, "It's Mischa, the Australian woman from this morning. I just thought I'd let you know they have a substitute."

I heard him tell Melissa. I heard Melissa say something, and then he said, "Let her fight the substitute."

"What? Let her fight the substitute?" I said, a little shocked. Then, after a pause, I said, "OK, just letting you know."

The response seemed too quick and ill considered. I walked around in circles a few times and then put my head down and ran the gauntlet of the casino while I tried to recall the room number.

The elevator doors opened to two security guards, and I could see a group of men standing near Melissa's room down the hall. I walked toward them. One of the men was Fresquez, a small white-haired man with whom I'd only exchanged a few words. As I approached I heard Bionic Brian say in a raised voice, "It's not about money. Money wouldn't make any difference."

And then Fresquez walked past me. "What's happening?" I asked.

"She's chickening out," said Fresquez and kept walking.

When I arrived at the room, the door was open and Melissa was right there. "Please don't shoot the messenger," I said, "but it's going to look bad for you. Sue Fox is pissed off. You should know that, you're going to get a lot of flak."

"OK. That's fine," she said. "Why I gotta do what everyone else wants me to do instead of what I want?"

"She doesn't need this," Bionic Brian interrupted. "She's already upset." And he made like he was going to eject me from the room, but Melissa stopped him. "No, no, Mischa's our buddy," she said. "Let her stay."

At that point I dropped any notion of being an impartial observer, but because everyone seemed to be forming opinions on what was happening way too fast, I tried not to form any strong ones of my own.

It seemed that Fresquez had offered to cut the wraps and redo them. But by now Melissa was unfocused, upset, beyond persuading. She wasn't going to fight now, no matter what heat she took as a result.

I decided to go back down and watch the substitute. I also wanted to hear what everyone was saying about the situation.

Once again I worked my way through the toxic air and into the venue. This time I joined the VIPs, none of whom I recognized, up on the stage so I could get a good view. I arrived there just as the substitute was getting into the ring. She looked familiar. Her red shorts did, too, and they had the name Sanchez on the back. Surely not . . . After fighting four tough rounds against Amanda Crespin, Jessica Sanchez was now going to take on Holm? Wait a minute, she was as tall as Sanchez but heavier set. It wasn't Sanchez, it was Victoria from the gym, the girl who had sparred Belinda. I sent Melissa a text message, but there was no reply.

When Holm came into the ring the crowd roared.

When the fight began, it became apparent that the crowd would have gone wild even if Holm was fighting a burlap sack. They just wanted to see her fight somebody.

And while it wasn't really competitive, it was certainly action packed. Victoria was giving it her all in every round and by the third round had inched ahead of Holm briefly. She did a lot better against Holm than she had against Belinda in the gym, although she took some solid shots that spun her head around. But she also blocked a lot of them and came in ducking down as if she had worked it out before, which actually she had, because she'd sparred Holm before. She crossed herself before each round, the same way she had in the car when she took us back to the hotel that night. Whatever it is about boxers and crossing themselves, it never helps them win.

Holm was so lean she looked flayed. You could see the sinews and tendons around the back of her shoulders like nuts and bolts on a machine. She was as carved and cut as it was possible for a woman to be. Her success was strongly tied to her natural physical attributes, her southpaw stance, her height, her movement. She came out early at the start of each round and jumped up and down on the spot like a Masai warrior until the bell sounded. In the corner she jiggled her leg like a nervous adolescent boy. And when she was in there she had the ability to keep throwing once she was in range.

But take away her gas tank, and I don't know how effective she would be. Her style was ugly to watch. Great boxers can still move when they're out of shape. The unwell Belinda could still make someone look bad even if she couldn't breathe. Others depend on their stamina. And Holm was one of these. She didn't have Herbie Hancock inside her. She had a marching band playing in 4-4 time. I wondered how Melissa's Latin rhythms would have worked against that stiff Caucasian beat. Victoria was strong and tough and made it a crowd-pleasing fight because of her little glimmers of success, even managing to bloody Holm's nose at one point. But she was never really in the race. You couldn't help but be moved by her determination, though, and the fortitude it took to be literally a last-minute replacement against such a formidable opponent. It was a Cinderella story, one that was going to make Melissa look more and more like the sneaky, cowardly villain. It was bad news. Bad Blood, indeed.

I messaged Melissa about midway through, "Victoria's giving Holm a good fight."

I got a message back that simply read, "lol."

After the fight, everyone fell instantly in love with Victoria Cisneros. Her courage and determination had been on display. Holm, too, was heaping praise on her and why not? She won by such a shutout she could afford to be generous. But she also decided to have a dig at Melissa saying the crowd got a better fight than they would have with the original opponent.

"Everyone knows hurricanes never land in New Mexico," she said to wild applause.

I went over to Terri Moss, and before I could open my mouth she stood up and pronounced, "That was a set-up. That girl knew she was going to fight tonight. You can't fight ten hard rounds like that without being fully prepared. I've fought for world titles five times, and I'm telling you, you need six to eight weeks to prepare for that kind of thing."

"But she had to borrow shorts from Jessica Sanchez," I said.

That didn't wash with Terri, who would be suspicious of Mother Teresa's motives.

As soon as the fight was over, people began taking sides. Down in the venue, it was mostly those who were on the side of Holm and the brave Victoria who said, "It's just the love of boxing. That's why I did it."

The most obviously opportunistic of the bandwagon jumpers was Ryan Wissow, the sleazy little man who was president of the WIBA, a position that gave him carte blanche to salivate over young women and offer them the chance to fight for his belt. He'd slithered his way around the Florida Golden Gloves tournament with his pencil mustache and his long hair tied back in a tight pony tail, ostensibly hunting for talent.

When I asked him to recount what had happened that night, he told me Melissa's team had vanished when Holm's hands were being wrapped, "nowhere to be found," and then tried to shake down the promoter for more money to come back and fight when he offered to cut them and rewrap. That very quickly became the official line. Being in New Mexico suddenly felt like being in the Soviet Union in the 1970s. No one sought a comment from Melissa on the matter, ignoring one of the fundamental tenets of journalism—getting both sides of the story.

"Chicken Ducks The Rabbit" said the *Albuquerque Journal* sports section the next morning, carrying no comment from Team Hernandez, relying instead on the self-interested Wissow as their authoritative source.

"I think she just chickened out," he was quoted as saying.

I made my way back up to room 509, and when the elevator door opened I saw Jill Emery on the phone explaining everything to someone. I waited for her to finish her call. "What do you think?" I said.

"About her not fighting?"

I nodded.

"Well," she said, leaning against the wall. "I think she was right to leave. But I come from a theater background, you know. The show must go on. I think maybe she should have agreed to go back when they came up to her room."

Jill then rightly pointed out that if they had wanted a well-qualified substitute, they should have offered the fight to her. She'd been trying to secure a match with Holm since August when, inexplicably, negotiations had come to a halt.

Jill was such a contrast to the hot-blooded Latinas. For a fighter, she had an amazingly gentle manner. She had mixed feelings about the stand Melissa was taking and, like me, was hanging back a little. But she also couldn't help sticking by her regardless. Melissa inspired a certain loyalty.

"It's a disaster," she said finally.

"Yeah," I said. "I think it is."

While we were talking, Jennifer Czirr called me from New York, where they had all gathered to watch the webcast.

"Meesha," she said. "What's happening there? Why didn't Melissa fight?"

"It's a disaster," I said to Jennifer and Jill winked at me.

Then Jennifer repeated to the group, "It's a disaster."

"It's a complicated disaster," I said, and again she repeated, "A complicated disaster." And I went on to tell the story for about the fourth or fifth time that hour.

"OK," she said. "Well, we're disappointed. But tell her we still love her."

Then I made my way down the hall toward the room, where it appeared everyone was packing up to go. I asked Ronica what she thought, and she began a long and reasoned explanation about why it was important for Melissa to take a stand, particularly when it came to her safety, and that it took a lot of mental preparation to get ready for a fight like this, and the disruption had put her in a position in which she couldn't fight. And now she needed to make it clear that she wasn't going to be pushed around by promoters.

"It's not about her being chicken," she said. "Anyone who knows her and has seen her fight knows that it's not about that. And anyone who says so is a fucking cunt."

I walked into the room, and Melissa hugged me. "Mischa," she said. "I'm so sorry. You still didn't get to see me fight."

"Never mind," I said. "I might get to see you drunk now, and I haven't seen that before either."

In the room, the cutman and the Bionic Bull and his mate seemed to be caught in a loop, telling and retelling the story.

Soon after, Terri and the others arrived. "Why was she at the weigh-in?" Terri asked about Cisneros. "Why was she at the press conference? And she was driving you guys around, sparring with Belinda. She was in shape to fight ten rounds. Think about it. You wouldn't take a fight at the last minute like that, a ten-round title fight if you didn't know you were ready. She put everything into it until the last round. They knew. They knew. That girl's an opportunist."

The Bionic Bull and the cutman were still rewinding and replaying the sequence of events. I could hear the indignation in their voices building, particularly the cutman, whose height seemed to give him authority that he wouldn't otherwise have. But after a while they sounded like a bunch of teenagers who had been hauled into the principal's office over a schoolyard fight. Their voices became background music over the next few hours as people gathered in the suite to chew over the events.

"If there was nothing wrong with the wraps, they would have just cut them and redone them," the cutman said to me.

"I got that bit," I said, feeling a little exasperated. "It's OK, I got it."

As the night wore on, Melissa actually became more and more entertaining.

"You're a renegade," said Terri. "That's your problem. You know what they used to call Sugar Ray Robinson? They called him Run-Out Ray. You know why? Because he would have done exactly this sort of thing, and he was the best pound-for-pound fighter of all time. Men do this stuff, Melissa. Fights on ESPN and HBO are always delayed over something. You were acting just like Bernard Hopkins."

The next day, the Internet was awash with even more talk. Facebook, YouTube, boxing blogs. Opinions were extreme. Either Melissa was a coward or she was brave for standing up for herself.

One of the first people to come out in support of Melissa was Mia

"The Knockout" St. John, the former *Playboy* cover girl I'd once dismissed.

"I have been in a few fights where fighters did that same thing," she wrote on her Facebook page. "And when I complained, I was bullied into fighting. Now I regret not standing up for myself. I wish I had the guts you had!"

Maybe I'd underestimated The Knockout. I always thought that with her big boobs and her tiny pink pants, Mia had taken a wrong turn into boxing, too desperate for male attention in the conventional sense.

Sue Fox was upset. She wrote:

> I am sitting at ringside . . . I am so "Up," so "Happy," so "Proud" of these women boxers who are on this card . . . I am a past fighter from the late 1970s . . . I fought as a professional female boxer when we were more like the "plague" and not respected athletes in this sport. I was never offered such great opportunities as the women boxers of today, and would have probably given anything at the time that I boxed to have such opportunities. *So while I am sitting at the ringside apron this night, I have some real feelings and emotions about what is going on.* I am, first, feeling deeply embarrassed for the sport, embarrassed for WBAN, for what I would end up having to write about this incident—wishing I were somewhere else . . . *I am also upset*—upset that I flew all the way from Portland, Oregon, to Albuquerque, New Mexico (anyone who knows me, knows that I do not like to fly), and so to take this flight to New Mexico it would have been for a fight card I genuinely wanted to see.

I sympathized with Sue. In the context of her experience it seemed petulant of Melissa to look a gift horse in the mouth. But it was a sign of how far things had come. In terms of behaving badly, Melissa had a mighty long way to go before she matched the men, actually.

I was jarringly reminded of this soon after the Albuquerque disaster while reading *A Year at the Fights*, a collection of Thomas Hauser's articles on boxing. In one of his pieces, he recounts the famous press conference before the 2002 fight between Lennox Lewis and Mike Tyson:

> Tyson was introduced first. Dressed in black, he strode onto the stage and took his place, as planned, on a small platform. Lewis was introduced next. At this point, Tyson left his platform and walked in a menacing fashion towards Lewis. Lewis's bodyguard stepped between them. Tyson threw a left hook at the bodyguard, Lewis retaliated with an overhand right, and all hell broke loose. Tyson was the instigator, plain and simple. During the scuffle, Tyson bit through Lewis's pants and into his thigh, causing significant bleeding. Once semi-order had been restored, Tyson moved to the front of the stage, grabbed his crotch, thrust his hips back and forth, and began screaming obscenities at the media. Someone in the crowd hollered, "Get him a straight jacket." At that point, Tyson shouted back, "Fuck you, you white faggot. I'll fuck you up the ass, white boy. I'll fuck you till you love me," and other obscenities.

Melissa's actions were the mildest of growing pains, part of a generational shift, perhaps, from those who were grateful just to be in the ring to those who are willing to be in the ring only on their own terms. If girls fight like guys, then maybe they have the right to act like them as well. Just a little bit.

EPILOGUE

AT THE women's world boxing championships in Bridgetown, Barbados in the fall of 2010, a precursor to the 2012 Olympics, I watched in a kind of mesmerized awe as the boxers' gender began to recede from view.

Dressed in the international amateur boxing uniforms of shirts and knee-length shorts, their long hair and fine, feminine features hidden beneath regulation head guards, sometimes even I had to remind myself that these were women I was watching.

In bout after bout, over the ten days of competition, women's boxing skills were becoming indistinguishable from those of men and in some cases, surpassed them. I had never seen anything like it, on such a scale, in my life. And it wasn't just wishful thinking. I was clearly witnessing a seismic shift, an accumulation of all that I had been part of over these past fifteen years, escalating rapidly towards some kind of peak. It was a rejoinder to all the skeptics and doubters, a final resonating and comprehensive statement that this sport had come of age and would never go backwards again.

They came from everywhere: Russia, Ukraine, Poland, Sweden, Germany, Turkey, India, China, Costa Rica, Kenya, Thailand, the Philippines, Great Britain, USA, Wales, Ireland, and even my native Australia fielded a team. Many of these countries had fostered the talent, created opportunities, and ensured a high standard—especially China, which had hosted and dominated the previous championships in 2008.

In the training tent, a makeshift facility with three full-sized rings, I watched as boxers who had been eliminated in the preliminary bouts took the opportunity to improve by sparring each other in morning sessions. There I could see up close how much punching power was being delivered, how much resilience was on display, how much hunger and ambition was fueling these fighters who had the historic London Olympic Games in their sights. And the mix grew as the tournament edged towards the finals and more boxers were eliminated. At times the tent was wall to wall with women boxers, their trainers shouting in many different languages, setting up sparring between them like horse traders at a market as the girls shadowboxed around them, trying to stay focused in the chaos, trying to win the spar despite losing the bout and perhaps even more ferocious because of it. The intensity shook the walls and vibrated in the muggy Caribbean air. It was loud and competitive and at times, totally wild, boxers wearing ten-ounce competition gloves and holding back nothing.

For many days I bit my lip, wondering should I or shouldn't I, enter the fray. Even with my experience and my reasonably reliable survival instincts, I wasn't sure if sparring these killers would be an entirely wise move. Peter's words, for the first time, shifted to the forefront of my mind. "Don't bite off more than you can chew."

Many of the women were less than half my age, clearly accomplished and talented athletes in their prime, as well as being seasoned boxers who'd had to fight to win a place on their own national teams. In this tournament—the sixth and the biggest women's world championships ever to be hosted by the International Boxing Association—there were 267 boxers in total. Of the ten weight classes represented at the tournament, only three will be included in the 2012 Olympics: 51-kg., 60-kg., and 75-kg. There were more than forty boxers in each of the 51-kg. and 60-kg. divisions, along with twenty-seven in the 75-kg. division. I'd heard that in Russia alone there were two hundred girls in the 60-kg. division.

One of the most anticipated contenders in the tournament, aside from India's four-time world champion flyweight Mary Kom, was the Irish two-time world champion lightweight Katie Taylor. She was a superstar in her own country, and had even met the Obamas at the White House on St. Patrick's Day in 2010. In a tiny media contingent, the Irish had sent photographers, journalists, and TV crews who told me that if she won the world championship for a third time it would be a front-page story and the lead news item at home. She was a celebrity in Ireland, where she also played for the national soccer team, seemingly both adored and respected. Taylor had won 95 of her 101 bouts coming into the competition and was expected to win her third world championship with little resistance. She hovered around the Barbados Beach Club Hotel where the athletes stayed, slightly removed from the rest, in a kind of exclusive bubble reserved for the supremely gifted. Yet she was physically unassuming, neither bulky nor particularly muscular or especially tall for her weight class.

The twenty-four-year-old had been boxing since the age of eleven and was trained by her father Peter Taylor, who was also the national coach. The world of women's boxing had long been abuzz with how good she was but I had seen only short clips of her on YouTube and was looking forward to seeing her in the flesh. And once the first bell sounded for her fight against India's Neetu

Chahal in the preliminaries, I understood what all the fuss was about. I'd never seen such blistering combinations, such dart-like precision and such smart and swift ring-craft. Neetu didn't manage to score more than 2 points against Taylor's 12. And it was more of the same against Brazil's formidable Adriana Araujo (20-5) and Russia's Anastasia Belyakova (16-1).

Then came the semifinal.

Taylor headed into her ninety-ninth bout against Quanita Lee, better known as Queen Underwood, a twenty-five-year-old from Seattle, Washington who had already been beaten twice by Taylor— once on points and once via a stoppage, both times in Ireland despite winning the US national championship with relative ease.

And in the first round it looked like Taylor could make it a hat trick, notching up a 6-0 lead.

And even though Underwood scraped together 2 points to Taylor's 10 in the second round, nothing looked like it could upset the anticipated outcome.

But in round three, the tables turned. Underwood started to rob Taylor of breathing space, catching her with a punch that knocked her to the ground and saw her hang on for dear life, losing two points for the foul of holding. The scores shifted to 17-8, still in Taylor's favor but the Irish woman seemed rattled. Underwood, with a most impressively muscular back and a killer's cold focus in her eyes, kept on pushing through round four, finding Taylor's weakness and turning the bout into one of the most electrifyingly of the tournament.

Taylor lost two more points for another foul, bringing the scores to 15 even in the last minute. Digging deep into her champion's heart, Taylor threw so many punches in that last stanza that she edged to an 18-16 finish. She scraped through to a final against China's Cheng Dong by the skin of her teeth to win the gold 18-5 boxing in her signature style.

But it was Queen, who I'd first heard of from Melissa Roberts at the Florida Golden Gloves in 2009, who showed the rest of the 60-kg. fighters how they might be able to conquer the almost unbeatable Taylor. More importantly though, the performance brought the crowd to the edge of their seats and women's amateur boxing to a new and exciting level. Almost everyone at the Garfield Sobers Arena forgot they were watching women—somewhat ironically, since the fighters were wearing new skirts that had been unveiled for the semi-finals. The skirts had been deemed necessary by AIBA's president, Ching-Kuo Wu, who felt the need to distinguish the women from the men since it was getting harder to do so from watching them fight. Just when gender was becoming irrelevant, the officials were trying to bring it back on the agenda again. It was a mystifying move, regarded by some as simple, old-fashioned sexism.

Meanwhile, with only three days to go, I was running out of time so I asked the Australian coach, Ruben 'The Cuban' Sanchez, who I had been training with, if I should spar. He shrugged and pointed to a Venezuelan flyweight named Cara who was preparing to get in the ring. I rushed to get my mouth guard, borrowed some gloves and headgear, and jumped in.

The 50-kg. girl didn't kill me, so I sparred some more with another flyweight, an eighty-fight veteran from Canada named Jackie. But I still felt that I should at least get within spitting range of my own weight class.

So the next day, feeling slightly more confident, I moved up to the 60-kg. division, which would probably be my own if I were twenty years younger. I did two rounds with the German two-time national champion Tasheena Bugar. Two rounds turned into four and the next day I sparred again with her and two different Mexican fighters. I'd like to think I held my own and, at the very least, didn't disgrace myself. Of course I regretted that I hadn't started sparring sooner and that I had spent too much time worrying that

I might be out of my depth. I guess that's the difference between me and the genuine, elite athletes in this sport.

Surviving, it seems, really is enough for me. Anything more than that has always exceeded my wildest dreams.

ABOUT THE AUTHOR

MISCHA MERZ is a journalist and author of fiction and creative non-fiction. She began training as an amateur boxer in 1995 and is the 2001 Australian Amateur Boxing League women's welterweight champion. Her book *Bruising*, about her experiences as a boxer, was published to critical acclaim by Picador Australia in 2000 and was shortlisted for the Dobbie Award. Her journalism has appeared in numerous publications, including *The Age*, the *Sunday Age*, and the *Herald Sun*.

ABOUT SEVEN STORIES PRESS

SEVEN STORIES PRESS is an independent book publisher based in New York City, with distribution throughout the United States, Canada, England, and Australia. We publish works of the imagination by such writers as Nelson Algren, Russell Banks, Octavia E. Butler, Ani DiFranco, Assia Djebar, Ariel Dorfman, Coco Fusco, Barry Gifford, Hwang Sok-yong, Peter Plate, Lee Stringer, and Kurt Vonnegut, to name a few, together with political titles by voices of conscience, including the Boston Women's Health Collective, Noam Chomsky, Angela Y. Davis, Human Rights Watch, Derrick Jensen, Ralph Nader, Loretta Napoleoni, Gary Null, Project Censored, Ted Rall, Barbara Seaman, Alice Walker, Gary Webb, and Howard Zinn, among many others. Seven Stories Press believes publishers have a special responsibility to defend free speech and human rights, and to celebrate the gifts of the human imagination, wherever we can. For additional information, visit www.sevenstories.com.